The Beloved World of
Sonia Sotomayor

The Beloved World of

Sonia Sotomayor

Sonia Sotomayor

DELACORTE PRESS

All rights reserved. Published in the United States by Delacorte Press,
an imprint of Random House Children's Books,
a division of Penguin Random House LLC, New York.

This work is based on *My Beloved World*, copyright © 2013 by Sonia Sotomayor.
Published in hardcover by Alfred A. Knopf, an imprint of the Knopf Doubleday
Publishing Group, a division of Penguin Random House LLC, New York, in 2013.

Delacorte Press is a registered trademark and the colophon is a trademark of
Penguin Random House LLC.

All photos are from the author's personal collection, except for the last photo in
the photo section, which is by Steve Petteway, courtesy of the Supreme Court
of the United States.

Visit us on the Web! rhcbooks.com

Educators and librarians, for a variety of teaching tools, visit us at
RHTeachersLibrarians.com

Library of Congress Cataloging-in-Publication Data
Names: Sotomayor, Sonia, author. | Delacorte Press, editor.
Title: The beloved world of Sonia Sotomayor / Sonia Sotomayor.
Description: New York : Delacorte Books for Young Readers, 2018.
Identifiers: LCCN 2018014386 (print) | LCCN 2018015211 (ebook) |
ISBN 978-1-5247-7116-4 (ebook) | ISBN 978-1-5247-7114-0 (hardback) |
ISBN 978-1-5247-7115-7 (library binding)
Subjects: LCSH: Sotomayor, Sonia | Hispanic American judges—Biography—
Juvenile literature. | Hispanic American women—Biography—Juvenile literature. |
Judges—United States—Biography—Juvenile literature. | United States. Supreme
Court—Officials and employees—Biography—Juvenile literature. | BISAC:
JUVENILE NONFICTION / Biography & Autobiography / Cultural Heritage. |
JUVENILE NONFICTION / Biography & Autobiography / Women. | JUVENILE
NONFICTION / Family / Parents.
Classification: LCC KF8745.S67 (ebook) | LCC KF8745.S67 A33 2018 (print) |
DDC 347.73/2634 [B]—dc23

The text of this book is set in 11-point Berling.
Interior design by Trish Parcell

Bottom photo on spine and bottom middle photo on front cover
copyright © by Elena Siebert

Printed in the United States of America

10 9 8 7 6 5 4 3 2 1
First Edition

To my cousin and dear friend, Miriam Ramirez Gonzerelli, a brilliant middle school teacher, whose work in bilingual education and advocacy for kids inspires my interactions with them

Family Members in this Book

PATERNAL SIDE

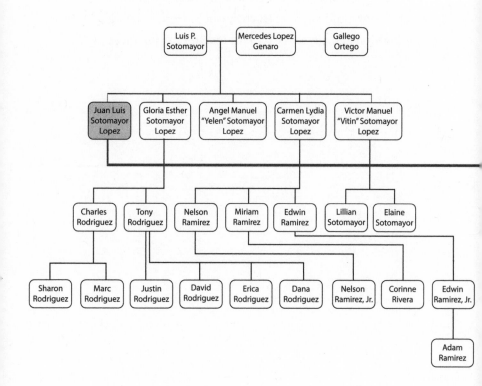

MATERNAL SIDE

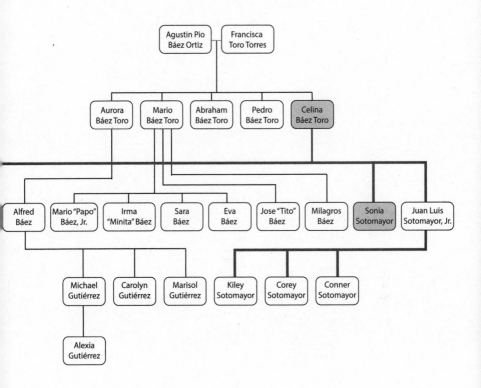

Introduction

I have been asked by people of all ages, but especially by middle school students, if I ever imagined being on the highest court of the United States, the Supreme Court. "No," I answer, because when I was a child my family was poor and we knew no lawyers or judges and none lived in our neighborhood. I knew nothing about the Supreme Court and how much its work in interpreting the Constitution and the laws of the United States affected peoples' lives. You cannot dream of becoming something you don't even know about. That has been the most important lesson of my life. You have to learn to dream big dreams. Only an education can expose you to what the world has to offer. So much of my life story is about how education opened my eyes to the many possibilities of what I could become.

When I wrote an adult version of this book, I realized

that I wanted to create another version for schoolkids. This book was inspired by kids asking me questions. I want kids to understand that dreams, even ones you cannot first imagine, can come true. Despite hardships and challenges in my life, I have been able to succeed beyond my wildest dreams, and I know you can too. Is there a secret you will discover in my book? Yes. Here it is: You should never give up trying. Doing anything new in life is scary and hard. Many times you will fail when you first try. You have to get up and try and try again. Every mistake teaches you something new. Every failure teaches what you did wrong and have to practice more, what you need to avoid doing the next time, where you need help, and how to change to become better at what you want to do. If you fail, it means you tried. If you don't try at all, you will never be in a position to succeed or to experience the joy of triumphing.

The chapters in this book are not only about how I ultimately succeeded, but also about how uncomfortable I was learning new things in my life, how hard I had to work to figure things out, and how often I had to try to get things right. My life circumstances did not naturally promise success. My story may resonate in ways that many of you will relate to. You may feel the way I felt. The challenges I have faced—including material poverty, chronic illness, struggling to learn English, and being raised by a single mom—are not uncommon. For many, it is a source of hope to see someone realize her dreams while bearing such burdens. People who live in difficult circumstances need to know that happy endings are possible.

A young student once asked me: "Given that there are only nine Supreme Court Justices, each with life tenure, can anyone realistically aspire to such a goal? How do we hold on to dreams that statistically are almost impossible?" I admit that not everyone's exact dreams can come true. But experience has taught me that the value of dreams does not depend on the odds of their coming true. Their real value lies in stirring within us the will to aspire. That will, wherever it leads, moves you forward. After a time you may recognize that the proper measure of success is not how much you've closed the distance to some far-off goal, but the quality of what you have done today and how hard you tried.

I hope you will enjoy reading how an ordinary person like me, with strengths and weaknesses like yours, has managed an extraordinary journey. I look forward to you writing to me and telling me how hard you tried and how far you went in life.

Prologue

I was barely awake, and my mother was already screaming. I knew Papi would start yelling in a second. That much was routine, but the substance of their argument was new, and it etched that morning into my memory.

"You have to learn how to give it to her, Juli. I can't be here all the time!"

"I'm afraid to hurt her. My hands are trembling." It was true. When my father had made his first attempt at giving me the insulin shot the day before, his hands were shaking so much I was afraid he would miss my arm entirely and stab me in the face. He had to jab hard just to steady his aim.

"Whose fault is it your hands tremble?"

Uh-oh, here we go.

"You're the nurse, Celina! You know how to do these things."

Actually, when Mami gave me the shot my first morning home from the hospital, she was so nervous that she jabbed me even harder, and hurt me even worse, than Papi would the next day.

"That's right, I'm the nurse. I have to work and help support this family. I have to do everything! But I can't be here all the time, Juli, and she's going to need this for the rest of her life. So you better figure it out."

The needles hurt, but the screaming was worse. It was bad enough when they were fighting about the milk, or the housework, or the money, or the drinking. The last thing I wanted was for them to fight about me.

"I swear, Juli, you'll kill that child if you don't learn how to do this!"

As usual, Mami walked away and slammed the door behind her, so she had to scream even louder to continue the fight.

If my parents couldn't pick up the syringe without panicking, an even darker prospect loomed: my grandmother wouldn't be up to the job either. That would be the end of my weekly sleepovers at her apartment and my only escape from the gloom at home. It then dawned on me: if I needed to have these shots every day for the rest of my life, the only way I'd survive was to do it myself.

The first step, I knew, was to sterilize the needle and syringe. Not yet eight years old, I was barely tall enough to see the top of the stove, and I wasn't sure how to perform the tricky maneuver with match and gas to light the burner. So

I dragged a chair the couple of feet from table to stove—the kitchen was tiny—and climbed up to figure it out. The two small pots for Mami's *café con leche* were sitting there, getting cold while they fought, the coffee staining its little cloth sack in one pot, *la nata* forming a wrinkled skin on top of the milk in the other.

"Sonia! What are you doing? You'll burn the building down, *nena*!"

"I'm going to give myself the shot, Mami." That silenced her for a moment.

"Do you know how?" She looked at me levelly, seriously.

"I think so. At the hospital they had me practice on an orange."

My mother showed me how to hold the match while turning the dial, to make the flame whoosh to life in a blue ring. Together we filled the pot with water, enough to cover the syringe and needle and some extra in case it boiled down. She directed me to wait for the bubbles and only then to start counting five minutes by the clock. I had learned how to tell time the year before, in first grade. After the water had boiled long enough, she said, I would still need to wait for the syringe to cool. I watched the pot and the invisibly slow creep of the clock's hand until tiny, delicate chains of bubbles rose from the glass syringe and the needle, my mind racing through a hundred other things as I marked the time.

Watching water boil would try the patience of any child, but I was physically restless as I was mentally and had well earned the family nickname Aji—"hot pepper"—for my eagerness to jump headlong into any mischief impelled by equal parts curiosity and rambunctiousness. But believing that my life now depended on this morning ritual, I would soon figure out how to manage the time efficiently: to get dressed, brush my teeth, and get ready for school in the intervals while the pot boiled or cooled. I learned self-discipline from living with diabetes. Fainting in church was how it all started. We had just stood up to sing, and I felt as if I were suffocating. The singing seemed far away, and then the light from the stained-glass windows turned yellow. Everything turned yellow, and then it went black.

When I opened my eyes, all I could see was the principal, Sister Marita Joseph, and Sister Elizabeth Regina, their worried faces upside down and pale inside their black bonnets. I was lying on the tile floor in the sacristy, shivering cold from the water splashed all over my face. And scared. So they called my mother.

Although I went to Mass every Sunday, which was obligatory for students at Blessed Sacrament School, my parents never did. When my mother arrived, the Sisters of Charity made a big fuss. Had this ever happened before? Come to think of it, there was the time I'd fallen off the slide, the sudden dizziness as I stepped over the top of the ladder before the ground came rushing up to me in a long moment of panic . . . She had to take me to the doctor, the nuns insisted.

Dr. Fisher was already firmly established as a family hero. All of our relatives were under his care at one time or another, and his house calls did as much to ease fears and panics as they did aches and pains. A German immigrant, he was an old-fashioned country doctor who just happened to be practicing in the Bronx. Dr. Fisher asked a lot of questions, and Mami told him I was losing weight and always thirsty and that I had started wetting the bed, which was so mortifying that I would try not to fall asleep.

Dr. Fisher sent us to the lab at Prospect Hospital, where my mother worked. I didn't see trouble coming, because I perceived Mr. Rivera in the lab to be a friend of mine. I thought I could trust him, unlike Mrs. Gibbs, my mother's supervisor, who had tried to hide the needle behind her back when I'd had my tonsils out. But when he tied a rubber tube around my arm, I realized this was no ordinary shot. The syringe looked almost as big as my arm, and as he got closer, I could see that the needle was sliced off at an angle with the hole gaping like a little mouth at the end of it.

As he approached, I screamed, "No!" Knocking the chair back, I ran across the hall and right out the front door. It seemed as if half the hospital were running right behind me, shouting "Catch her!" but I didn't turn around to look. I just dove under a parked car.

I could see their shoes. One of them bent down and stuck his nose into the shadow of the undercarriage. Shoes all around now, and hands reaching under the car. But I scrunched up like a turtle, until someone caught me by the foot. I was hollering so loud as they dragged me back to the lab that I couldn't have hollered any louder when the needle went in.

When we went back to Dr. Fisher after they took my blood, it was the first time I'd ever seen my mother cry. I was outside in the waiting room, but his office door was open a crack. I could hear her voice break and see her shoulders quaking. The nurse closed the door when she noticed I was watching, but I'd seen enough to understand that something was seriously wrong. Then Dr. Fisher opened the door and called me in. He explained that there was sugar in my blood, that it's called diabetes, and that I would have to change the way I ate. He reassured me that the bed-wetting would end when we had things under control: it was just the body's way of getting rid of excess blood sugar. He even told me that he also had diabetes, although I understood later that he had the more common type 2, while I had the rarer juvenile diabetes, or type 1, in which the pancreas stops producing insulin, making daily injections of insulin necessary.

Then he took a bottle of soda from the cupboard behind him and popped the top off. "Taste it. It's called No-Cal. Just like soda but without sugar."

I took a sip. "I don't really think so." Poor Dr. Fisher. My mother insisted that we always be polite even if that meant softening a strong opinion, a lesson that stuck with me.

"Well, there are lots of other flavors. Even chocolate."

I thought to myself: This doesn't add up. He's making it sound as if it's no big deal. Just skip dessert and drink a different soda. Why is my mother so upset?

We went straight from Dr. Fisher's office to my grandmother's home. Abuelita tucked me into her bed, even though it was the middle of the afternoon and I had long outgrown naps. She closed the curtains, and I lay there in the half dark listening as the front door kept opening and voices filled the living room. I could hear my father's sisters, Titi Carmen and Titi Gloria. My cousin Charlie was there too, and Gallego, my step-grandfather. Abuelita sounded terribly upset. She was talking about my mother as if she weren't there, and since I didn't hear Mami's voice at all, it was clear that she had left.

"It runs in families, *como una maldición.*"

"This curse is from Celina's side, for sure, not ours."

There was speculation about whether Mami's own mother had died of this terrible affliction and talk of a special herb that might cure it. Abuelita knew all about healing with herbs. The least sniffle or stomachache had her brewing noxious potions that would leave me with a lifelong aversion to tea of any sort. Now she was scheming with my aunts to get word to her brother in Puerto Rico. She would tell him where to find the plant, which he was to pick at dawn before boarding a flight from San Juan the same day so she could prepare it at the peak of potency. He actually pulled it off, but sadly, Abuelita's herbal remedy would prove ineffective, and this failure of her skill in a case so close to her heart would disturb her deeply.

Abuelita's obvious anxiety that afternoon, and the talk of my other grandmother's death, did achieve one thing: it made me realize how serious this situation was. Now my mother's crying made sense to me, and I was shaken. I was even more shaken when I learned that I had to be hospitalized to stabilize my blood sugar levels, which was routine in those days.

In 1962, when I was first diagnosed, the treatment of juvenile diabetes was primitive by today's standards, and life expectancy was much shorter. Nevertheless, Dr. Fisher had managed to locate the best care for the disease in New York City, and possibly in the entire country. He discovered that the Albert Einstein College of Medicine, a leader in juvenile diabetes research, ran a clinic at Jacobi Medical Center, a public hospital, which by luck happened to be in the Bronx. The vastness of Jacobi Medical Center awed me. It made Prospect Hospital seem like a dollhouse.

Every morning, starting at eight o'clock, they would draw my blood repeatedly for testing. Hourly, they used the thick needle with the rubber tube on my arm, and every half hour they would slice my finger with a lance for a smaller sample. It continued until noon, and the next day they did the same thing again. This went on for an entire week and part of the next. I didn't holler and I didn't run, but I have never forgotten the pain.

But even more than the clinical procedures, it was my absence from school for so long that set off my inner alarm. I knew I had to be seriously sick for my mother to allow it. School was just as important as work, she insisted, and she never once stayed home from work. Equally worrying, she brought me a present almost every day I was in the hospital: a coloring book, a puzzle, once even a comic book, which meant she was thinking hard about what I would like instead of what she wanted me to have.

My very last day at the hospital started again at eight o'clock with the big needle and the lances. My arm was aching and my fingers were burning right from the very beginning. I made it through the first two hours, but just as they were lining up their instruments for the ten o'clock torture, something inside me broke. After all those days of being brave and holding it in, I started crying. And once I started, I couldn't stop. My mother must have heard me because she burst in, and I flew sobbing into her arms. "Enough!" she said, fiercer than I'd ever seen her. Fiercer even than when she fought with my father. "We stop now. She's done." She said it in a way that nobody—not the lab technician standing there with the syringe in his hand, not any doctor in Jacobi Medical Center—was going to argue with her.

"Do you know how much to give, Sonia?"

"Up to this line here."

"That's right. But do it carefully. You can't give too little and you can't give too much. And you have to be careful, Sonia, not to let any bubbles get into the needle. That's dangerous."

"I know how to do this part. But it doesn't make sense to say I'm *giving* it, Mami. I'm the one who's *getting* the shot."

"Whatever you say, Sonia."

"I'm doing both."

And I did. I held my breath, and I gave myself the shot.

One

The world that I was born into was a tiny microcosm of Hispanic New York City. A tight few blocks in the South Bronx bounded the lives of my extended family: my grandmother, matriarch of the tribe, and her second husband, Gallego, her daughters and sons. My playmates were my cousins. We spoke Spanish at home, and many in my family spoke virtually no English. My parents had both come to New York from Puerto Rico in 1944, my mother, Celina Baez, in the Women's Army Corps, my father, Juan Luís Sotomayor, with his family in search of work as part of a huge migration from the island, driven by economic hardship.

My brother, now Juan Luis Sotomayor Jr., MD, but to me forever Junior, was born three years after I was. I found him a nuisance as only a little brother can be, following me everywhere, mimicking my every gesture, eavesdropping on every conversation. In retrospect, he was actually a quiet child who made few demands on anyone's attention. My mother always said that compared with me, caring for Junior was like taking a vacation. Once, when he was still tiny and I wasn't much bigger, my exasperation with him inspired me to lead him into the hallway outside the apartment and shut the door. I don't know how much later it was that my mother found him, sitting right where I'd left him, sucking his thumb. But I do know I got walloped that day.

But that was just domestic politics. On the playground, or once he started school at Blessed Sacrament with me, I watched out for him, and any bully thinking of messing with him would have to mix it up with me first. If I got beat up on Junior's account, I would settle things with him later, but no one was going to lay a hand on him except me.

Around the time that Junior was born, we moved to a newly constructed public housing project in Soundview, just a ten-minute drive from our old neighborhood. The Bronxdale Houses sprawled over three large city blocks: twenty-eight buildings, each seven stories tall with eight apartments to a floor. My mother saw the projects as a safer, cleaner, brighter alternative to the decaying tenement where we had lived. My grandmother Abuelita, however, saw this move as a venture into far and alien territory, *el jurutungo viejo* for all practical purposes. My mother should never have made us move, she said, because in the old neighborhood there was life on the streets and family nearby; in the projects we were isolated.

I knew well enough that we were isolated, but that condition had more to do with my father's drinking and the shame attached to it. It constrained our lives as far back as my memory reaches. We almost never had visitors. My cousins never spent the night at our home as I did at theirs. Even Ana, my mother's best friend, never came over, though she lived in the projects too, in the building kitty-corner from ours, and took care of my brother, Junior, and me after school. We always went to her place, never the other way around.

The only exception to this rule was Alfred. Alfred was my first cousin—the son of my mother's sister, Titi Aurora. And just as Titi Aurora was much older than Mami, and more of a mother to her than a sister, Alfred, being sixteen years older than I, acted more as an uncle to me than a cousin. Sometimes my father would ask Alfred to bring him a bottle from the liquor store. We counted on Alfred a lot, in part because my father avoided driving. This annoyed me, as it clearly contributed to our isolation—and what's the point of having a car if you never drive it? I didn't understand until I was older that his drinking was probably the reason.

My father would cook dinner when he got home from work; he was an excellent cook and could re-create from memory any new dish he encountered, as well as the Puerto Rican standards he no doubt picked up in Abuelita's kitchen. I loved every dish he made without exception, even his liver and onions, which Junior hated and shoveled over to me when Papi's back was turned. But as soon as dinner was over, the dishes still piled in the sink, he would shut himself in the bedroom. We wouldn't see him again until he came out to tell

17

us to get ready for bed. It was just Junior and I every night, doing homework and not much else. Junior wasn't much of a conversationalist yet. Eventually, we got a television, which helped to fill the silence.

My mother's way of coping was to avoid being at home with my father. She worked the night shift as a practical nurse at Prospect Hospital and often on weekends, too. When she wasn't working, she would drop us off at Abuelita's or sometimes at her sister Aurora's apartment and then disappear for hours with another of my aunts. Even though my mother and I shared the same bed every night (Junior slept in the other room with Papi), she might as well have been a log, lying there with her back to me. My father's neglect made me sad, but I intuitively understood that he could not help himself; my mother's neglect made me angry at her. She was beautiful, always elegantly dressed, seemingly strong and decisive. She was the one who moved us to the projects. Unlike my aunts, she chose to work. She was the one who insisted we go to Catholic school. Unfairly perhaps, I expected more from her.

However much was said at home, and loudly, much also went unsaid, and in that atmosphere I was a watchful child constantly scanning the adults for cues and listening in on their conversations. My sense of security depended on what information I could glean, any clue dropped inadvertently when they didn't realize a child was paying attention. My aunts and my mother would gather in Abuelita's kitchen, drinking coffee and gossiping. "*¡No me molestes!* Go play in the other room now," an aunt would say, shooing me away, but I overheard much regardless: how my father had broken the lock on Titi Gloria's liquor cabinet, ruining her favorite piece of furniture; how whenever Junior and I slept over with our cousins, my father would phone every fifteen minutes all night long, asking, "Did you feed them? Did you give them a bath?"

When my mother wasn't present, the gossip would take a familiar turn, my grandmother saying something like "Maybe if Celina ever came home, he wouldn't be drinking every night. If those kids had a mother who ever cooked a meal, Juli wouldn't be worrying about them all night." As much as I adored Abuelita—and no one resented my mother's absence more than I did—I couldn't bear this constant blaming. And often my mother's efforts to please Abuelita—whether a generously chosen gift or her ready services as a nurse—went dimly acknowledged. Even being Abuelita's favorite, I felt exposed and unmoored when she criticized my mother, whom I struggled to understand and forgive myself.

One overheard conversation had a lasting effect, though I now remember it only vaguely. My father was sick: he had passed out, and Mami took him to the hospital. Tío Vitín and Tío Benny came to get Junior and me, and they were talking in the elevator about how our home was a pigsty, with dishes in the sink and no toilet paper. They spoke as if we weren't there. When I realized what they were saying, my stomach lurched with shame. After that I washed the dishes every night, even the pots and pans, as soon as we finished dinner. I also dusted the living room once a week. Even though no one ever came over, the house was always clean. And when I went shopping with Papi on Fridays, I made sure we bought toilet paper. And milk. More than enough milk.

The biggest fight my parents ever had was because of the milk. At dinnertime, Papi was pouring a glass for me, and his hands were shaking so badly the milk spilled all over the table. I cleaned up the mess, and he tried again with the same result. "Papi, please don't!" I kept repeating. It was all I could do to keep myself from crying; I was utterly powerless to stop him. "Papi, I don't want any milk!" But he didn't stop until the carton was empty. When my mother got home from work later and there was no milk for her coffee, all hell broke loose. Papi was the one who had spilled the milk, but I was the one who felt guilty.

Two

Abuelita was going to cook for a party, and she wanted me to come with her to buy the chickens. I was the only one who ever went with her to the *vivero*.

I loved Abuelita, totally and without reservation, and her apartment on Southern Boulevard was a safe haven from my parents' storms at home. I was determined to grow up to be just like her, to age with the same ungraying, exuberant grace. Not that we looked much alike: she had very dark eyes, darker than mine, and a long face with a pointed nose, framed by long straight hair—nothing like my pudgy nose and short, curly mop. But otherwise we recognized in each other a twin spirit and enjoyed a bond beyond explanation, a deep emotional resonance that sometimes seemed telepathic. We were so much alike, in fact, that people called me Mercedita—little Mercedes—which was a source of great pride for me.

Nelson, who among my many cousins was closest to me in age as well as my inseparable coconspirator in every adventure, also had a special connection with Abuelita. But even Nelson never wanted to go with Abuelita to the *vivero* on Saturday mornings because of the smell. It wasn't just the chickens that smelled. They had baby goats in pens and pigeons and ducks and rabbits in cages stacked up against a long wall. The cages were stacked so high that Abuelita would climb up a ladder on wheels to see into the top rows. The birds would all be squawking and clucking and flapping and screeching. There were feathers in the air and sticking to the wet floor, which was slippery when they hosed it down, and there were turkeys with mean eyes watching you. Abuelita inspected all the chickens to find a plump and lively one.

"*Mira*, Sonia, see that one in the corner just sitting there with droopy eyes?"

"He looks like he's falling asleep."

"That's a bad sign. But this one, see how he's ready to fight the others when they come close? He's feisty and fat, and I promise you he's tasty."

After Abuelita picked out the very best chicken, it was my job to watch them butcher it while she waited in line for eggs. In a room all closed up in glass, a man stood breaking necks, one after another, and a machine plucked the feathers. Another man cleaned the birds, and another weighed each one and wrapped it up in paper. It was a fast-moving line, as in a factory. I had to watch carefully to make sure that the chicken we'd chosen was the one we got in the end. I was supposed to tell Abuelita if they mixed them up, but it never happened.

We would walk back under the crisscrossed shadows of the train tracks overhead, up Westchester Avenue toward Southern Boulevard and home—which is what Abuelita's house felt like to me. Of course Abuelita's house wasn't a real house like the one her daughter Titi Gloria lived in, in the far northern part of the Bronx, with a front porch and rosebushes. Abuelita lived in a five-story tenement, three apartments to a floor, with a fire escape that zigzagged up the front, like our old building on Kelly Street, where we lived before moving to the projects.

As we walked back, Abuelita would stop to choose vegetables from the crates that were lined up on the sidewalk. For almost every meal she fried *tostones,* so we'd buy green plantains, and also peppers, some green ones and some little sweet ones, and onions, tomatoes, *recao,* and garlic to make *sofrito.* She would always haggle, and though she made it sound as if she were complaining about the quality and how expensive everything was, by the end she'd be laughing with the *vendedor.* All these years later, an open market still stirs in me the urge to haggle the way I learned from Abuelita.

"¿Sonia, quieres una china?"

Abuelita loved oranges, but they were expensive most of the year, so we would buy just one to share as a treat, and she'd ask me to choose. My father taught me how to choose fruit—how to make sure it's ripe by smelling its sweetness. My father had shown me how to choose good meat, too, with enough fat for flavor, and how to recognize if it's not fresh. I went grocery shopping with Papi on Fridays, which was payday. Those shopping trips were the best times of the week for me, not counting my days at Abuelita's. Papi and I would walk to the new Pathmark that was built on the empty lot near our projects and come home with our cart filled. I'd pull the cart while Papi toted the extra bags that didn't fit.

With Abuelita, our shopping trip would conclude with a final stop to pick up bread and milk at the bodega a few doors down from her place. The bodega, a tiny grocery store, is the heart of every Hispanic neighborhood and a lifeline in areas with no supermarkets in walking distance. In those days, the bread they sold was so fresh that its warm smell filled the store. Abuelita would give me *la tetita*, the crunchy end, even though she liked it too, I knew. The bodega was always crowded with the same guys. They sat in the corner, reading *El Diario* and arguing about the news. Sometimes one of them would read the *Daily News* and explain to the others in Spanish what it said. I could tell when he was improvising or embellishing the story; I knew what news sounded like in English. The stairs up to Abuelita's third-floor apartment were narrow and dark, and Abuelita didn't have an elevator to rely on as we did. But in the projects, the elevator was more than a convenience: Junior and I were absolutely forbidden to take the stairs, where my mother had once been mugged and where addicts regularly shot up, littering the scene with needles and other paraphernalia. I can still hear Mami's warning that we should never, but never, touch those needles or take that junk: if we did, we would surely die.

Mami and my aunts would often be at Abuelita's when we got back, crowded into the kitchen for coffee and gossip. Abuelita would join them while I joined Nelson and my other cousins at the bedroom window to make faces at the passengers zipping by on the elevated train that ran just at the height of Abuelita's apartment. Gallego, my step-grandfather, would be busy with his own preparations for the party, choosing the dance music. His hands trembled slightly with Parkinson's disease, still in its early stages then, as he lined up the record albums.

Once a month, my mother and aunts would help Abuelita make *sofrito*, the Puerto Rican vegetable and spice base that enhances the flavors in any dish. Abuelita's kitchen would turn into a factory, with all of the women cleaning and peeling, slicing and chopping. They would fill up jars and jars of the stuff, enough for a month's worth of dinners in each of their homes, and enough for the Saturday parties, too. On the table, waiting for their turn in the blender, were big piles of chopped peppers, onions, tomatoes: my target.

"Sonia, get your hands out of there!"

"Give me that! *¡Te vas a enfermar!* You'll get sick; you can't eat it raw!" Oh yes I can. I inherited adventurous taste buds from Papi and Abuelita, and I'll still happily eat many things more timid palates won't venture.

When we went to Abuelita's for the parties that happened most Saturdays, Mami made the hopeless effort to have me get dressed up. My dress would get wrinkled or stained almost immediately, and ribbons never stayed put in my hair. By contrast, my cousin Miriam—Nelson's sister and Titi Carmen's daughter—always looked like a princess doll in a glass case, no matter the occasion. It would take me most of my life to feel remotely put together, and it's still an effort.

As soon as the door opened, I would catapult into Abuelita's arms. Wherever in the apartment she was, I would find her first.

"Sonia, careful!" Mami would say to me. "We just got here and already you're a mess." And then, to Abuelita, "Too much energy, too much talking, too much running around. I'm sorry, Mercedes, I don't know what to do with her."

"*Para*, Celina. Let the child be. There's nothing wrong with her except too much energy." Abuelita was on my side, always, and Mami was always apologizing to Abuelita. Sometimes even I wanted to say "*¡Para, Mami!*"

Next I would run to find Nelson, who would invariably be lying on the bed reading a comic book while waiting for me. Nelson was a genius, and my best friend on top of being my cousin. I never got bored talking to him. He could figure out how anything worked, and together we pondered mysteries of the natural world, like gravity. He was up for any game I could devise, including jousting knights, which involved charging at each other across the living room, each carrying on his or her back a younger brother armed with a broom or a mop. Miriam tried to stop us, but it didn't prevent Eddie, her little brother, from falling off Nelson and breaking a leg. When the screams of pain brought my aunt running, the blame was assigned, as usual, before any facts were established: "Sonia! What did you do now?" Another walloping for that one.

Tío Benny, who was Nelson, Miriam, and Eddie's dad, was determined that Nelson would grow up to be a doctor. In my eyes, Tío Benny was the ideal father. He spent time with his kids and took them on outings, which occasionally included me, too. He spoke English, which meant he could go to parent-teacher conferences. Best of all, he didn't drink. I would have traded fathers with Nelson in a heartbeat. But sadly, for all his brilliance, Nelson wouldn't live up to Tío Benny's dreams, and I would do well despite a less than perfect father.

Abuelita's apartment was small enough that wherever we settled down to play, the warm smells of her feast would find us, beckoning like cartoon ribbons in the air. Garlic and onions calling, still the happiest smells I know.

"Mercedes, you should open your own restaurant."

"Don't be shy, there's plenty."

The dominoes never stopped for dinner. The game was serious. Someone would have to lose the whole match and give up the seat before even thinking about food. "*¿Tú estás ciego?* It's right in front of your eyes!" They'd yell a lot and pretend to be angry.

"Benny, wake up and look at what you have!" Mami would

counter. She was good at this and could keep track of every bone played.

"Hey, no cheating! How many times are you going to cough? Somebody get this man a drink, he's choking!"

"Don't look at me, I'm honest. Mercedes is the one who cheats."

"I know you have that *ficha*, so play it!"

"Nice one, Celina."

Gallego would be out of the game, calling foul as he went. He'd pick up his *güiro* and strum a ratchety rhythm on the gourd, playing along with the record, as if he wished someone would show up with a guitar. Instead, sooner or later someone would lift the needle off the record, cutting off Los Panchos mid-song. The voices in the living room would settle to a hush, and all eyes would turn to Abuelita, resting on the couch, having cleaned up and taken a turn at dominoes. When the music stopped, that was the cue for those in the kitchen to crowd in the doorway of the living room. Nelson and I would scramble to a spot under the table where we could see. It was time for poetry.

Abuelita stands up, closes her eyes, and takes a deep breath. When she opens them and begins to recite, her voice is different. Deeper, and vibrant in a way that makes you hold your breath to listen.

> *Por fin, corazón, por fin,*
> *alienta con la esperanza . . .*

I couldn't understand the words exactly, but that didn't matter. The feeling of the poem came through clearly in the music of Abuelita's voice and in the look of faraway longing in the faces of her listeners.

Her long black hair is tied back simply and her dress is plain, but to my eyes she looks more glamorous than anyone trying to be fancy. Now her arms stretch wide and her skirt swirls as she turns, reaching for the whole horizon. You can almost see green mountains, the sea and the sky unfolding, the whole world being born as she lifts her hand. As it turns, her fingers spread open like a flower blooming in the sun.

> . . . *y va la tierra brotando*
> *como Venus de la espuma.*

I look around. She has the whole room mesmerized. Titi Carmen wipes a tear.

> *Para poder conocerla*
> *es preciso compararla,*
> *de lejos en sueños verla;*
> *y para saber quererla*
> *es necesario dejarla.*
> *¡Oh! no envidie tu belleza,*
> *de otra inmensa población*
> *el poder y la riqueza,*
> *que allí vive la cabeza,*

y aquí vive el corazón.
Y si vivir es sentir,
y si vivir es pensar . . .

The poems that Abuelita and her listeners loved were often in the key of nostalgia and drenched in rosy sunset hues that obscured the poverty, disease, and natural disasters they had left behind. Not that their yearnings were unfounded. As the poet says, "To know it, you need to see it in dreams from afar. To learn how to love it, you need to leave it." Even those of the generations following who were born here, who have settled decisively into a mainland existence and rarely have reason to visit the island—even we have corners of our hearts where such a nostalgia lingers. All it takes to spark it is a poem, or a song like *"En Mi Viejo San Juan."*

The parties always wound down late. The stragglers had to be fed; Charlie and Tony, Titi Gloria's sons, might stop by after their Saturday-night dates. Most others would say their good-byes and go home, like Tío Vitín and Titi Judy, who typically left carrying their kids, my cousins Lillian and Elaine, fast asleep, drooped over a shoulder.

But for those who remained, what often happened next was the climax of the evening. The *velada* was something that no one ever talked about; adults would change the subject casually if a kid asked a question. The kitchen table would be cleared and moved into the living room. A couple of neighbors from downstairs would appear, joining the party quietly.

My mother and Titi Gloria would retire to the kitchen. Mami thought the whole business was silly and didn't want any part of it. Titi Gloria was actually scared of the spirits.

The remaining kids—Nelson, Miriam, Eddie, Junior, and I—would be corralled in the bedroom and ordered to sleep. We knew that nothing would happen until the adults believed we were snoozing, and they were dead serious about this. Somehow they failed to reckon with the power of my curiosity, or how easily I could impose my will on the other kids. We all lay on the bed in watchful silence, perfectly still, waiting.

There was just enough light coming from the street and through the curtains on the glazed doors separating the bedroom from the living room to make the atmosphere cozy or spooky, depending on your mood. I could hear the fading rumble of the El train going by. I could hear by their breathing when Junior and Eddie both conked out.

As we lay there, my mind would rehearse what Charlie had told us: how Abuelita and Gallego called the spirits to ask them questions; how they were not evil but they were powerful, and you had to develop your own powers if you wanted their help; how Abuelita's spirit guide was called Madamita Sandorí and spoke with a Jamaican accent. His eyes got wide just talking about it. Charlie and Tony were Alfred's age, an in-between generation much older than the rest of the cousins. Charlie was adult enough that they let him sit at the table for the *velada*. Gallego, who was as skilled an

31

espiritista as Abuelita, wanted to teach Charlie, but Charlie did not want that responsibility. It was one thing to have the gift, quite another to dedicate yourself and study it.

As strange as they were, Charlie's reports of the supernatural made sense. They weren't like Alfred's unbelievable stories, about the ghosts of dead *jíbaros* riding horses around San Germán, intended only to scare us. I knew that Abuelita used her magic on the side of good. She used it for healing and for protecting the people she loved. Of course I understood that a person with a talent for engaging the spirit world could equally put it to work for darker ends—*brujería*, or witchcraft. In Abuelita's own building one of the neighbors was known to put curses on people. I was forbidden to go near her door on penalty of getting smacked, which was something Abuelita had never done, so I knew she meant it.

Finally, the little bell would ring very softly. That was the cue. Nelson, Miriam, and I would climb off the bed and sneak up to the glazed doors. We'd stick our noses to the panes, peering through the tiny gaps at the edge of the curtain stretched and pinned over the glass. All I could see was the backs of chairs, the backs of heads, shoulders hunched by candlelight in a tight circle around the table. The bell would tinkle again, but except for that one clear note it was impossible to make out any sounds through the door.

I would carefully open the door a tiny crack, and we would huddle to listen. It was good to be close together, just in case. Gallego would always be the first to talk, and not in his usual voice. It didn't sound like Spanish, but it wasn't

English, either. It sounded like someone chewing words and swallowing them. Choking on them. Then the voice coming out of Gallego would moan louder until the table moved, seeming to rise off the floor, signaling the spirits' arrival. Miriam, trembling, would scoot back into bed fast. I wouldn't give up so easily. But no matter how hard I tried, I couldn't decipher the garbled words. After Nelson and I got tired of trying, we'd join Miriam in bed. Nelson would pull the blanket over his head and whisper in mock exasperation, "How do they expect us to sleep with a house full of spirits?" We'd all lie still for a minute. Then Nelson would pretend to snore very softly, and Miriam and I would start giggling.

Except for my very earliest memories, when we still lived on Kelly Street in the same tenement as Abuelita, my father hardly ever came along to the parties. It was easier that way. On the rare occasions when he did come—on Mother's Day or Thanksgiving—I was nervous, watching and waiting for the inevitable signs of trouble. Even in the midst of the wildest mayhem that Nelson and I could concoct, even sinking my teeth into Abuelita's irresistible crispy chicken, even when everyone else was lost in music and laughter, I would be watching my father from the corner of my eye. It would start almost imperceptibly. His fingers would slowly curl up into claws. Then his face gradually scrunched up, just slightly at first, until finally it was frozen into a contorted grimace.

I usually noticed the early signs before my mother did,

and for an agonizing interval I watched them both, waiting for her to notice. As soon as she did, there would be sharp words. It was time to go home, while he could still walk. I didn't have a name for what was happening, didn't understand what alcoholic neuropathy was. I only knew that I saw my father receding from us, disappearing behind that twisted mask. It was like being trapped in a horror film, complete with his lumbering Frankenstein walk as he made his exit and the looming certainty that there would be screaming when we got home.

Best were the times when I didn't have to go home. Most Saturday nights I stayed over at Abuelita's. When there was a party, Mami would take Junior home; Tío Benny and Titi Carmen somehow managed to get Nelson, Miriam, and Eddie down the street and into their own beds.

When I woke up in the morning, I would have Abuelita all to myself. She would stand at the stove in the housecoat she always wore for an apron, her pockets full of cigarettes and tissues, making the thick, fluffy pancakes she knew I loved. Those mornings were heaven. When Mami came to take me home later, I would kiss Abuelita good-bye. *"Bendición, Abuelita."* She would hug me and say without fail every time we parted, *"Que Dios te bendiga, te favorezca y te libre de todo mal y peligro."* May God bless you, favor you, and deliver you from all evil and danger. Just her saying it made it so.

Three

"This is my mother, Sonia, your *bisabuela*," said Abuelita. "Give her a kiss." The cheek that was my target was wrinkled and translucent, so fragile that I feared my lips would bruise it. Her eyes were blank. As I leaned in to kiss her, she seemed to pull away, but it was just the rocking chair easing back from my weight. There was no spark of awareness or curiosity. I don't know if I was more disturbed by this absence that gave no hint of how I should relate to her or by the shadow of Abuelita's features that I could see arranged inanimately on her mother's face.

Bisabuela Ciriata was in her nineties, though she looked two hundred years old to me. Her rocking chair of carved wood and woven cane tilted between this world and another that was beyond imagining.

We were in an area of San Juan called Santurce. Abuelita

visited with her sisters and brothers while I played on the balcony or in half-hidden gardens. There had been ten of them all together, she said (Diezilita, Piatrina, Angelina, Eloys . . .), but I couldn't keep track or tell sisters and brothers from cousins and uncles and aunts. We were in a city, but it seemed to teeter on the edge of dissolving into nature. Vines snaked under iron fences and up balustrades. Chickens scrabbled under hibiscus bushes and bright yellow canario flowers. I watched the afternoon rains pour down like a curtain enclosing the balcony, rutting the street below with muddy streams, pounding on the corrugated roofs and wooden walls until Abuelita called me inside to a treat for *merienda*—maybe a *tembleque*, a gelatin made of coconut milk and sweetened condensed milk, or fruits that I'd never seen in New York: guavas with their sharp perfume, *quenepas* with pits as big as grapes and a thin layer of featherlight flesh that puckered your mouth when you sucked on it, and mangoes of a melting sweetness unlike any I had tasted back home. At night, I slept with Abuelita in a room crowded with sisters and cousins, and the mosquito nets transformed our bed into a cozy hideaway among gauzy clouds. The traffic noise gave way to the rickety rhythm of the ceiling fan and *coquís*—the tiny musical frogs that are a symbol of the island—chirping in the shadows as I drifted to sleep.

On my earliest trips to Puerto Rico, when I was small—including my first as a toddler—it was just Abuelita and I. My mother was determined that she would never, ever go back to the island, but then she changed her mind. Some of the best summer vacations I remember were traveling with my mother and Junior to Mayagüez to visit her family.

In Mayagüez, we usually stayed at Titi Maria's house. She was the first wife of Tío Mayo, my mother's eldest brother. Titi Maria helped to look after my mother when she was small, and their family bond outlasted the marriage. My mother is close to Tío Mayo's later families, too; she has a talent for not taking sides, which is handy in a complicated extended family. It is a trait I've adopted, trying never to lose contact with cousins and second cousins whose parents have separated or divorced. We visit with everybody.

At Titi Maria's house, my cousin Papo always prepared a special welcome. Waiting for me under the sink would be two whole shopping bags of mangoes that he'd gathered from under the trees up the hill in anticipation of our arrival. I ate them all day long, in spite of constant warnings that I would get sick. Looking back, I suspect I was getting a higher dosage of insulin than I needed—not uncommon for juvenile diabetics in that day—making the added sugar manageable. In any case, I hated the sluggish feeling that high blood sugar brought on, and I didn't need reminding. I might have had to eat less of something else, but I could indulge my lust for mangoes.

At lunchtime, the whole family came home from work, and Titi Maria cooked a big meal for all her kids—my adult cousins—and some of their kids, too. Even those who lived elsewhere would often come for that meal. After lunch we settled down for a siesta. I would read a book—sleep wouldn't come to me easily—but I loved this time when everyone was gathered at home and quietly connected.

Papo had a job designing window displays for a number of big stores on the island. He claimed to be the first person doing this work as a professional designer in Puerto Rico, and he often traveled to New York to gather ideas. Charo was a high school teacher. Minita was the senior executive secretary for the newspaper *El Mundo*. Evita worked in a government office. It was clear to me even then that the people I knew on the island had better jobs than the Puerto Ricans I knew in New York. When we walked down the street in Mayagüez, it gave me a proud thrill to read the little signs above the doors, of the doctors, the lawyers, and the other professionals who were Puerto Rican. It was not something I had often seen in New York. At the hospital where my mother worked, there were Puerto Rican nurses but only one Puerto Rican doctor. At the larger shops and businesses in the Bronx, there were Puerto Rican workers but rarely managers or owners.

Tío Mayo's *panadería* was my favorite place to visit. They called it a *panadería*, but it was much more than a bakery. There were loaves of bread and rolls that Tío Mayo started making while it was still dark outside, kept warm in a special case with a heat lamp. There were cases full of cakes and pastries filled with cream, homemade cheese, and guava jam. My uncle's then wife, Titi Elisa, also got up early to make lunch and snacks to sell to the workers who sewed in the factory across the street. She fried the chicken and roasted the pork, made stews and meat pies and pots of rice and beans. The smells of her cooking mixed with the yeasty smell of the bread, and the coffee, and the whole amazing cloud of flavors spread down the street and up into the balconies.

When the noon whistle blew at the factory, the bakery would fill up in minutes. I helped with serving, and I loved the two-handed challenge of the lunch hour rush. I knew the price of every item, and I knew how to make change—I was discovering that I had a facility with numbers, which I inherited from Papi—and Titi Elisa would let me work the cash register when my uncle wasn't around. Although he had seen me in action, he couldn't quite believe it. He wasn't comfortable with the idea of girls handling money.

When I wasn't busy helping, I played with my cousin Tito in the alleyway behind the bakery, reenacting scenes from *The Three Stooges*. Tito was Moe and I was Curly. We could usually convince Junior or someone else to be Larry, the third *chiflado*, but only Tito and I knew all the moves and the right sound effects: a twang for a fake eye poke, a ratchety sound for an ear twist, and the all-purpose "Nyuk! Nyuk! Nyuk!"

Before she left Puerto Rico, my mother had lived in Lajas and San Germán and had seen very little of the island beyond the neighborhoods of her childhood. She was eager to show us places that she'd heard about but had never seen herself. We went to the beach at Luquillo. It was nothing like Orchard Beach in the Bronx, which was the only beach I knew. There were no traffic jams in Puerto Rico, no waiting for hours packed in a hot car to get there, no dirty sand, no standing in line for the bathroom. Progress has caught up with the island since my childhood, and it has its share of traffic jams, but the water is still warm and clear, and the sand is perfectly white. When you look down into the water, you can see the bottom, and it rolls out blue until it meets the blue of the sky.

Of all the sights, the art museum in Ponce left the deepest impression. I had never been to a museum before. The building is beautiful and seemed to me then as grand as a castle with its staircase that sweeps in a big circle on two sides. It was so magnificent that I just had to run up and down the stairs to see what it felt like. It felt horrible when the guard yelled at me. So I walked slowly and looked at the paintings one by one.

I figured out that portraits were pictures in which a person from olden times just stood there or sat, wearing fancy clothes and staring very seriously. I wondered who these people were. Why did an artist choose *them* to be in a picture? How much work was it to paint this? How long did he have to stand there like that? Other paintings were more like stories, though I didn't know what the story was. Why did she cut off his head? I could tell that this dove was not just an ordinary dove that happened to be flying by. I could see that it had a meaning, even though I didn't know what the meaning was. When I got tired of not understanding the stories, I noticed other things: Sometimes you could see the brushstrokes and the thickness of the paint; other times it was smooth, without texture. Sometimes things in the distance were smaller, and it felt as if you could reach into the space; other times it was flat like a map. I wondered, were these the things I *should* be noticing? I could tell that there was more going on than I could describe or understand.

"Sonia, we're going to visit your grandfather. My father." This got my attention. My mother had never so much as mentioned his existence before. When I questioned her, she answered in a voice that sounded as if she were reading aloud from the small print on the back of a package of medicine. "I don't know the man. He left when I was born. I haven't seen him since then. But Tío Mayo and Titi Aurora want me to come with them to the hospital to see him, and they say you should come too." The unknown grandfather was not the whole mystery. I usually knew what Mami was thinking from the flash in her voice, the speed of her smile, as rare as it was then, the telltale arch of her brows. This woman speaking with such flat indifference was not the mother I knew.

Tío Mayo led us to the bed at the far end of the room, by the window. As we walked the length of the ward, I hardly saw the patients in the other beds, so intently was I focused on my mother and our looming destination. Nothing was going to slip by me, though I had no idea what to expect or even what I should be wondering about. Would she greet him with a kiss? How do you relate to a father you don't know?

He had Mami's light eyes. Framed by the white of his hair, the white mustache, the white of the sheets, their sea-green color seemed even lighter, bluer, more startling. He was a handsome man but gaunt. His arms were just sticks poking from the sleeves of the hospital gown. A thousand questions ran through my head, but I didn't dare speak any of them out loud: Why did you leave Mami behind? Who are you? Do you have a wife? Do you have other kids? Where have you been living?

I climbed onto the chair and watched. My mother walked up to the bed and stood looking down at the old man. In an ice-cold voice she said, *"Yo soy Celina."* That was it. He didn't say anything to her. He didn't ask how her life had been, what it was now. There were no tears, no revelations.

Titi Aurora, who often went to Puerto Rico to visit friends and sort out family problems, led me by the hand to the bedside and introduced me. I got barely a nod from him. I retreated, climbed back onto the chair, and watched as Titi Aurora chattered about nothing and fluffed his pillows. Tío Mayo was there and not there, talking to the nurses, taking care of business. But in all this nothing, I understood something: that my mother had been wounded as deeply as a human being could be.

Four

It was in April of the year that I turned nine. I was heading straight home after school that day because Papi had stayed home sick from work. Usually, Junior and I would go to Ana's first and then play outside till Papi got home. I didn't need to check in with Ana, because she would know that Papi was home. My mother had coffee with Ana every day before she went to work; there was nothing about each other's lives that they didn't know instantly.

When we came around the corner, I could see Moncho, Ana's husband, hanging out the window on the third floor of their building, washing the windows but also looking intently at passersby. That was odd, I thought. When he saw me, he waved at me. He didn't stop. He kept on waving furiously, signaling to me, and then he yelled "Sonia! Junior! Come upstairs!" in a voice that meant business. Junior bounced ahead of me, happy to see Moncho.

But when Ana opened the door, something was terribly wrong. Her eyes were puffy from crying, and her face was pale. This wasn't some everyday fuss that just happened to reach the level of tears; something had shaken her deeply. She wouldn't explain, but she started to cry and made us wait while she phoned Mami, saying to Moncho, "Celina should tell them." Moncho was quieter than I'd ever seen him. This was all so strange that I was scared but also riveted as I watched to see what would happen next. Ana said, "Let's go," and we walked downstairs and across the way to our building. It was the shortest of walks, but it took forever. It was hard to move my legs, as if dread were weighing them down.

Alfred opened the door to our apartment. His eyes too were red. Tío Vitín was there, and I could hear other voices. I looked into the living room and saw many faces looking back at me with the same teary gaze. Mami was sitting in the chair by the telephone in the hallway, staring into space, her eyes wide and wet. Junior said to her, "Where's Papi?"

"Dios se lo llevó."

God took him. I could see that Junior didn't understand. I did. She meant that Papi had died. But what did *that* mean? Had he become a spirit? I didn't know what I was supposed to feel, or say, or do. As if from a far distance, I could hear my own voice joining all the other voices crying. I ran down the hall and threw myself on the bed. I was sobbing, pounding my fists, when Ana entered the room.

"Sonia, you have to be a big girl now. Your mother's very upset; you can't cry anymore. You have to be strong for your *mami*."

So that's what I'm supposed to do? I stopped crying. "I'm okay, Ana." She left me alone. The stillness in the room was louder than the noise down the hall. I remembered that morning how Papi had called out from the bathroom, saying that since he wasn't going to work, he wanted to make us a Sunday breakfast, even though it was a weekday. Mami had yelled: "Go back to bed if you're sick, the kids don't have time, they have to get to school, and why are you taking so long shaving?"

We had been at the funeral home for hours. It felt like forever, but my mother and Abuelita and my aunts had been there even longer, for days. It was important not to leave the body alone, and they all had to keep one another company. Mami didn't want Junior and me to come, but Titi Aurora insisted, because the nuns and Monsignor Hart were coming from Blessed Sacrament. It wouldn't be respectful if Junior and I weren't there when they showed up.

The room smelled of flowers, cologne, and perfume masking a mustiness. People were speaking in whispers, looking at the floor, shaking their heads. There was talk of premonitions, a greeting or casual word exchanged with my father over the last few days that now took on greater significance; the way he had shaved and dressed up that morning, even though he

45

was home sick. As if he had known. Everyone agreed that he was a good man, a family man, and that forty-two was a tragically young age to go. And Celina so young, too, a widow at thirty-six with two young kids!

My aunts took turns crying. Abuelita never stopped. I sat down next to her on the couch and held her hand. Abuelita's crying was unbearably painful to me. I couldn't even tell if I had any sadness of my own, because I was so full of Abuelita's sadness. I worried that her spirit had been torn apart so painfully by Papi's death that she might never be happy again. What would happen to me if she died too?

The nuns and Monsignor Hart came and went. Dr. Fisher came too, and some people from the factory where Papi worked. All the while, Mami just sat there. Her eyes were open, but she was not really present, not even answering when people talked to her. Titi Aurora had to tell her to say thank you to Monsignor Hart.

What happens next is that I'm supposed to say good-bye to Papi, Titi Aurora says. She wants me to kiss him. I want to scream "No!" but I swallow it because I don't want to upset Abuelita any more than she's upset already. "*No tengas miedo*, Sonia. Touch his hand." I'm not afraid, but I'm not okay, either. This thing with a powdery white face resembles my father, but it's not him, and it's certainly not something I want to touch. But I close my eyes and get it over with.

A part of me was not surprised by what happened then. A knot that had been tied tight inside me for longer than I can remember began to come loose. Deep down, I'd known for a while that this was where Papi was heading. Looking at this thing that was not Papi, I realized that he was not coming back. From here, Mami, Junior, and I would be going along without him. Maybe it would be easier this way.

We had been sleeping at Abuelita's every night since Papi died, because my mother couldn't bear to go back to our apartment. That meant getting up very early in the morning so Mami could get us to school on time, after which she would go to Ana's. They would drink coffee and talk and cry together until school was out, and then she would take us back to Abuelita's. Fortunately, the building manager at Bronxdale Houses let us move into a different apartment very quickly. It was over on Watson Avenue on the second floor—much better than the seventh floor if you'd rather not see what happens in the stairwells. It was much closer to Blessed Sacrament, too. Best of all, my mother was able to change her schedule at the hospital. She didn't have to work nights anymore, so she could be at home after school.

Tío Vitín and my cousin Alfred helped us with the move. They cleaned out Papi's room and carried out a big bag of clanking empty bottles. They found those flat half-pint bottles, drained of Seagram's Seven, under the mattress, in the closet, behind the drawers, in his coat pockets, his trousers, his shirts, in every jacket. There was even one hidden inside the lining of a coat.

It occurred to me that every day when he came home from work and sent us off with pennies for candy and fifteen minutes more to play, my father was keeping us outside just long enough to have a drink before starting dinner. Junior, who had slept in the same room with Papi, in the other twin bed, and sometimes only pretended to be asleep, now confessed that he had known all along about the bottles under the mattress. I always slept with my mother in the other room, and nothing ever woke me up once I fell asleep. I wondered what else I had missed.

I do know that my father loved us. But as much as he loved us, it wasn't enough to stop him from drinking. To the end, Abuelita and my aunts blamed my mother for Papi's drinking. It's true that Mami could say all the wrong things; neither of them knew how to stop an argument once they started. But I knew too that my mother didn't make him drink any more than she could make him stop. I knew he did this to himself; even as a child, I knew he was the only one responsible.

All those hours that he sat by the window looking out . . . I treasured those times when I stood beside him, inhaling the scent of Old Spice up close and of rice and beans bubbling in the background, and he told me what he imagined the future would be: all the different stores they would build on the empty lots around us, or how one day a rocket ship would carry a man to the full moon that was rising, low and yellow, over the South Bronx. The truth is, though, that for each of those moments, there were so many more long hours of sadness, when he stared in silence at the vacant lots, at the highway and the brick walls, at a city and a life that slowly strangled him.

On the day we moved in, it smelled of fresh paint. The view from the new apartment on Watson Avenue was different. You could see the school yard at Blessed Sacrament from our window. The kids had left for the day, but there were still two guys practicing shots on the basketball court. Farther back, one of the nuns was walking along by the buildings, but I couldn't tell who it was under the black bonnet. . . . As I looked out the window, a memory came to me of something that had happened the day Papi died, which I'd almost forgotten in all the commotion that followed. I was down in the school yard at recess, standing by the fence, looking this way toward the projects—and I thought about him. It wasn't a normal thought that pops into your head or one that's connected to the thought that came before it. More of a feeling than a thought, but almost not even a feeling: like the barest shadow of a mood passing over, or a breeze so perfectly soft that nothing moves. I didn't know yet what had happened, but maybe that was Papi himself, saying good-bye.

Five

In the days and weeks following the funeral, the release and relief I felt from the end of the fighting gave way to anxious puzzlement. At nine, I was equipped to understand loss, even sadness, but not grief, not someone else's and certainly not my own. I couldn't figure out what was wrong with Mami, and it scared me.

Every day Junior and I came home from school to find the apartment quiet and dark, with the curtains drawn. Mami would come out just long enough to cook dinner, leaving the back bedroom, where she passed hour after hour with the door closed and the lights out. (Junior and I shared the front bedroom in the new apartment on Watson Avenue, using the twin beds that had been in Papi's room in the old place.) After serving dinner like a zombie, hardly saying a word, she would go right back into her room. So even though she was working the early shift now and getting home in the afternoon before us, we saw no more of her than when she'd been working late. We did homework. We watched TV. We did homework and watched TV.

On weekends, I was able to rouse Mami to go grocery shopping, retracing my father's steps. I remembered what Papi used to buy, and that was what I put in the basket, though I wasn't sure Mami would know what to do with everything. I missed Papi's cooking. I missed Papi. Somehow, when he died, I had taken it for granted that our lives would be better. I hadn't counted on this gloom.

I wasn't the only one who was worried about my mother. I overheard some of her friends talking to Ana, and they decided one of them would pay a call at Blessed Sacrament to ask Father Dolan to come visit Celina. His refusal, as reported over coffee at Ana's, enraged me, all the more so because of the reason: my mother didn't go to church on Sunday.

It was true, but she did send her kids to church and always with money for the offering basket. And she worked long hours at the hospital so we could go to school at Blessed Sacrament. Shouldn't Father Dolan be forgiving if she needed help? Even if he thought she wasn't Christian enough, I reasoned, shouldn't he be more Christian?

Another week passed in darkness and silence. Another friend of my mother's, Cristina, asked the pastor at her church to visit Mami. He'd never even met her before, and of course she'd never been to his church, which was Baptist. But that didn't stop him from coming. They talked quietly together for hours. I was impressed that he spoke Spanish; whether or not he had anything to say that could help, at least he cared enough to try. That I respected.

As spring turned to summer, Mami stayed shut in her darkened room, and I found myself on summer vacation longing for school to start. I didn't feel like playing outside. I couldn't articulate exactly what I feared, but I knew I should stay close by and keep an eye on things.

My solace and only distraction that summer was reading. I discovered the pleasure of chapter books and devoured a big stack of them. The Parkchester Library was my haven. To thumb through the card catalog was to touch an infinite bounty, more books than I could ever possibly exhaust. My choices were more or less random. There was no one in my family who could point me toward children's classics, no teacher who took an interest, and it never occurred to me to ask the librarian for guidance. My mother had subscribed to *Highlights* for Junior and me, and *Reader's Digest* for herself, but by now I was reading whole issues of the *Digest* myself, cover to cover.

My favorite book was one that Dr. Fisher had lent me. I had seen it, bound in burgundy-red leather, on the shelf in his office and asked about it. He pulled the heavy volume down and said I could keep it as long as I liked. Those stories of Greek gods and heroes sustained me that summer and beyond. The heroes were admirable if flawed, as compelling as any comic book superhero to a kid who was hungry for escape, and there was grandeur in their struggles that the Flash could not match. Riven by conflicting impulses, these immortals seemed more realistic, more accessible, than the singular, all-forgiving, unchanging God of my Church. It was in that book of Dr. Fisher's too that I learned that my own name is a version of Sophia, meaning wisdom. I glowed with that discovery. And I never did return the book.

Usually, when I didn't understand what was going on with someone, I could listen carefully and observe until I figured things out. But with my mother, still sitting alone in darkness behind her closed door, there were no clues. As far as I knew, when Papi was alive, they did nothing but fight. If they weren't screaming, they were putting up a stone wall of bitter silence between them. I couldn't remember ever having seen them happy together. And so her sadness, if that's what it was, seemed irrational to me.

Abuelita's terrible pain seemed less mysterious, if only because I was so attuned to her feelings. And yet it had been years since I'd seen her talking to Papi as her beloved firstborn, with that glow of adoration that lit up her face. On holidays when he came with us to Abuelita's house, he would sit silently, looking out the window, the same way he did at home. He might warm up if there was a ball game on TV. Before we got our own set, he might even come just to watch the game, then one of his few real pleasures. Those baseball games, with some good shouting for a change, were such a rare semblance of normal family life that on those nights I would fall asleep with a smile that wouldn't go away.

But still, looking at it rationally—and I was a very rational child—why should the parties stop when Papi hardly ever came anyway? Why would his not being there make a difference now when it hadn't before? Why was even Titi Carmen so overcome with grief at the funeral that she tried to jump into the grave and had to be dragged out? I never once saw her eager to spend time with Papi when he was alive.

What was all this adult misery about? I had my theory. They must all feel guilty. If Papi had slowly poisoned himself to death, then of course it must be Mami's fault (as had long been the theory), or maybe Abuelita now blamed herself and the failure of her spirit powers. Titi Carmen, too, might have faulted herself for not interceding. And how many times had I heard Titi Judy criticized for Tío Vitín's failure to visit the family more often—even though Tío Vitín was Abuelita's son and Titi Judy was just his wife? That was how their minds worked: if a man did something wrong, there was a woman to blame, whether wife, mother, sister, or sister-in-law. I recognized that it must be horribly painful to imagine you could have stopped him but didn't. But I also knew all that was nonsense. There was no saving Papi from himself.

It is a day like any other, and the door is still closed. My rational self hasn't yet noticed it, but I can't take another minute of this. Before I know what's happening, I'm pounding with both fists on that stupid, blank, faceless door, and when she opens it, I'm screaming in her face, "Enough! You've got to stop this! You're miserable and you're making us miserable."

Such screaming hasn't been heard in the house in months. She's just standing there, blinking at me. I can't help myself, I'm still screaming. "What's wrong with you? Papi died. Are you going to die too? Then what happens to me and Junior? Stop already, Mami, stop it!"

I turn around and march up the hall to the front bedroom, slamming the door behind me as hard as I can. I grab a book and lie down on the bed. But with my hands trembling and my eyes full of tears, there's no way I can read. I close the book and sob for a very long time. I haven't done that in ages. Crying like a stupid baby.

Six

When I woke up the morning after I'd screamed at my mother, she had already left for work as usual. Ana fixed breakfast for Junior and me and got us off to school as on any other day. But when we came home that afternoon, I could feel a change as soon as I opened the door. The window shades were up for the first time in many months, and Radio WADO was playing. "We're home, Mami!" Junior shouted, and then she appeared. She had on a black dress with white polka dots, and it seemed so vivacious I didn't then register that she was still technically wearing black. She also had on makeup and perfume. I felt my smile spreading, my whole body filling up with relief.

The silence of mourning was over finally, but more important, the constant, bitter conflict that had filled our lives was over too. Of course Junior and I still found plenty of reasons to yell at each other, provoking my mother's familiar warning call—her *la la la la* that rose ominously in tone, step by step, until we got the message that we had gone too far and that justice would be swift if we didn't immediately make ourselves scarce. We were still not like a family on television, but the screaming fights that had worn me down with sadness were no more.

My mother still often worked six days a week, but she was no longer trying to escape from us. Home was now a good place to be, and so she worked the early shift at Prospect Hospital, leaving at six in the morning in order to be home by the time we finished at Blessed Sacrament. Ana came over in the mornings to fix breakfast and get us off to school. I could have managed by myself, but Junior was such a sleepyhead that we'd never have gotten to school on time without help.

The apartment was always immaculate, but it was no longer my doing. I quit my compulsive cleaning and left it to my mother, who cared about the place now. With the bit of insurance money left over after Papi's burial, she even bought a mirror that covered one wall of the living room, making it seem bright and spacious.

I didn't entirely trust this new reality, my mother's transformation included. Once in a while, not often, she would date: a friend's brother, or someone's divorced son. I wondered what would happen to Junior and me if she got married again. Would she leave us behind? Would the fighting resume with a new combatant? My anger still lingered at what I had perceived for so long as her abandonment and her coldness toward us. It would take me many years to let go of that anger completely, and just as long for her to lose the last of her chill. It just wasn't in my mother's nature at that time to show affection, give you a hug, or get down on the floor to engage with a kid. She had been deprived of the formative security that nurtures such impulses. Besides, they would have mussed up her outfit.

My mother always dressed with effortless style, which seemed almost magical given her modest means. Even now in her eighties, she still looks flawless, camera ready, perfectly put together at all times. She would never understand why I lacked this talent that came so naturally to her. There was always some fault in my appearance that was glaring to her and invisible to me, and she badgered me constantly for being sloppy.

However undemonstrative, Mami cared about people, and she served as the unofficial visiting nurse on twenty-four-hour call for family, friends, and neighbors throughout Bronxdale and beyond. She took temperatures, gave shots, changed dressings, and called the doctor with any questions she couldn't answer herself. She grumbled only when people took advantage—"Titi Celina! I need some suppositories for my hemorrhoids!" Perhaps they assumed she could pick up supplies for free at the hospital. The staff there would often help themselves, but my mother wouldn't dream of it. "You think I'm going to steal a bottle of aspirin or a box of disposable needles, even for you, Sonia?" She hardly had extra money to pay for them, but it scared her to see my needles, reused to the point of bending when I tried to inject myself.

The healing wasn't limited to physical aches and pains. Some of her best medicine involved listening to people's troubles, which she could do with full attention and sympathy, while reserving judgment. Her compassion impressed me. In turn, the role of confidante to friends has come naturally to me, and I credit the example of my mother, who, left on a park bench, could probably get a tree to tell her its woes.

One memory of my mother's comforting sneaks up on me in the night sometimes. The bedroom I shared with Junior on Watson Avenue, with its one little window, was not just tiny but unbearably hot in summer. We had a little electric fan propped up on a chair, but it didn't help much. Sometimes I would wake up miserable in the middle of the night, with the pillow and sheets drenched in sweat, my hair dripping wet. Mami would come change the bed, whispering to me quietly in the dark so as not to wake Junior. Then she'd sit beside me with a pot of cold water and a washcloth and sponge me down until I fell asleep. The cool damp was so delicious, and her hands so firmly gentle—expert nurse's hands, I thought—that a part of me always tried to stay awake, to prolong this blissful taken-care-of feeling just a bit longer.

While my mother seemed to find new confidence and strength after the loss of my father, Abuelita would never emerge from her *luto* at all. She had always dressed simply, but now it was simply black, as if all color had vanished from her life. The parties ended. There was no more music and dancing, no more dominoes and poetry. No more shopping for chickens. I still went to see her often, especially after she moved to the projects, just a block away from us. But her eyesight was beginning to fail, and she didn't go out unless it was absolutely necessary. Our visits became more sedate, just the two of us talking, spending time together comfortably. I would bring my homework or read a book while she cooked; it was always quieter at her house.

That year of my father's death had been incredibly hard on her. Her mother, my *bisabuela*, would die very soon after Papi. Abuelita didn't even go to Puerto Rico for the funeral, she was so overwhelmed with grief for her son. She never spoke about my father after he died, at least not in my hearing, but my aunts and uncles understood the transformation that came over her: Juli was the firstborn, the protected one. If he could be taken away from her, then nothing in the world was safe. Something in the fabric of her universe was torn beyond repair.

Her husband's Parkinson's disease had been steadily claiming more and more of him for a long time. By the time my father died, Gallego's speech was fading, and within a few months he was completely bedridden, another reason Abuelita rarely left the house. My mother went every week on her day off from the hospital to bathe him and help change the sheets. Perhaps my grandmother was mourning prospectively for her husband, too, the sadness heaving back and forth between Papi and Gallego like a trapped wave. When Gallego died a few years later, she would move to the seniors' home at Castle Hill within days. In the same way that my mother refused to go back into the old apartment after my father died, Abuelita couldn't bear to be in that space where memories and emptiness collided. And so we did the *rosario* for Gallego in a brand-new, subsidized senior citizens' home.

Things had changed at school, too. My fourth-grade teacher, Sister Maria Rosalie, made an effort to be kinder, and I enjoyed an unofficial respite from reprimand from April, when Papi died, until summer vacation. Not coincidentally, by the time fifth grade started, school had become for the first time something to look forward to. Until then, I had been struggling to figure out what was going on, especially since my return from being in the hospital. Now suddenly lessons seemed easier. It certainly didn't hurt that I had spent the entire summer vacation with my nose in a book, hiding from my mother's gloom, but there was another reason too. It was around that time that my mother made an effort to speak some English at home.

As early as kindergarten, Mami once told me, a teacher had sent a letter home saying that we should speak English in the house. But that was easier said than done. My mother's

English was accented and sometimes faltering, though she could manage well enough at the hospital, even working an occasional weekend shift on the telephone switchboard. At home, however, she felt awkward speaking in front of Papi in a language that he didn't know well.

I don't know if my father spoke any English at all. Perhaps he was too shy to speak it badly in front of us. I'm guessing he would have picked up a few phrases to get through his days at the factory, though I never actually heard him say a word. I know that Abuelita couldn't manage in English, because my mother interpreted for her whenever she had to deal with officialdom. In any case, our family life was conducted entirely in Spanish.

It sounded odd when my mother first started speaking English at home, addressing Junior and me as if she were talking to a doctor at the hospital. But as soon as she found the words to scold us, it began to seem natural enough. In time I hardly noticed which language we were speaking. Still, as easily as Junior and I shifted gears into English with the flexibility of youth, at the age of thirty-six my mother could not have steered that change without a mighty effort. Only her devotion to our education could have supplied such a force of will. "You've got to get your education! It's the only way to get ahead in the world." That was her constant refrain, and I could no more get it out of my head than a commercial I'd heard a thousand times.

One day the doorbell rang, and my mother opened the door to a man carrying two big briefcases. It wasn't the man who made the rounds of the projects selling insurance. It wasn't the old man who came to collect two dollars every Saturday for the drapes he'd sold us months before. My mother sat down with the salesman at the kitchen table, and they talked for a very long time, looking at books, adding up numbers. I was in the other room, overhearing bits and pieces: "priceless gift of knowledge . . . like a library of a thousand books . . . easy monthly payments . . ."

When the two big boxes labeled *Encyclopaedia Britannica* arrived, it was Christmas come early. Junior and I sat on the floor surrounded by piles of books like explorers at the base of Everest. Each of the twenty-four volumes was a doorstop, the kind of book you'd expect to see in a library, never in someone's home and certainly not twenty-four of them, including a whole separate book just for the index! As I turned the densely set onionskin pages at random, I found myself wandering the world's geography, pondering molecules like daisy chains, marveling at the physiology of the eye. I was introduced to flora and fauna, to the microscopic structures of cells, to mitosis, meiosis, and Mendel's garden of peas. The world branched out before me in a thousand new directions, pretty much as the salesman had promised, and when it became overwhelming, all I had to do was close the book. It would wait for me to return.

There was one more reason, beyond the pleasure of reading, the influence of English, and my mother's various interventions, that I finally started to thrive at school. Mrs. Reilly, our fifth-grade teacher, unleashed my competitive spirit. She would put a gold star up on the blackboard each time a student did something really well, and was I a sucker for those gold stars! I was determined to collect as many as I could. After the first As began appearing on my report card, I made a solemn vow that from then on, every report card would have at least one more A than the last one.

A vow on its own wasn't enough; I had to figure out how to make it happen. Study skills were not something that our teachers at Blessed Sacrament had ever addressed explicitly. Obviously, some kids were smarter than others; some kids worked harder than others. But as I also noticed, a handful of kids, the same ones every time, routinely got the top marks. That was the camp I wanted to join. But how did they do it?

It was then, in Mrs. Reilly's class, under the allure of those gold stars, that I did something very unusual for a child, though it seemed like common sense to me at the time. I decided to approach one of the smartest girls in the class and ask her how to study. Donna Renella looked surprised, maybe even flattered. In any case, she generously divulged her technique: how, while she was reading, she underlined important facts and took notes to condense information into smaller bits that were easier to remember; how, the night before a test, she would reread the relevant chapter. Obvious things once you've learned them, but at the time deriving them on my own would have been like trying to invent the wheel. I'd like to believe that even schools in poor neighborhoods have made some progress in teaching basic study skills since I was in the fifth grade. But the more critical lesson I learned that day is still one too many kids never figure out: don't be shy about making a teacher of any willing party who knows what he or she is doing. In retrospect, I can see how important that pattern would become for me: how readily I've sought out mentors, asking guidance from professors or colleagues, and in every friendship soaking up eagerly whatever that friend could teach me.

At the time, all I knew was that my strategy worked. Soon Mrs. Reilly had moved me to the row next to the window, which was reserved for the top students. My pleasure was diluted, however, when I found out that Junior's teacher had assigned him to the farthest row from the window, where the slowest kids sat. Naturally, Junior was upset, and the unfairness irked me, too. It's true that I called him stupid, but that was a big sister's prerogative, and I knew that he wasn't really. He studied almost as hard as I did. He was quiet, but he listened and paid attention; nothing slipped by him.

"He's a boy," said Mami. "He'll get there when he does." The Sisters of Charity held a pessimistic view of male children: they were trouble for the most part, often in need of a good thrashing, and unlikely to amount to much. There was more wisdom in my mother's open-ended encouragement. She would never push Junior and me to get better grades, never crack the whip regarding homework or lecture us about setting our goals high, the way Tío Benny did with my cousin Nelson. When I brought my report card home for her to sign, I could tell she was delighted to see that I was getting As. That same proud smile greeted the news in later years that

I'd made valedictorian or was graduating summa cum laude. It didn't matter that she didn't understand exactly what I'd accomplished to earn her pride. She trusted me, and Junior, too. "Just study," she would say. "I don't care what grade you get, just study. *No me importa si trabajan lavando baños. Lo importante es hacerlo bien.*" I don't care if you clean toilets, just do it well. Achievement was all very well, but it was the process, not the goal, that was most important.

On that first Christmas without Papi, Alfred helped me carry the tree home. He held the base and I supported the top as we walked it all the way, retracing the expeditions my father had led in years past. People always used to stop him to ask where he found such a perfect tree. No one stopped Alfred and me, but it wasn't until we got that sorry specimen up the elevator and into the apartment that we noticed how much it leaned to one side. It was a lesson I'd always remember, if only seasonally: make sure the trunk is straight.

I was in charge of decorating now. I did remember how Papi always said you couldn't have two lights of the same color next to each other, or two identical ornaments side by side, and you had to drape each icicle of silver tinsel separately over a branch. No tossing clumpy handfuls, which disqualified Junior from helping, since he just didn't have the patience to do it right. But what I couldn't figure out was how Papi always managed to string the lights so cunningly that the wires were invisible. I spent hours at it without success. He'd always fussed over it a long time, too. So I knew it wasn't easy, but obviously it involved some particular trick that he had never let me in on.

As the string of lights turned into a hopeless cat's cradle in my hands, Mami walked in and I gave her a desperate look of distress, but she just shook her head and said, "Juli always did the tree. I don't know how."

Finally, one way or another, the tree was finished. The cotton skirting around the base became a snowy setting for the *Nacimiento* with its tiny manger. The picture was complete, soft sparkle and twinkling color, lights peeping shyly from behind the veil of tinsel, the crowning star aglow.

A hug from Papi would have been nice just then. I couldn't deny that our life was so much better now, but I did miss him. For all the misery he'd caused, I knew with certainty that he'd loved us. Those aren't things you can measure or weigh. You can't say: this much love is worth this much misery. They're not opposites that cancel each other out; they're both true at the same time.

Seven

Dr. Elsa Paulsen intrigued me. She was tall and very polished, even regal, in her white coat. She spoke with a hint of an accent that was not from New York, but not foreign, either. When she walked into the pediatric diabetes clinic at Jacobi Medical Center, everybody—interns, residents, nurses—came to attention. You could tell that they wanted to please her, that she was the boss, though she was also warm and friendly. When she checked in on me, she actually talked to me, not just to my mother.

Dr. Paulsen was the first woman in a position of real-world authority I'd encountered. At Prospect Hospital, where my mother worked, all the doctors were men. The nursing supervisors were women, but that's as far as it went. Even at Blessed Sacrament, the nuns wielded power only over kids. To Monsignor Hart and Father Dolan the Sisters deferred.

At the clinic, the nurse would weigh me and take urine samples. If I was lucky, she took my blood, too. If I was unlucky, I'd have to face one of the interns doing this for the first time. Feeling now and then like a guinea pig was in retrospect a small price to pay for the benefit of the cutting-edge treatment being developed there by the Albert Einstein College of Medicine. They had a research program on juvenile diabetes, and considering how rare the disease was then, it was amazing good fortune that the clinic happened to be located in the Bronx, even though we still had to take a long subway ride and then a bus to get there.

With a strong focus on patient education, the clinic was pioneering much that is now standard practice: child-friendly lessons on how to live with diabetes, on nutrition, and on what's going on in your body. Since I'd first begun treatment, my disease had progressed to the point where my pancreas was producing no insulin at all. Without my shots, I'd have been dead within days, if not sooner. The insulin available then was long acting, a single dose given in the morning, but there were sometimes unexpected fluctuations in blood sugar throughout the day. So you had to eat on a rigid schedule and keep snacks or juice at hand in case of a sudden drop. It wasn't true that I couldn't eat sweets, or that mangoes would kill me, as my aunts warned. Fortunately, my mother had a better understanding, and we celebrated after each visit to the clinic by sharing a piece of cherry cheesecake from the hospital cafeteria.

For the most part, moderation with sweets came naturally

to me because I so disliked the sensation caused by a spike in blood sugar. I could recognize the first hints of that slow-motion heaviness, that feeling of trying to get out of the chair with a thousand-pound barbell on my lap. Low blood sugar felt just as bad but in a different way. I would start to sweat and get dizzy; I would lose patience, and my thinking became fuzzy. Complicating matters, there was then no easy, accurate way to test your own blood sugar, no glucose meter, only urine strips that reflected what your levels had been hours earlier. So to keep track of my blood sugar, I cultivated a constant mindfulness of how my body felt. Even now, with much more precise technology at hand, I still find myself mentally checking physical sensations every minute of the day. Along with discipline, that habit of internal awareness was perhaps another accidental gift from my disease. It is linked, I believe, to the ease with which I can recall the emotions attached to memories and to a fine-tuned sensitivity to others' emotional states, which has served me well in the courtroom.

But even if I took the shots like clockwork and watched my diet carefully, there was the grim reality of the disease then: I would still probably die sooner rather than later from complications. Given the advances in treatment since I was a child, a shortened life span is no longer as likely as it was. But that was the reality at the time, and it explains why my family had received my diagnosis as a catastrophe of tragic dimensions. My mother's biggest fear was the threat of amputations, blindness, and a panoply of other complications that were then typical. As collected and professionally cool as she was in the emergency room, as confident and reassuring when helping a sick neighbor, she would fall apart when I was the patient. If I stubbed my toe, she'd be yelling about gangrene. Sometimes I would vent my annoyance through reckless antics on the playground, just to scare her. And always, since that first day, I had asserted my independence by giving myself my own shots.

My cousin Alfred was the only one who refused to believe that diabetes was a terrible disability. Perhaps that explained his drill sergeant's determination to toughen me up. It was Alfred who would get me up on a pair of skis and even put me on a horse two or three times. When he took Junior and me to the Statue of Liberty, he made us climb all the way to the crown. I was spent by the time we had scaled the pedestal, but no: "Onward and upward! All the way to the top!" The last flights were torture, my legs in such pain that I couldn't stop tears from coming. But no way was I going to let Alfred see me cry, which meant I had to stay ahead of him, and that's how I made it to the top.

Eventually, I would translate my family's fatalism into an outlook that better suited my temperament: I probably wasn't going to live as long as most people, I figured. So I couldn't afford to waste time. Once in school, I would never contemplate taking a semester or year off. Later might never come, so I'd better get to work right now. That urgency has always stayed with me, even as the threat has receded.

Sitting in the waiting room at the clinic, I wondered, did it never occur to anyone at the Albert Einstein College of Medicine that kids who might not have long to live shouldn't have to wait endless hours with nothing to read but stacks of old *Highlights*? I should have brought my Nancy Drew book, I grumbled.

But when my turn came, they gave me something else to read—a pamphlet about choosing a profession. I am ten years old, I thought. Isn't it a little early to be worrying about this? *You can be a famous actress*, the pamphlet assured me, *like Mary Tyler Moore. You can be a professional athlete. You can be:*

> *a doctor*
> *a lawyer*
> *an architect*
> *an engineer*
> *a nurse*
> *a teacher* . . .

The list of possibilities for a diabetic didn't seem very long. And then, more darkly, there was a list of professions that were out-of-bounds. You couldn't be an airline pilot or a bus driver. Fair enough, I thought: you don't want someone flying a plane who might pass out. You couldn't serve in the military. Fine: I'd had enough of boot camp for a lifetime, thanks to Alfred. And you couldn't be a police officer . . . uh-oh. That one stopped me like a slap in the face.

You couldn't be a police officer? That meant you couldn't

be a detective. This was a catastrophe! It's true that Nancy Drew manages without being a police officer, but she is an exception. She is also fictional. I knew enough about the real world to know that detectives are normally cops and not eighteen-year-old girls with charmed lives. And yet Nancy Drew had a powerful hold on my imagination. Every night, when I'd finished reading and got into bed and closed my eyes, I would continue the story, with me in Nancy's shoes, until I fell asleep.

I was convinced I would make an excellent detective. My mind worked in ways very similar to Nancy Drew's, I told myself: I was a keen observer and listener. I picked up on clues. I figured things out logically, and I enjoyed puzzles. I loved the clear, focused feeling that came when I concentrated on solving a problem and everything else faded out. And I could be brave when I needed to be.

I could be a great detective, if only I weren't diabetic.

"Junior, change the channel! *Perry Mason*'s on." Okay, so I couldn't be a police officer or a detective, but it occurred to me that the solution to my quandary appeared on that small black-and-white screen every Thursday night.

Perry Mason was a lawyer, a defense attorney. He worked alongside a detective, Paul Drake, but even so it was Perry Mason who untangled the real story behind the crime, which was never what it seemed. And it was once the trial started that things got really interesting. You assume, of course, that

Perry Mason is the hero. He's the one the show is named after, the one who gets the close-up shots, who wins the case almost every time and gets the hugs and tears of gratitude at the end. But my sympathies were not entirely monopolized by Perry Mason. I was fond of Burger, the prosecutor, too. I liked that he was a good loser, that he was more committed to finding the truth than to winning his case. If the defendant was truly innocent, he once explained, and the case was dismissed, then he had done his job, because justice had been served.

Most of all it was the judge who fascinated me. A minimal but vital presence, he was more of an abstraction than a character: a personification of justice. At the end of the hour, when Perry Mason said, "Your Honor, I move to dismiss the charges against my client and release him," it was the judge who made the final decision—"case dismissed" or "motion granted"—that wrapped up the episode. You had to watch carefully because it was over in a flash, but I knew that was the most important moment in the show. And even before that final decision, it was the judge who called the shots, who decided whether it was "overruled" or "sustained" when a lawyer said, "Objection!"

There was a whole new vocabulary here. And though I wasn't sure what every detail meant, I followed the gist of it. It was like the puzzles I enjoyed, a complex game with its own rules, and one that intersected with grand themes of right and wrong. I was intrigued and determined to figure it out.

I could be a great lawyer, I decided. But a part of me, I knew, would have preferred to be the judge rather than Perry Mason. At the time, with no knowledge of what either aspiration might entail, the one didn't seem any more outlandish than the other.

Eight

I was beginning to find my own role in the social scene of middle school, and Carmelo had a lot to do with it, especially his nickname for me: Computer-Head, or Compy for short. He meant it as a compliment: I was rational and methodical. When my mind went to work, he imagined, lights blinked and tapes whirred, men in white coats with clipboards feeding me punch cards for breakfast. Carmelo saw the benefit of being friends with a nerd and would always sit beside me for every quiz and test, even though I didn't make it easy for him. He must have pulled his share of neck muscles trying to get decent grades. But he was still grateful: in turn, he looked out for me and wouldn't let me be bullied by anyone.

Carmelo was one of the most popular kids at school. He had the special ease of a cute boy: tall, with close-cropped curly hair and a dimple on one side when he smiled. He and

Eileen, another one of the cool kids, were both good friends of mine, which did wonders for my social standing. Both lived in the Rosedale Mitchell-Lama co-op on the other side of the highway, a notch up from the Bronxdale Houses. (Or several notches, if you listened to Titi Judy and Tío Vitín, who lived there too.)

The gang liked to hang out at my place because my mother, happy to have her kids nearby and under her surveillance, made everyone feel at home. There was never a hint of disapproval about anyone I might choose to invite: all were welcome, with plenty of rice and beans to go around. Often, Eileen's stepsisters, Solangela and Myra, came too, even though they were older, in high school. They were Mami's friends as much as mine, endlessly discussing their love lives with her.

"Mami, if I invite some kids over tomorrow, can you make your *chuletas*?" I stuck my nose in the refrigerator, taking stock of what we had, what we needed to buy. My mother gave me a look as if I'd just asked her to address the United Nations General Assembly in five minutes. For all her willingness to welcome my friends, she remained convinced that she was a lousy cook, ever since the Thanksgiving after Papi died, when she roasted her first turkey with the paper packet of giblets left inside. It was a mystery how someone who never enjoyed cooking made such heavenly pork chops.

I was more than happy to handle the shopping and the rest of the preparations. Hosting a party came naturally to me. I loved it when the apartment was full of talk and laughter, music and cooking smells. It reminded me of Abuelita's parties, even if it was just a bunch of middle school kids. I tried to remember how Abuelita had made it happen and translate that for seventh graders. No rum but plenty of Coke and heaps of rice and beans and Mami's pork chops.

Junior stuck his head in the kitchen door and chanted a whiny taunt, "Sonia's in love with Ringo, nyeah, nyeah, nyeah . . ."

Junior was still my cross to bear, perpetual pest of an unshakable little sibling. When my friends came over, he listened to every word we said, pretending to be doing homework or watching TV. Sooner or later anything I said, even a confession of my favorite Beatle, would be used against me.

At that age, we fought routinely, and our fights were physical. At least that's how it worked at home. Outside, at school or on the street, I was still Junior's protector, and I took it as a grave responsibility, suffering lots of bumps and bruises on his behalf. For these I would settle with him later, privately. We continued in that manner until the day I recognized the beginning of a growth spurt I knew I could never match. He would always be three years younger, but he was a boy, with all that entailed hormonally, and a boy who spent hours every day on the basketball court. The time had come for war by other means: "Junior, we're too old for this. Let's be civilized, we can talk things out and"—though I don't remember saying this last bit in so many words—"we can always blackmail each other." Henceforth that was the form our hostilities took. We tracked each other's trespasses, we snitched to Mami, or threatened to, whichever availed the greater advantage. Our snitching often entailed phone calls to the hospital that must have driven my mother nuts, not to mention her supervisors, bless their forbearance. I've always believed phone calls from kids must be allowed if mothers are to feel welcome in the workplace, as anyone who has worked in my chambers can attest. Eventually, in high school, Junior and I outgrew our warring ways, and over time we've become very close. We don't talk all that often, but when something really matters, each of us naturally reaches out to the other before anyone else. Still, to this day my brother claims a deep resentment that he spent his childhood waiting to get big enough to beat me up and on the threshold of his triumph I changed the rules.

When Pope Paul VI came to New York in the fall of 1965, Monsignor Hart arranged for a group of students from Blessed Sacrament to go see him. I wanted more than anything to be included. This wasn't just a field trip—not that we ever went on field trips at Blessed Sacrament. It was history in the making, the first time a pope had visited the United States. And Paul VI wasn't just any pope. He was elected the summer after my father died, when I had spent so much time reading. Everything I'd read about him inspired me, and now once again there were magazine and newspaper articles appearing almost daily, describing the plans for his visit and the ideas he had—about ending the war in Vietnam and using the money from disarmament to help poor countries, about dialogue between religions, and about continuing the work of Vatican II to make the Church more responsive and open to ordinary people.

I was often moved and excited by books, but how often does a newspaper article give you chills? I had to look up unfamiliar words—"ecumenism," "vernacular"—but all his impulses resonated deeply with me. I loved this pope!

So I was especially upset and disappointed at not being allowed to see him—though not surprised: only kids who had attended church regularly were included. Ever since Father Dolan had refused to pay a call on my mother in her misery, my Sunday attendance at Blessed Sacrament Church had faltered. I often went to St. Athanasius with Titi Aurora instead. That didn't count at Blessed Sacrament, though. And so I would conclude that I had to figure out for myself what really counted.

"So what was it like? Did you shake hands? Did he talk to you?" I interrogated my classmates. Despite the bitterness of exclusion, I was hungry for details. It was a relief to learn that I hadn't missed much. The kids from Blessed Sacrament were among a crowd of thousands, and they saw less than I did on television. The cameras had followed the pope through the thronged streets of Manhattan, into St. Patrick's, to a meeting with President Johnson, and to a Mass at Yankee Stadium.

Best of all, they had captured his address to the UN General Assembly: "No more war, never again war. Peace, it is peace that must guide the destinies of people and of all mankind." All in one amazing day.

It occurred to me that if I was going to be a lawyer—or, who knows, a judge—I had to learn to speak persuasively and confidently in front of an audience. I couldn't be a quivering mess of nerves. So when they asked for volunteers to do the Bible reading in church on Sunday, I spied an opportunity to test myself. Girls reading was a new thing, a small ripple from Vatican II along with the tidal wave that had changed the Mass from Latin to English. We couldn't be altar servers, though; that was still for boys only.

Doing the Bible reading was not the same as giving a speech, of course, because you didn't need to worry about what you would say or even memorize it. It was a long way from arguing a case in a trial, but a small step in the right direction. And I had to start somewhere.

As I walked up the few stone stairs to the pulpit, my knees were buckling. I watched my hand tremble as it came to rest on the banister, as if it belonged to someone else. If I couldn't even keep my hands still, what would happen when I opened my mouth to speak? Every pew was packed, rows and rows of faces looking at me, waiting, it now seemed, for me to make a fool of myself. I could feel a faint gagging reflex. Suppose I threw up right there, all over the Bible? I had practiced the night before, read the passage aloud so many times—would it all be for nothing?

Wobbly at first, my voice soon steadied, and so did my knees. The words started to flow. I knew it was important to look up at the end of each sentence, but I didn't dare. The faces terrified me. If I looked in their eyes, I'd be lost, maybe even turn into a pillar of salt. So at the end of each sentence I looked at the ceiling instead: the wooden beams marking off rectangular coffers, gold spiral edges, lamps hanging from black metal rings. But soon the weirdness of looking up made me even more self-conscious, and I began to worry how this was coming across: "Does this kid think she's reading to God?" Fortunately, after the next verse or two came inspiration: to avoid the trap of their eyes, I would focus on their foreheads . . .

Before I knew it, I made it down the stairs and back to my seat. I had done it, and I knew I could do it again.

I spent eight years at Blessed Sacrament School, far more than half my life by the time the last bell of eighth grade rang. Ted Shaw, a high school friend who later became the legal director of the NAACP Legal Defense and Educational Fund, describes Catholic school as his salvation and damnation: it shaped his future and terrified his heart. I identify with this depiction. The Sisters of Charity helped to shape who I am, but there was much that I wouldn't be sad to leave behind.

In the mimeographed pamphlet that was our eighth-grade yearbook, each child wrote a "last will and testament" to the life being left behind at Blessed Sacrament; the Sisters responded in turn with a few words of "prophecy" about each child. Looking over those pages, I am struck by how low were their expectations for their young charges. Of one girl, for instance, it is written that she had "hopes of becoming a fashion designer but we think she'd make a better mother with six children." Sadly, such discouragement, directed even at the many girls who aspired to more traditional occupations like secretaries, was not unusual. And yet for a tiny school with very limited resources, in a poor neighborhood where many young lives were fatally seduced by drugs and alcohol or cut short by violence, Blessed Sacrament launched so many of my classmates toward a productive and meaningful existence, success often well beyond those mimeographed prophecies. There is no denying that credit is due to the Sisters of Charity and the discipline they instilled, however roughly.

My own yearbook entry surprises me with its self-assurance. I was confident by then of my own intellect:

> *I, Sonia Sotomayor, being of sound mind and body,*
> *do hereby leave my brains, to be divided evenly, to*
> *the incoming class of 8-1, so they will never have to*
> *know the wrath of Sister Mary Regina because of*
> *lack of knowledge.*

And here, less confident but still hopeful, is what Sister Mary Regina wrote:

> *This girl's ambitions, odd as they may seem, are to become an attorney and someday marry. Hopefully, she wishes to be successful in both fields. We predict a new life of challenges in Cardinal Spellman, where she will be attending High School, we hope she will be able to meet these new challenges.*

I recently returned to Blessed Sacrament for a visit. It has many fewer students and much smaller classes than when I attended. It is also clear that the teachers, now more lay-people as well as nuns, subscribe to a more nurturing approach since abandonment of the rod. Every generation has its own way of showing it cares.

Nine

Cardinal Spellman High School was a good hour's ride from the Bronxdale Houses, assuming the trains and buses were running on time. The school building was divided right down the middle by a crack in the wall, girls on one side and boys on the other. On each floor, a nun stood guard at the crack to make sure that neither sex crossed over into the other's side without a teacher's permission slip. The nuns were Sisters of Charity, the same as at Blessed Sacrament, but by the time I entered high school in 1968, many had shed the black bonnets and long black habits, looking a lot less menacing than they used to.

Girls and boys were allowed to mix in the lunchroom, but we had separate classes, except for religion and a very few upper-level courses, mostly Advanced Placement. Another exception was freshman Spanish. All the kids who spoke

Spanish at home were in one accelerated class, taught by a nun recently arrived from Spain. It was her plan, she told us, to condense three years of high school Spanish into one month of "review" and then start teaching us literature.

We were only a week into the semester when the class was on the verge of mutiny. A desperate mob surrounded Eddie Irizarry and me—the two biggest mouths—asking us to plead the class's case.

"Tell her we aren't Spanish, we're American."

"Forty-five minutes and nobody understood a word that she said!"

Our teacher was totally unaware that Puerto Rican kids raised in the Bronx would have had no formal instruction in their native language. As for the acquired tongue, many of us had struggled in earlier years through a sink-or-swim transition in schools that had provided no support for kids who'd first enrolled speaking little or no English. And so I started high school having never studied Spanish grammar, conjugated a verb, or read more than a few sentences at a time: an advertisement, or a newspaper headline, maybe a very short article. I had certainly never read a book in Spanish. None of us could understand the teacher's proper Castilian accent or her elegant diction. We looked on blankly, unable even to follow her instructions, let alone do the assignments.

My Spanish was so deficient that I wasn't even pronouncing my own name properly. She called me on it. "You have the most regal of Spanish names," she said. "Don't you ever let anybody mispronounce it. You are *Sonia Sotomayor*—

Soh-toh-mah-yor—and anything less is disgraceful. Say it correctly, and wear it with pride."

I could tell that her heart was in the right place. And sure enough, when Eddie and I explained the situation, she was very understanding and accommodating. The very next day she came back with a gentle apology and a new plan that was much more realistic: we would still go twice as fast as the regular Spanish class, but we'd cover the basics and learn grammar first, then start Spanish literature the second year. It was a good lesson in the value of learning to express your basic needs and trusting you will be heard. Teachers, I was finally realizing, were not the enemy.

Not most of them, anyway. There was the geometry teacher nicknamed Rigor Mortis. Word had it she'd been at Cardinal Spellman since before the invention of the triangle, standing before eons of freshman classes, like a prehistoric scarecrow, skinny and wrinkled with a bright thatch of red hair.

I was shocked when she called me into her office and accused me of cheating. The basis for her accusation was my perfect score on the Regents geometry exam. No one in all her centuries of experience had ever scored a hundred on the Regents, New York State's standardized tests.

"So who did I cheat from?" I asked indignantly. "Who else got a hundred that I could have copied from?"

She looked flummoxed for a moment. "But you've never scored higher than eighties or low nineties on the practice tests. How could you get a hundred?"

The truth, as I explained, was that I'd never once got an answer wrong on the practice tests; points had been deducted only because I hadn't followed the steps she had prescribed. I had reasoned out my own steps, which made sense to me, and she had never explained what was wrong with them. On the Regents exam we only had to give the answer; no one was checking the steps.

What happened next truly amazed me. She dug out my old tests and reviewed them. Acknowledging the validity of my proofs, she changed my grades. Even Rigor Mortis, it turned out, wasn't quite as rigid as all that.

Perhaps the most improbable turn of events in those first months: my cousin Miriam and I signed up to be maritime cadets, a neighborhood after school program. On Friday nights, we went to P.S. 75 at Hunts Point and marched around the gym. We wore uniforms. We memorized nautical terms and learned how to tie knots. We would never actually set foot on a boat, but we did march in the Puerto Rican Day Parade.

Our ulterior motive for joining the cadets was to chaperone her brother Nelson, who played trumpet in their marching band. Nelson, my childhood accomplice, my genius sidekick, had grown into a girl magnet. He was incredibly handsome, as smart as ever, with a wicked sense of humor. He'd also become an impressively talented musician. In fact, he was desperate to pursue this love, even though Tío Benny had always wanted him to be a doctor. He'd only agreed to let

Nelson join the marching band because he thought the discipline was good for him and it would keep him off the street.

The seductions of girls and music weren't the only reasons Tío Benny felt someone had to keep an eye on Nelson. Nelson had started at Bronx High School of Science the same year I entered Cardinal Spellman, and already he was struggling. There was no question of his scientific aptitude. By the time he got to high school, he'd won several prestigious awards for his science fair projects, and his teachers had recognized him as a prodigy, equally talented at science and music. No, Nelson's real difficulties were not intellectual but emotional: Tío Benny and Titi Carmen were breaking up.

I couldn't imagine what the split was doing to Nelson, Miriam, and little Eddie, too.

Especially Nelson.

When we were little, Miriam always found a thousand reasons to say no to any new game or plan that I suggested. Eventually, she would agree, but it was such an effort cajoling her. We would have a lot of fun together in high school, but she'd been one prissy little kid growing up. Nelson, on the other hand, never said no to me. He was game for anything, sticking his neck out for a friend without thinking twice. Those were qualities that I loved in him when we were little, but those same qualities would leave him vulnerable to the worst temptations, especially in a neighborhood that was drowning in drugs.

Sometimes when I watched Nelson practice for the band, I'd imagine him standing on the bow of a boat, blowing his trumpet with all his heart, only for that boat to drift slowly out to sea and leave me standing on the dock.

The summer vacation between freshman and sophomore years, I was working my way through the summer reading list when *Lord of the Flies* brought me to a halt. I wasn't ready to start another book when I finished that one. I'd never read anything so layered with meaning: it haunted me, and I needed to think about it some more. But I didn't want to spend the whole break doing nothing but reading and watching TV. Junior was happy shooting baskets all the daylight hours, but there wasn't much else going on around the projects if you were too old for the playground and not into drugs. Orchard Beach still beckoned, roasting traffic and all, but getting there was a trek you couldn't make every day.

So I decided to get a job. Mami and Titi Carmen were sitting in Abuelita's kitchen over coffee when I announced my plan. There were no shops or businesses in the projects, but maybe I could find someone to hire me in Abuelita's old neighborhood. Titi Carmen still lived on Southern Boulevard and worked nearby at United Bargains. The mom-and-pop stores under the El wouldn't hire kids—leaning on family labor rather than paying a stranger—but the bigger retailers along Southern Boulevard might. I proposed to walk down the street and inquire in each one. "Don't do that," said Titi Carmen. "Let me ask Angie." Angie was Titi Carmen's boss.

My mother meanwhile looked stricken and bit her lip. She

didn't say anything until Titi had gone home. Then, for the first time, she told me a little bit about her own childhood: about sewing and ironing handkerchiefs for Titi Aurora since before she could remember, for hours every day. "I resented it, Sonia. I don't want you to grow up feeling like I did." She went on to apologize for being unable to buy us more things but still insisted it would be even worse if I blamed her one day for depriving me of a childhood.

I hadn't seen that coming. Nobody was forcing me to work. Sure, a little pocket money would be nice, but that wasn't the main motivation. "Mami, I *want* to work," I told her. She'd worked too hard all her life to appreciate that leisure could mean boredom, but that was what I knew I'd be facing if I sat home all summer. I promised never to blame her. In that moment, I began to understand how hard my mother's life had been.

Titi Carmen reported back that Angie was willing to hire me for a dollar an hour. That was less than minimum wage, but since I wasn't old enough to work legally anyway, they would just pay me off the books. I would take the bus, meet Titi Carmen at her place, and then we'd walk over to United Bargains together. That became our routine. It wasn't a neighborhood where you walked alone.

United Bargains sold women's clothing. I pitched in wherever needed: restocking, tidying up, monitoring the dressing rooms. I was supposed to watch for the telltale signs of a shoplifter trying to disappear behind the racks, rolling up merchandise to stuff in a purse.

On Saturday nights the store was open late, and it was dark by the time we rolled down the gates. Two patrol officers would meet us at the door and escort us home. I don't know how this was arranged, whether it was true that one of the saleswomen was dating one of these cops, but I was glad of it anyway. As we walked, we could see the SWAT team on the roofs all along Southern Boulevard, their silhouettes bulging with body armor, assault rifles bristling. One by one the shops would darken, and we could hear the clatter of the graffiti-covered gates being rolled down, trucks driving off, until we were the only ones walking. At Titi Carmen's, you wouldn't run into any neighbors. I would spend the night there, talking the night away with Miriam. I wished Nelson were there too, but he was never home anymore.

The next morning, in daylight, Southern Boulevard was less threatening. The street vendors were out, shop fronts were open, people were coming and going. On the way home I stopped at a makeshift fruit cart to buy a banana for a snack. I was standing there peeling my purchase when a police car rolled up to the curb. The cop got out and pointed here and there to what he wanted—there was a language barrier—and the vendor loaded two large shopping bags with fruit. The cop made as if to reach for his wallet, but it was only a gesture, and the vendor waved it off. When the cop drove away, I asked the man why he didn't take the money.

"*Es el precio de hacer negocios.* If I don't give the fruit, I can't sell the fruit."

My heart sank. I told him I was sorry it was like that.

"We all have to make a living," he said with a shrug. He looked more ashamed than aggrieved.

Why was I so upset? Without cops the neighborhood would be even more of a war zone than it was. They worked hard at a dangerous job with little thanks from the people they protected. We needed them. Was I angry because I held the police to a higher standard, the same way I did Father Dolan and the nuns? There was something more to it, beyond the betrayal of trust, beyond the corruption of someone whose uniform is a symbol of the civic order.

How do things break down? In *Lord of the Flies*, the more mature of those lost boys start off with every intention of building a moral, functional society on their island, drawing on what they remember—looking after the "littluns," building the shelters, keeping the signal fire burning. Their little community gradually breaks down all the same, battered by those who are more self-indulgent, those who are driven by ego and fear.

Which side was the cop on?

The boys need rules, law, order, to keep their worst instincts in check. The conch they blow to call a meeting or hold for the right to speak stands for order, but it holds no power in itself. Its only power is what they agree to honor. It is a beautiful thing, but fragile.

When I was much younger, on summer days I would sometimes go along with Titi Aurora to the place where she worked as a seamstress. Those must have been days when Mami was working the day shift and, for some reason, I couldn't go to Abuelita's. That room with the sewing machines whirring was a vision of hell to me: steaming hot, dark, and airless, with the windows painted black and the door shut tight. I was too young to be useful, but I tried to help anyway, to pass the time. Titi Aurora would give me a box of zippers to untangle, or I'd stack up hangers, sort scraps by color, or fetch things for the women sewing. All day long I'd keep an eye out for anyone heading toward the door. As soon as it opened, I'd race over and stick my head out for a breath of air, until Titi saw me and shooed me back in. I asked her why they didn't just keep the door open. "They just can't," she would say.

Behind the closed door and the blackened windows, all those women were breaking the law. But they weren't criminals. They were just women toiling long hours under miserable conditions to support their families. They were doing what they had to do to survive. It was my first inkling of what a tough life Titi Aurora had had. Titi never got the schooling that Mami got, and she'd borne the brunt of the father Mami was spared from knowing. Her married life would have many challenges and few rewards. Work was the only way she knew to keep going, and she never missed a day. And though Titi was also the most honest person I knew—if she found a dime in a pay phone, she'd dial the operator to ask where she should mail it—she broke the law every day she went to work.

One evening at United Bargains, the women were making crank calls, dialing random numbers out of the phone book.

If a woman's voice answered, they acted as if they were having an affair with the woman's husband, then howled with laughter at their poor gull's response. Titi Carmen would join in, taking her turn on the phone and laughing as long and hard as any of them. I couldn't understand how anyone could be so cruel—so arbitrarily, pointlessly cruel. What was the pleasure in it? Walking home, I asked her, "Titi, can't you imagine the pain you're causing in that house?"

"It was just a joke, Sonia. Nobody meant any harm."

How could she not imagine? How could the cop not imagine what two large shopping bags full of fruit might measure in a poor vendor's life, maybe a whole day's earnings? Was it so hard to see himself in the other man's shoes?

I was fifteen years old when I understood how it is that things break down: people can't imagine someone else's point of view.

Ten

Three days before Christmas and midway through my freshman year at Cardinal Spellman High School, we moved to a new apartment in Co-op City. Once again, my mother had led us to what seemed like the edge of nowhere. Co-op City was swampland, home to nothing but a desolate amusement park called Freedomland, until the cement mixers and dump trucks arrived barely a year before we did. We moved into one of the first of thirty buildings planned for a development designed to house fifty-five thousand. To get home from school, I had to hike a mile—down Baychester Avenue, across the freeway overpass, and through the vast construction site of half-built towers and bare, bulldozed mud—before reaching human habitation. An icy wind that could lift you off your feet blew from the Hutchinson River. Flurries of snow blurred the construction cranes against an opaque sky of what seemed like Siberia in the Bronx.

At least now we lived close enough for me to walk to school, and I was glad of that. The hour-long trek by bus and train from Watson Avenue had been tedious. Poor Junior, who was only in sixth grade when we moved, would make the commute in reverse from Co-op City to Blessed Sacrament for another two and a half years. No one we knew had ever heard of Co-op City. My mother learned about it from some newspaper article on the city's plans for building affordable housing. The cost of living there was pegged to income, and at the same time you were buying inexpensive shares in a cooperative, so in theory there was a tax break.

My mother was eager to get us into a safer place because the Bronxdale projects were headed downhill fast. Gangs were carving up the territory and each other, adding the threat of gratuitous violence to the scourges of drugs and poverty. A plague of arson was spreading through the surrounding neighborhoods as landlords of crumbling buildings chased insurance. Home was starting to look like another war zone.

It was Dr. Fisher who made the move possible. When he died, he left my mother five thousand dollars in his will, the final and least expected of the countless kindnesses that we could never repay, although we tried. When Dr. Fisher was hospitalized after his wife died, Abuelita made Gallego stop on the way to work every morning to pick up Dr. Fisher's laundry and deliver clean pajamas to him.

Yes, Co-op City was the end of the earth, but once I saw the apartment, it made sense. It had parquet floors and a big window in the living room with a long view. All the rooms were twice the size of those cubbyholes in the projects, and the kitchen was big enough to sit and eat in. Best of all, my mother's friend Willy, a musician who did handyman work, too, was able to partition the master bedroom into two little chambers, each big enough for a twin bed and a tiny bureau, so Junior and I could finally have separate rooms. Each had its own door, and Willy even let us each choose our own wallpaper. Junior chose something neutral, in a restrained shade of beige. Mine had constellations, planets, and signs of the zodiac in an antique style, as if a Renaissance cartographer had drawn a map for space travel.

I was reading a lot of science fiction and fantasizing about travel to other worlds or slipping through a time warp. It had been only the summer before, in July 1969, that two astronauts had walked on the moon, and I was awestruck that it had happened in my own lifetime, especially when I remembered that Papi had once predicted this.

I started a new job at Zaro's Bakery, in the small shopping center right across the street from our building in Co-op City. On the days that I worked the morning shift, I would open the shop along with the manager and her assistant. I'd fire up the machine that boiled the bagels and fill the display cases with the pastries and breads. Then, while waiting to open, we all settled down together for coffee and a snack, always a chocolate-covered French cruller for me, offset by a low-starch lunch, of course. I loved those few minutes every day, laughing over the stories amid the smells of fresh bread and coffee. It carried me back to Tío Mayo's bakery in Mayagüez.

Soon the customers would be lining up for the familiar ritual of making change and small talk. I would shake my head when they tried to engage me in Yiddish. "What, no Yiddish? A nice Jewish girl like you?" I heard that so often that I knew the routine: my boss would explain with a bit of Yiddish I did recognize. "Shiksa" was technically derogatory, but she said it so affectionately that I couldn't fault it. At least it wasn't "spic"—elsewhere I'd get that often enough too.

Co-op City gradually transformed from a construction site to a community. When the harshest days of winter had passed, you could see young couples strolling, little kids playing, senior citizens watching from the benches. A fair portion of the residents were Jewish, as the bakery's clientele indicated, but you saw people of every imaginable background, drawn from across the five boroughs, a slightly more prosperous population than we were used to in the projects: teachers, police officers, firefighters, and nurses like my mother. The buildings were pristine and flawless then, the shoddiness of their construction not yet apparent. The grounds were landscaped with trees and flowers, and the whole place was lit up at night.

Once Mami planted the flag in Co-op City, it started to look like a good idea to everyone else. Alfred, married and with kids by then, ended up in a building not far from us. Eventually, Titi Carmen arrived with Miriam and Eddie; Charlie with his new wife, Ruth; and finally Titi Gloria and Tío Tonio came too. Titi Aurora had beaten them all to the punch: as soon as we were settled, my mother's sister moved in with us.

As fond as I'd always been of Titi Aurora, this was not good news. No sooner had we finally acquired enough space to breathe than we were overcrowded once again. Titi slept on a daybed in the foyer. She was an early riser and grumbled if Junior and I stayed out past ten. If we had friends over, she would retire to my mother's bedroom. Titi was also a bit of a pack rat. I couldn't open a closet to grab a towel without triggering an avalanche on my head. And to say Titi Aurora was frugal would be an understatement. I don't think she ever spent a penny on her own pleasure or bought anything that wasn't strictly necessary. She wore the same clothes year after year and mended them expertly until mending was a lost cause. The very idea of eating out in a restaurant, of spending a dollar for eggs and toast, was deeply upsetting to her. Titi's frugality, in turn, was deeply upsetting to my mother, who took pride in dressing well and delighted in splurging on small pleasures. Mami never saved, never put money away, and she would overextend herself for something that really mattered—like the encyclopedias or keeping us in Catholic school. She often had to go into debt, but she worked long and hard to pay off those commitments.

They were an odd couple, those two sisters. Neither of

them showed affection, and Titi especially could be austere and forbidding, but it was also clear that they were bound to each other in a way that I didn't entirely understand. They were like two trees with buried roots so tangled that they inevitably leaned on each other, and also strangled each other a bit. The sixteen-year difference between them made them more like mother and daughter, which was how they'd begun and how they would remain.

Just as in the projects, our home was still my friends' favorite hangout. And even with Titi grumbling, the party continued, my mother coming in for a cup of coffee at regular intervals, just to remind us of her presence. If we got too noisy, though, one of the neighbors was bound to call Co-op City security. The first time that happened and a uniformed guard was banging at the door, we scrambled, looking for somewhere to hide two whole six-packs of beer. But the next thing I knew, Mami came bounding out of her bedroom like a tigress, fire in her eyes. She threw open the door and yelled into the hallway, "You tell those neighbors that these are young kids having fun in my house! That's why kids get into trouble, because people don't let them have fun at home!" Then, louder still, "If anyone has a problem with that, they can come talk to me! Not call security!" When she was done shouting, she invited the guard in for coffee and told the kids already gathering their stuff that they could stay, but just keep the volume down, please.

And so, thanks to Mami, our home became party central as well as campaign headquarters for student council elections. We threw poster-making parties, painting slogans on banners stretched all the way down the halls. We threw victory parties when we won and consolation parties when we lost. Throughout my high school years, apartment 5G, 100 Dreiser Loop, was the place to be.

Marguerite Gudewicz and I both had a crush on Joe. He was messing around with both of us, being straight with neither. What did he think, that girls don't talk? When he dumped us both for someone else, Marguerite and I became best friends.

There was something about going to Marguerite's house that stirred memories of Abuelita's when I was small. The place was like a village, with grandparents living downstairs, Marguerite and her brother and parents upstairs, and Uncle Walter in the basement apartment. I felt right at home.

Marguerite's father, John Gudewicz, was not one to censor himself, but at least he made an effort to tone down his remarks when I was in earshot. He still had his views on "those Puerto Ricans," but his kindly laugh made it impossible to take offense. In 1971, when the bigoted Archie Bunker first appeared on *All in the Family*, we all joked that Mr. Gudewicz could sue CBS for copyright infringement. Still, when push came to shove, he stood up for me. One night at a party, his brother asked pointedly, "Who's the spic?"

"She's a guest of ours, and if you don't like it, you can get the hell out," Mr. Gudewicz said. And he wasn't just being a good host. I learned that when Marguerite's parents married, in their communities a match between a German and a Pole was virtually miscegenation. What's more, Marguerite's mother, Margaret, a modest woman who never talked about herself, had hidden Jews in wartime Germany. The Gudewiczes were not people who needed any lessons on the evils of prejudice.

Beyond the very circumscribed world of my family and our few blocks of the South Bronx, a much wider world was opening up to me, if only in a New York sort of way. If you grow up on salsa and merengue, then polkas and jitterbugs look as if they'd jumped off the pages of *National Geographic*. To Puerto Rican taste buds, the blandness of German, Polish, and Irish food left something to be desired, but it did seem we had a lot to learn about preparing vegetables. I noticed too that the *mishigas* on display in the hallways of Co-op City or at Zaro's more than matched the volubility of Puerto Rican family life, but if we'd slung the kinds of insults that our Jewish neighbors regularly did, the dishonor and acrimony would have stuck for generations. I was always amazed to hear them laughing together again within minutes of a flare-up.

The differences were plain enough, and yet I saw that they were as nothing compared with what we had in common.

Just as my emotional world was growing in Co-op City, my intellectual horizons were beginning to expand at school.

Miss Katz, who taught us history my junior year, was different from any teacher I'd had before, different, in fact, from anyone I had ever known. Compared with the nuns, she seemed young and vibrant. She warned us against getting stuck in rote learning, about how we needed to master abstract, conceptual thinking. The meaning of all this would be revealed once we'd written our first essays. Our first what? There we sat, rows of blank faces in our regulation navy skirts, white blouses, and sweater vests. Eleven years of memorization had molded our minds to be no less uniform. Essay? Somehow we had reached junior year in high school without having written anything beyond book reports. The nuns had always fed us facts, and we had always parroted them back. I was very good at it. I prided myself on being able to soak up vast oceans of facts. No teacher had ever asked anything more in exchange for an A.

Miss Katz asked something more. Her pronouncements and challenges intrigued me. What would it mean to think critically about history? How do you analyze facts? At least I'd learned by then the value of asking for help. If I went to talk to her after class, she wouldn't slam the door on me.

In fact, the door was wide open, and we had several long and fascinating conversations. She told me about her boyfriend, a Brazilian she described as a freedom fighter working on behalf of the poor and oppressed under the military dictatorship. I asked how, being Jewish, she'd come to work at a Catholic school, and she told me she was inspired by the nuns and priests she'd encountered in Latin America. They put their lives at risk for the sake of helping the poor.

Miss Katz was the first progressive I'd ever encountered up close. There certainly weren't many others at Cardinal Spellman High School in those days, and she would last there only one year. I remember wondering what made her so intriguing. How could one become an interesting person? It wasn't just having a boyfriend you could describe as a hero, though that certainly got my attention. It had more to do with her questioning the meaning of her existence, thinking in terms of a purpose in life. She was a teacher but still educating herself, learning about the world and actively engaged in it. I began to have an intimation that education could be for something other than opening the doors of job opportunity, in the sense of my mother's constant refrain.

I wish I could say that the same kind of reflection that lit up my conversations with Miss Katz had thrown some light on the problem of writing a history essay. Somehow her prescription for critical thinking and analysis remained abstract, if tantalizing. Though I did well enough in her class, I would have to wait till college before I could really understand what she meant.

It had been established that Sonia Sotomayor was not much to look at. I had a pudgy nose. I was gawky and ungraceful. I barreled down the halls of Cardinal Spellman, headfirst, unlike those who knew how to amble with a sexy sashay. My own mother told me that I had terrible taste in clothes.

I did get asked out occasionally. Usually, a friend's boyfriend had a friend, and they were looking for a fourth to double-date. Sometimes he would ask me again, and sometimes it would last for a while but never as long as going steady. Once I was the one to put an end to it: as his contribution to a meal that some friends were making at my house, my date decided to shoplift the bacon for the BLTs. Making matters worse, it wouldn't have happened except that Mami didn't have enough money to put together a meal for us that day. She was terribly ashamed, but she would have been horrified to learn about the shoplifting. I wanted nothing more to do with that guy.

Mostly, I felt like everybody's second choice, which is why a compliment could catch me off guard, especially an unconventional one. For instance, according to Ana and Moncho's daughter, Chiqui, who was a few years older than me, I had "baseball bat legs." Thanks a lot, Chiqui.

"No, that's good! You see how your ankles are small and the calves curve? You've got good legs."

I would hear worse: Kevin told me that Scully's dad said I was "built like a brick outhouse."

"It's a compliment, Sonia."

"What kind of compliment is that?"

"It's just an expression," Kevin insisted. "It means you're well-built. Not like some flimsy wooden job." I couldn't believe my ears. Was that what they meant by Irish wit?

106

Apart from dubious flattery, the truth was that Kevin Noonan made me feel attractive in a way that was new to me and not unwelcome. I, in turn, was entranced by his blue-gray eyes. I found myself scanning the hallway on the far side of Cardinal Spellman's divisive crack to catch a glimpse of that frizzy halo of sandy curls that made his slight figure stand out in the uniformed crowd.

On our first date, we took the train down to Manhattan. We walked the entire city, walked for hours, talking as he showed me his favorite spots. The first place he took me was a tiny park on East Fifty-Third Street where a curtain of water still runs down a stone wall. The sound of the fountain makes the city seem far away and turns the vest-pocket park into a private cove.

From that first date, we were inseparable. For the first month that I knew Kevin, he brought me a rose every single day. One time after school I was walking with him to the stop where he caught the bus home to Yonkers. We passed by Titi Gloria's house, and I dragged Kevin in to meet her and Tío Tonio. Really, I just wanted to postpone our parting, but as soon as we got there, Kevin turned pale and clammed up. I thought maybe he was put off because Titi Gloria and Tío Tonio kept switching to Spanish, even though they were making quite an effort, welcoming us with cake and cookies and sodas. But Kevin remained stony, and I was more than a little upset by this.

The next day when I got to school, there was no rose. I was getting seriously worried that things were over between us. But finally Kevin confessed: he had been stealing my daily roses from Tío Tonio's garden! He looked at me with a hang-dog expression that didn't go with his sparkling eyes and said, "There's a lot of them, Sonia." It was true: Tío Tonio's rose-bushes were magnificent. I laughed so hard I almost choked. I was happy to accept that the rose-colored phase of our romance was over. Now we were just a couple.

Kevin practically moved in with us, except, of course, that my mother made him go home at night. We couldn't afford much dating beyond the local pizzeria. Instead, we hung out at home, studying together or watching TV. He loved reading as much as I did, and we might silently turn the pages side by side for hours at a time. We went for walks, or visited my family, or worked on Kevin's car. And we talked constantly about everything imaginable.

We didn't go over to his house much, because his mother had a hard time accepting me. She wouldn't say it to my face, but the message came through with a tightening of the lips, a slant of the eyebrow, a slam of the door. She would have been happier if I were Irish, or at least not Puerto Rican. I'd seen this before. One guy I'd dated before Kevin had ducked a teacup thrown at his head when his mother found out I was Puerto Rican. Kevin's mom was not so kinetic about her distress, seeking the counsel of her priest. He either shared her opinion of my people or else lacked the backbone to tell her that it was not a very Christian view. Kevin defended him. The parish in Yonkers was 100 percent Irish, he rationalized, and the priest had no choice but to affirm his community's values. I disagreed. Bigotry is not a value.

At some point I introduced Kevin to Abuelita, which made the relationship official. From then on it was taken for granted that we would get married. Whatever the differences between Puerto Ricans and Irish, among our friends and families a common expectation prevailed: you married your first sweetheart. The only question was whether we would do it right after high school or wait till we finished college.

Eleven

*Cerveza Schaefer es la mejor cuando se toma más de una. . . .*ᵃ

Kenny Moy was sitting next to Titi Aurora in front of the TV, belting out the beer jingle. That was pretty much the extent of his Spanish, but it didn't prevent him from bonding with Titi Aurora. They conducted bizarrely bilingual conversations while watching pro wrestling together. Titi would be bobbing up and down, screaming at the referee, cheering on her favorite of the day. I loved to watch her: wrestling was the only thing that made her loosen up and enjoy herself. It reminded me of Papi's periodic emergence from his mournful silence to root for the Yankees on Abuelita's little black-and-white TV. But the Sheik? The Crusher?

ᵃ "Schaefer is the one beer to have when you're having more than one."

Killer Kowalski? Gorilla Monsoon? How could Titi believe this was for real?

Ken Moy was the student coach of the girls' team of the Forensics Club at Cardinal Spellman. I signed up as part of my self-imposed preprofessional program in public speaking, which advanced whenever an opportunity presented itself. The dozen or so girls on the team were an especially interesting bunch of self-selected high-functioning nerds, and Kenny coached us in debate and extemporaneous speech. He was brilliant at debate. His mind was an analytic machine that could dismantle an opponent's position, step by inexorable step. His affirmative arguments would make a concrete bunker look like a house of cards. And he was utterly untainted by emotion. I aspired to Ken's unflappable, rational cool, though I feared that I came across more like Titi Gloria in the usual nervous tizzy that accompanied her every mundane decision—red dress or blue?

"Sonia, I don't care if you have to cut off your hands, get that gesture out of your repertoire!" That was Kenny ringside. Tell a Puerto Rican not to talk with her hands? Ask a bird not to fly.

Ken should have gone to Bronx Science, but his mother made him come to Cardinal Spellman to keep an eye on his sister. Janet was a radical individualist with a completely uncensored approach to the world, a ticking time bomb in a Catholic school. She even cursed the principal to his face in the cafeteria when he caught her holding hands with her boyfriend. Ken had to tax his mighty rhetorical powers to win her a reprieve. But the truth was that if Janet had been expelled, Ken would have left too, and the school would have lost a star pupil.

They lived in East Harlem, where their parents ran a Chinese hand laundry. I never visited Ken's home or met his parents. His dad was trouble three ways, he said—heroin, gambling, and a violent temper—and since they lived almost an hour away by subway, we hung out at my place. Ken claimed they were the only Chinese family in the barrio, and he was a barrio kid through and through, slamming down dominoes with the best of them. He was skinny as a knife blade, but he could eat more of Mami's rice and beans and *chuletas* in one sitting than the rest of us together.

In philosophy class, we were studying logic. I'm not sure what I expected of philosophy, but formal logic took me by surprise. I loved it. I perceived beauty in it, the idea of an order that held under any circumstances. What excited me most was how I could immediately apply it down the hall in debate practice. I was amazed that something so mathematically pure and abstract could transform into human persuasion, into words with the power to change people's minds.

Forensics Club was good training for a lawyer in ways that I barely understood at the time. You got handed a topic, as well as the side you had to argue, pro or con. It didn't matter what you believed about the issue; what mattered was how well you argued. You not only had to see both sides; you had to prepare as if you were arguing both in order to anticipate your opponent's moves. In your allotted five minutes, you had to use language carefully to paint a picture for those who would decide the match. Then you had to listen. "Half a debate is listening to what the other person says," Ken advised. It was easy to present your own points, much harder to listen well enough to respond effectively to your opponent.

Listening was second nature to me. My friends confided in me, unloaded their problems, and leaned on me for advice, the same way my mother's friends leaned on her. When I was little, listening and watching for cues had seemed like the key to survival in a precarious world. I notice when people hesitate or get defensive, when they care more about what they're saying than they'll admit, or when they're too quick about brushing something off. So much is communicated in tone of voice, in subtleties of expression, and in body language.

What Ken taught us was a different way of listening, more formal than my own intuitive skill. He taught us to pay attention for the vulnerable links in a chain of logic, the faulty assumptions and the supposed facts that you know you can challenge when your turn comes. But even as I absorbed Ken's logical strategies, I knew instinctively that emotion doesn't disappear. Much as you had to keep your own in check, there was still that of your listeners to consider. A line of reasoning could persuade, but so could a sequence of feelings. Constructing a chain of logic was one thing; building a chain of emotions required a different understanding.

I've made it to the finals of the extemporaneous speech competition. The timer starts, and I pick a slip of paper blindly. Three topics based on current events: choose one. I have fifteen minutes to brainstorm and organize a five-to-seven-minute speech. Two of the three are so loud with the din of the nightly news—outrage at My Lai, the killings at Kent State, the Vietnam War spreading across borders, the protests spreading across campuses—that it's hard to hear myself think. The third topic catches my eye: the cold-blooded murder of Kitty Genovese and the neighbors who witnessed it but did nothing. Closer to home—Queens instead of Cambodia—and it touches a nerve.

The clock is running. What can I recall of the news reports? Where do I want to take this? What's my purpose? What's the best point of entry? I'll start by painting a picture . . . and remember to keep my hands still.

"On a cold night in early spring, six years ago, a young woman drove home from the bar where she was working to her apartment in Queens. It was around three a.m. She parked her car in a nearby parking lot and was walking up the alley toward her building when a stranger appeared out of the shadows and approached her. Frightened, she ran, but he caught up with her. He stabbed her in the back. She screamed and cried for help. Several neighbors heard her cries and the struggle that ensued as Winston Moseley assaulted Kitty Genovese."

I look out and observe a rapt stillness in the room. I've got them.

"But the night was cold, and windows were closed. Those who heard thought it was probably just a lovers' quarrel or a couple of drunks getting rowdy. Kitty Genovese screamed and screamed for help as her assailant punched her and beat her over the head, stabbed her repeatedly, and bruised her all over her body. Finally, he raped her as she lay dying. When it was all over, one of the neighbors called the police. They arrived within minutes, but Kitty Genovese died in the ambulance on the way to the hospital.

"Winston Moseley got away that night. He was apprehended later on a burglary charge and confessed to the murder. He's locked up for life. That's not what I'm concerned with today. No, what concerns me is this: thirty-eight neighbors also confessed. Each one of them heard or witnessed some part of the attack, which lasted over half an hour. Thirty-eight neighbors did nothing to intervene. They looked on and let this young woman die a horrible death."

When I pause to look at the faces before me, I see an opening: these are the bystanders, I imagine, sitting right here in the auditorium. How do I get past whatever it is that paralyzes them? How do I get them to step up and take responsibility?

"Thirty-eight neighbors did nothing. How does this happen? It happens when we become apathetic about our roles in society. It happens when we forget that we are a community, that we are connected to one another and have an obligation to engage with other human beings." Okay, I have to unpack this a bit, cover the bases, then circle back. "A crime like what happened to Kitty Genovese may be the act of a deranged individual. Other crimes may be different in their causes, pointing to broader failures of society. But in the moment of opportunity, when a criminal grabs his chance and a victim is suffering, our own responsibility is the same. When the criminal finds his victim in a dark alley, an observer, too, has a moment of opportunity. Will you see the victim not as a stranger or a statistic but as another human being like yourself? Will you be fully human in that moment and feel the obligation to care, to act, to get involved? Will you be fully a citizen and rise to the responsibility?"

They're still with me, every one of them. So I start to sum up and come in for a landing . . . "There was a young woman at the threshold of her life, a budding flower ready to open." And there's my hand, almost as if it doesn't belong to me, the fingers cupped and opening in bloom, then closing to a hard fist: "We destroyed that flower."

The applause carries me down the steps. Ken is grinning broadly, proudly. They announce that I've won first prize! A little cocky, I tell Ken that sometimes talking with your hands is fine. It's who I am, where I come from.

I was doing my homework at the kitchen table and Junior was doing his, as usual, in front of the TV, when the door opened. Mami made a dramatic entrance, slamming the stack of books in her arms straight down on the floor.

"I'm not going back!" she announced, her voice trembling. "It's too much for me. I'm sorry, I can't do it."

"Junior, get in here!" I yelled. He appeared in the doorway instantly. "If you can't do it, Mami, then we can't either. Take a break, Junior, no more school for us." With both hands I snapped shut the textbook I was reading—a very satisfying sound. I did glance at the page number first, though.

This mutiny was incited only a few months after my mother had sat Junior and me down at that same kitchen table and asked whether we would be willing to make some sacrifices so that she could study to qualify as a registered nurse. She had wanted years before to continue her schooling, but that hope was dashed when Papi died. Over time, the salary she earned as a practical nurse lagged further and further behind what registered nurses were earning. She was worried that with her Social Security survivors' benefits ending when Junior and I finished school, she wouldn't be able to manage on her own. She certainly didn't want to lean on us to support her. We would have to tighten our belts for a while, while she took leave from the hospital to attend school.

The money was not an insurmountable problem. My mother took a Saturday shift at a methadone clinic to make up a bit of lost income. I had worked the previous summer in the business office at Prospect Hospital, and they let me continue on weekends during the school year. Junior was working at Prospect too, in reception, and he had a second job as a sacristan at St. Patrick's Cathedral. All the little pieces added up.

No, the problem was not money. The problem was that my mother was scared out of her wits. Never mind that she was one very intelligent and ambitious woman. Never mind that Hostos Community College, where she enrolled, was specially created to serve the South Bronx Latino community with a bilingual program for students like my mother. Never mind that she had done the work of a registered nurse unofficially for years, if only because Prospect Hospital was so tiny and she was so well trusted there. Never mind even that she had nursed half the residents of Hunts Point, Bronxdale, and Co-op City at one point or another. Do I exaggerate? Not much.

My mother was tortured by lack of confidence in her own mental ability. She was especially terrified as soon as anything could be labeled a math problem, instead of just a matter of calculating a dosage. The word "quiz" was to her a stun gun. Most of the time, she beat back her fear with furious effort. She would crack the books as soon as she walked in the door, and midnight would find her still studying. Occasionally, though, anxiety got the better of her, and it was then that a bit of reverse psychology—some might say emotional blackmail—was in order. The idea that Junior and I might quit too, however improbable, was far more terrifying than any quiz.

Seeing my mother get back to her studies was all the proof I needed that a chain of emotion can persuade when one forged of logic won't hold. But more important was her example that a surplus of effort could overcome a deficit of confidence. It was something I would remember often in years ahead, whenever faced with fears that I wasn't smart enough to succeed.

Twelve

As much as I aspired to Kenny's cool, dispassionate rationality, *Love Story* succeeded in sucking me in, along with every other high school girl in America. But there was something on the screen that mesmerized me even more than the heart-tugging story of Ali MacGraw's sickness or Ryan O'Neal's blue eyes. The college campus where the 1970 movie was set, supposedly Harvard, seemed a wonderland. Set among pristine snowy fields, here was a cathedral of learning whose denizens lived out what seemed like an antiquarian fantasy, debating under pointy arches, scaling book-lined walls, and lounging on leather couches. Apart from Camden, New Jersey, and the alternate reality of Puerto Rico, I had never traveled far from the Bronx, and I had certainly never seen anything like this. If I had known then that many scenes of *Love Story* were actually filmed at Fordham University in the borough where we lived, my future might have turned out very differently.

Until those darkened hours in a movie theater, I hadn't given much thought to what life at college might be like or how it might be different from high school. Then, in the fall of my senior year, the phone rang. It was Kenny, the familiar deep, steady voice calling long-distance from Princeton, where he was a freshman. As he fed coins into the box every few minutes, he described the strange new world he was navigating. He advised me that it was time for me, too, to be thinking about applying to college, and one thing he said sticks clearly in my memory, because I had no idea what he meant: "Try for the Ivy League." Ken was the first student we knew from Spellman ever to have crossed into that world, and it wasn't a term that had ever come up in conversation. He explained that this was the finest college education available and that it would open every door. I jotted down the names of the colleges as he rattled them off, tossing in Stanford for good measure.

The next day the guidance counselor had only one question as she was thumbing through the thick catalog she'd taken down from the shelf: "Have you thought about Fordham?" A couple of pages of the book were devoted to each college: a mission statement in blandly aspirational code, a few statistics, generic black-and-white photographs of students looking earnestly engaged. When I said no to Fordham, she offered the names of several more Catholic colleges.

I told her that I wasn't really interested in parochial colleges; I wanted to apply to Harvard, Yale, Princeton, Columbia, Stanford . . .

She looked at me. "Okay." And that was the extent of her guidance. This was an occasion when it would never have occurred to me to ask for advice. At a Catholic high school that served the kids of Irish and Italian immigrants, a focus on parochial colleges made perfect sense: just getting into college was already more than most students' parents had accomplished. I happened to be graduating on the cusp of a change that would soon see many of Spellman's students going on to the most highly competitive schools. But that fall, Kenny Moy at Princeton was pretty much the first Spellman student to walk on the moon.

I got the application forms and wrote my essays, scribbling in the dark with not a clue as to what might be a worthy subject or how to shape such a thing. I tackled the SAT in much the same way. The brochure that came with the registration form was the only hint I had of what to expect on the test. Anyway, I could not have afforded a prep course, even if I'd known there was such a thing.

Qualifying for financial aid was the easiest part. With my mother enrolled at Hostos Community College at the time, we were living mainly on the Social Security survivors' benefits, supplemented slightly by Mami's part-time work at the methadone clinic, her summer pay at Prospect Hospital, and the little that Junior and I contributed from our part-time and summer jobs. There were no assets to report. None of us even had a bank account. On paydays I would walk five blocks from Prospect Hospital to the check-cashing place near the train station to cash my paycheck, just as my mother had always done, just as the rest of the staff at the hospital did. To pay the phone bill, you could get a money order there too. Cash was good enough for everything else.

It's just as well I had no idea how selective the colleges I was applying to were. If I had known, I might have hesitated. I did understand enough to hedge my bets, though: City University of New York could serve as my safety school, since it was public admission. Among the alternatives, I figured it likeliest I would end up at the state university at Stony Brook, at which Kevin was aiming. I had quickly given up on Stanford as being too far away. Flying cross-country to have a look would have already cost more than I could afford, never mind coming home for Christmas.

Come November, a postcard arrived from Princeton with three boxes, a cryptic message beside each—"likely," "possible," and "unlikely." On my card, the first was marked with an X. This seemed more like communication from a Magic 8 Ball than from a university. I wasn't sure what I was expected to do with this occult clue, so I trooped off once again to the guidance counselor's office.

Behind the look of utter surprise that completely rearranged her features, the oracle pronounced: "'Likely' means just what it says. There's a very good chance you'll get in." I thought to myself, really?

I was still getting my head around this when a couple of days later I happened to walk by the school nurse's office. "I heard you got a 'likely' from Princeton," she called out to me as I passed.

I stopped in my tracks. "Yes, I did."

"Well, can you explain to me how you got a 'likely' and the two top-ranking girls in the school only got a 'possible'?"

I just looked at her. What did she mean by that? Not to mention that accusatory tone. My perplexed discomfort under her baleful gaze was clearly not enough; shame was the response she seemed to want from me.

Sometimes in such situations, an apt answer only occurs to you hours later: "Because of what I've accomplished on the forensics team and in student government. Because I work part-time during the school year and full-time during the summers. I may be ranked below them, but I'm still in the top ten, and I *do* much more than the others do." But even that undelivered comeback was far from complete. Her question would hang over me not just that day but for the next several years, while I lived the day-to-day reality of affirmative action. At the time I was applying to college, I had little understanding of how the admissions process functioned generally, let alone how affirmative action might affect it in particular. Barely a decade had passed since affirmative action had been implemented in government contracting. It was still experimental in Ivy League college admissions, and few of the first minority students to benefit from it had even managed to graduate yet.

Soon, those fat envelopes I came to recognize as acceptance packages stuffed the mailbox almost daily. Now that the choice was real and imminent, I sat down to more serious deliberation. Columbia, I realized, a mere subway ride away, was too close for comfort: I'd have no choice but to live at home, unable to justify the extra expense of a dorm room. That left Radcliffe (Harvard's sister school), Yale, and Princeton, each worth a visit.

With *Love Story* still lodged in my mind, I scheduled Radcliffe first. I was told that after an interview at the admissions office, a student group would show me around. But first I had to find my way to Massachusetts. As close as we had lived to Manhattan my whole life, I had only been there on special occasions—that first date with Kevin; the Christmas and Easter shows at Radio City Music Hall; Alfred's death march to the summit of Lady Liberty. On the miserable rainy day that my visit was scheduled, the cavernous hall of Grand Central station seemed cold shelter, its vault dark with decades of grime. The railways then were staggering back following a long decline, only recently rescued by the establishment of Amtrak and, in New York, the long reconstruction of Penn Station as Madison Square Garden. My nine dollars and ninety cents bought me a seat in a tattered car carpeted in cigarette butts.

A sooty rain fell uninterrupted from New York to Boston, and by the time I had navigated the Boston subway and walked the last few blocks to the admissions office, I was dripping like a sewer rat. I was also feeling a shade of disappointment. There was neo-Gothic architecture aplenty, but the campus was no idyllic haven set apart from the world. Harvard and Radcliffe were fused with Cambridge, densely urban, tangled with honking traffic.

Inside the waiting room, when the inner door finally opened, I found myself face-to-face with a creature such as I had never encountered: a woman with a hairdo of sculpted silver, in a perfectly tailored black dress, a pearl necklace and earrings, beautiful little pumps. This is different! I thought.

I followed this apparition into her office and was stunned again by what met my eyes. I had never before seen an Oriental rug, its intricate pattern the most gorgeous of puzzles meandering across the floor. And I had never before seen a white couch. To be honest, I had probably never seen a couch that wasn't covered in plastic. I was ushered into an elegant, high-backed, winged throne of a chair, in which I felt tiny, surprised to feel my feet touch the floor. I had never seen such a room with my own eyes, but I knew: This was good taste. And this was money.

That was when the yapping dogs shattered my trance. They must have been barking since I'd walked in, but now they were jumping up at me, all bare teeth and bony claws. They were just lapdogs, really, one black and one white, but they scared me. She called to them, and they scrambled onto the white couch and sat beside her, and there the three of them completed a surreal tableau, three pairs of eyes gazing at me, a vision in black and white.

That may have been the shortest interview of my life,

perhaps all of fifteen minutes. The flow of words that always came to me naturally, and still does whenever I meet a stranger, mostly dried up. When I found myself back in the waiting room, too early for the students who were to meet me, the numbness dissolved into a suffocating panic: I don't belong here! For the first and, so far, the last time in my life, I did the unthinkable: I fled. Asking the receptionist to leave word for the students who were coming to get me, I said, "I'm sorry, but I have to leave."

It was early evening by the time I retraced my journey in reverse. My mother looked up from her homework at the kitchen table. "What's wrong? You were supposed to be away for a couple of days."

"Mami, I don't belong there."

Her gaze seemed inclined to question this conclusion, but after a moment's thought she said, "You know best, Sonia." She would say it often thereafter, to confess the limits of her judgment in the world I was entering and acknowledge my having reached the stage of adult self-determination. And that was the last we would speak of Radcliffe. I was convinced they would retract their offer. They didn't, but my list was now shorter by one.

My visit to Yale was a very different story. When I arrived at the station in New Haven, an old hand at Amtrak by now, the two Latino students sent to pick me up said they were coming from a campus protest. Eager to jump back into the fray, they apologized, saying that they would just be dropping me off for now. They would give me the tour later . . . unless, perhaps, I'd like to come along to the protest?

My experience of the antiwar protests was limited to the television screen. Though friends worried plenty about their luck in the draft lottery and Vietnam would come up as a topic in Forensics Club, debates weren't boiling up spontaneously in my high school lunchroom.

That's not to say I didn't understand the reasons underlying the cause, but raising voice and fist against Yale's involvement in the war effort didn't seem a smart way to prepare for an interview there. Instead, I went for a walk. The inner city of New Haven was impoverished then, depressed and threatening, no better than the South Bronx and a lot less lively. Actually, it made Co-op City seem idyllic.

When my guides found me again, they were buzzing from the protest and eager for a rap session. We joined up with a larger group of Hispanic kids, some from New York, others from the Southwest, all of them more radical than anyone I had ever known before. For two days I camped in the dorm and scouted the campus in their company, listening to talk of revolution, Cuba, and Che Guevara and feeling generally uninformed. At least Fidel Castro was a familiar name, and news of the Cuban missile crisis had penetrated even the cocoon of my Catholic school childhood, where communism was deemed a godless threat, more cosmic than political. I could tell purgatory from limbo better than I could recognize the distinctions between socialism and communism that spurred the arguments during those two days at Yale. So embarrassed was I by my innocence that I would go to the library and read up on Che Guevara after I got home.

I was embarrassed, too, by all the "down with whitey" talk. It wasn't an attitude I shared, nor one I was eager to adopt. Many of my friends, most of my classmates, and virtually all of my teachers were white. Whether it was due to the indeterminate color of my skin or my very determined personality, I moved easily between different worlds without assuming disguises. Yes, I'd experienced prejudice aimed straight at me, from the blatant taunts of my street-fighting days to the cold shoulder of Kevin's mom, to the subtler barb from the school nurse more recently. But I couldn't see such narrow-mindedness as the workings of systemic forces of history and certainly not as fitting neatly into a master narrative of perpetual class struggle, the way these Yale kids did. This stuff simply didn't define me in any meaningful way: if somebody called me a spic, it told me a lot about them, but nothing about myself. And how could it help the situation to hurl a slur in reply?

It was difficult to picture myself spending four years in this environment, especially with Kevin coming to visit on weekends. I left Yale thinking: not here—though I didn't feel the same panicked urge to flee that I had felt at Radcliffe. Even if I didn't share their attitudes, I knew where these kids were coming from, and when they talked of family and home, I recognized how much we did share.

By the time I went to see Princeton, I was down to gathering loose change for bus fare, Amtrak now beyond my budget. When Kenny met me at the bus station, I was surprised to see his hair grown very long, an expression of his new freedom. We dropped my bag at his dorm before heading out to tour the campus.

As we entered the main gates from Nassau Street, the sunlight on that balmy spring day danced magically on the sandy Collegiate Gothic architecture and the emerald lawns and the surrounding woodlands, a prospect that has enchanted generations of Princeton students but that took me completely unprepared. Even the bronze tigers flanking the entrance to ivy-covered Nassau Hall, while reminding me of the stone lions that guard the New York Public Library, seemed more pensive and more elegant.

Kenny had gathered a very small group of friends. Like him, they were exceptionally bright but slightly offbeat inner-city kids, radical in their politics, though quietly so, who conducted their lives at arm's length from Princeton's preppy mainstream. We sat up late together in a dorm room that night, talking easily. "Socially, it's a wasteland here," Kenny said, his judgment affirmed by solemn nods from the other freshmen. "It's a bunch of very strange, privileged human beings, and you're not going to understand any of them. But intellectually, you can deal with these people. They're not *that* smart."

At my interview the next morning I felt just as comfortable chatting with the admissions officer in his tiny corner office. He was professorially tweedy, down to his leather elbow patches and little horn-rimmed glasses, but he was open and easy to talk to.

Before the weekend was over, my decision was firm. A full scholarship capped it.

When, at the end of summer, it finally came time to say good-bye, the women at Prospect Hospital had taken up a collection. "Sonia, go buy yourself some new shoes for college. Please!"

"But these shoes are comfortable," I said, my usual line. It wasn't the first time they had begged me to upgrade my footwear. My feet blistered easily in new shoes, so once I had broken in a pair, I would never give them up. Everyone in the office had heard me on the phone defending my raggedy shoes to my grandmother. "Buy some new shoes already! Make your grandmother happy" was an old story. New shoes for college was just the latest twist.

On Kenny's advice, I planned to get a bicycle once I got to Princeton. The only other purchase he advised was a raincoat. Mami offered to buy it and came shopping with me. We searched up and down Fordham Road without finding anything I liked. We even stepped into Loehmann's, my first time there. Though it was a discount house, and popular in Co-op City, the prices, to us, were a shock. So we went—where else?—to La Tercera, the Latino shopping heart of the South Bronx on Third Avenue.

No luck at Alexander's. I wasn't being fussy; I was just having a hard time picturing myself in that magical land of archways and manicured lawns wearing anything I saw on these racks. On the other side of the street, which was divided by the elevated train line rumbling overhead, were the slightly more upscale dress shops, places where you might shop for a wedding or some other very special occasion. In this case, a last resort.

There it was: glowing white with toggle buttons and a subtle flair of fake fur trim up the front and around the hood. As improbably white as a white couch, white as a blanket of snow on a college lawn.

"You like it, Sonia?"

"I love it, Mami." This was another first. Unlike my mother, or Chiqui, or my cousin Miriam, or many of my friends, I'd never cared enough to fall in love with a garment. But wrapped in this, I knew I wouldn't feel so odd. Unfortunately, it was a size too small. I tried on a couple of other coats, but my heart had been claimed, and Mami knew it.

I was ready to leave and try elsewhere, but she said, "*Espera* . . . Sonia, wait, maybe they can order it." She went to the counter and waited in silence as the saleswoman helped another customer. And then another and another. My mother is a very patient woman, so I knew what it took for her to finally say, "Miss, I need help."

"What do you want?" the saleswoman snapped without turning.

"Do you have this in a twelve?"

"If it's not on the rack, we don't have it."

"Do you have another store? Can you order it?"

The woman finally turned and looked at her. "Well, that would be a lot of trouble, wouldn't it?"

I was halfway to the door, fully expecting my mother to give up, but she stood her ground. "I know it's a lot of trouble, but my daughter's going away to college and she likes this coat. I want to give it to her as a gift. So would you please look to see if you can find this coat for my daughter."

The woman's silent shrug spoke loudly enough: You're a royal pain. But as she turned away, she asked indifferently, "So where's she going to college?"

"To Princeton."

I saw the saleswoman's head swing around as in a cartoon double take. The transformation was remarkable. She was suddenly all courtesy and respect, full of praise for Princeton, and more than happy to make a phone call in search of my coat, which, as it turned out, would arrive in a week. Mami thanked her profusely and left a deposit. It was a lot of money, but that coat would last me all four years of college. It had to.

As we were walking back to the station, I commented on the saleswoman's change of attitude. My mother stopped in the shadow of the elevated track and said to me, "I have to tell you, Sonia, at the hospital I'm being treated like a queen right now. Doctors who have never once had a nice word for me, who have never spoken to me at all, have come up to congratulate me."

Overhead, the train rumbled loudly, and I had to pause for a long moment before I admitted that I had never dreamed what a difference Princeton would make to people.

She looked at me steadily. "What you got yourself into, daughter, I don't know. But we're going to find out."

Thirteen

In the week since Alfred had driven off with Mami waving good-bye out the window, the collegiate fairy tale in my mind was becoming something more akin to science fiction. In part it was the record-breaking heat that summer of 1972, which silvered Princeton's leafy vistas, endowing everything with a more unearthly aura than I had remembered. But I was also finding that many of my classmates seemed to come from another planet and that that impression was reciprocated.

Waiting outside Dillon Gym, where we were to meet our advisers, I struck up a conversation with another freshman sitting beside me. She was from Alabama, she said. I had never before heard an accent like that in real life. I listened spellbound as she explained how her father, her grandfather, and her elder brother were all Princeton alums. She couldn't have been more delighted to be there representing her generation. "And it really is just the friendliest, most welcoming place you'll find," she gushed. "I mean, look at all the unusual people that come here!" She was indicating an approaching pair, their heads together, laughing loudly.

I recognized my roommate, Dolores, and our friend Teresa. Dolores was vaguely Mexican looking, with light brown skin and Indian-black hair. Teresa was barely a shade darker than I am, hardly dark at all, but her features were distinctively Latina. They both looked pretty normal to me. Without premeditation, I greeted them exuberantly in rapid-fire Spanish, though we usually spoke English together. I meant no malice toward the girl from Alabama, but my pulse was speeding with a sense of purpose. Nothing more needed to be said.

Dolores Chavez was from New Mexico. We must have been assigned to room together because someone had assumed two Hispanics would have a lot in common. But all Dolores knew of Puerto Ricans came from *West Side Story*, and I suspect that initially she was half afraid I'd knife her in her sleep. I knew even less of New Mexico than she knew of New York. Dolores seemed to me a country girl, sweet-tempered, shy, and very far from home. One night soon after we'd arrived, she got her guitar out and sang softly for a while before we went to sleep, such deep longing in her voice.

As social as I am, I was quiet in those early days, trying to make sense of the conversations flowing around me. One evening, I found myself with a group of girls sitting in our resident adviser's dorm room. One of them mentioned being invited to a wedding and that she'd decided just to choose a gift from the bridal registry. What in the world is a bridal registry? I wondered. Our adviser, a senior, allowed that her father sometimes received wedding invitations from people whose names he didn't even recognize, probably strangers hoping he would blame his memory and send a gift anyway, she figured. Who invites strangers to their wedding? For that matter, who sends them gifts? Where I came from, you handed the couple an envelope with money at the reception. Were people here so rich they could afford a wedding without gifts of cash?

Whenever I felt out of place or homesick, I took refuge at Firestone Library. Books had seen me through an earlier time of trouble, and their presence all around me was both a comfort and an answer to the question of why I had come here. From my first day on campus, I'd enviously eyed the carrels in Firestone, which were reserved for upperclassmen. One day, one of those would be mine! Meanwhile, I reveled in the vastness of the main catalog room, riffling through the drawers full of cards, rows and rows of cabinets running almost the full length of the ground floor. And above them, like cathedral spires, rose the stacks, shelf after shelf, carrying a book for every card below.

My grazing in Firestone that first week was not at random, however. The course offerings at Princeton seemed a bewildering buffet: so many unfamiliar subjects that whetted my appetite. I dug into the library catalog to get a taste of each subject that tempted me before committing to a whole meal. At the same time, I was already well aware that in our freshman class, some, like me, were far fresher than others. Many from across the United States and abroad had gone to high schools that sounded more like mini-colleges, with library buildings of their own and sophisticated electives. I had made it into Princeton but, in this way too, with far more meager resources than most. I was under no illusions about how much remedial education could be accomplished skimming a few books in the stacks.

That there was no official pre-law curriculum turned out to be a blessing of sorts. I had to decide for myself what would be the most useful way to fill in the wide blank areas in my understanding. Having negligible prior knowledge of practically everything, I planned with each course to gulp down as much as I could. And so introductory surveys seemed ideal. I was drawn to psychology and sociology, having always been interested in the patterns of individual behavior, as well as the structure of communities; history, especially American, seemed essential and promised to reveal how a larger scheme of things had developed over time. Moral philosophy sounded a lot like what I imagined legal reasoning to involve. And just from reading the newspaper since entering Spellman, I knew that one day I would need to grapple with economics. An art history survey seemed like just the way to answer the many questions that had lapped at my mind since my childhood visit to the Ponce museum. But I would err on the side of practicality for now, saving that one for a sophomore treat.

My adviser approved my course load without question,

and I felt I was on my way. But back at the dorm, deflation awaited. Everyone had returned from taking care of the same business, and the freshman floor was abuzz with talk of exotic upper-level courses my classmates were taking thanks to their Advanced Placement work in high school, which had allowed them to leapfrog ahead. By comparison, my course selections sounded boring, even lazy. Was I squandering an opportunity to really challenge myself? Maybe I just wasn't as smart as they were?

That tide of insecurity would come in and out over the years, sometimes stranding me for a while but occasionally lifting me just beyond what I thought I could accomplish. Either way, it would wash over the same bedrock certainty: ultimately, I know myself. At each stage of my life, I've had a pretty clear notion of my needs and of what I was ready for. The introductory surveys would involve just as much work, given their broad scope, as more specialized advanced courses and would allow me for the first time to cultivate the critical faculties that Miss Katz had tried to instill: understanding the world by engaging with its big questions rather than just absorbing the factual particulars.

I still had to choose a science lab course to meet a core requirement. Those in the natural sciences were known to be backbreakers, more appropriate for a pre-med or a budding scientist than an aspiring lawyer. I did notice, however, that Introductory Psychology included a lab that met the need. An introduction to Freud and other schools of thought, as well as an overview of brain function, seemed as if it might prove very handy over time. There was only one challenge to overcome, but one far more daunting than any rigors of organic chemistry or molecular biology labs: rats.

I have always had a deathly fear of anything that scurries or crawls: bugs, rodents, what have you. It isn't just the stereotypical fear of a lady standing on a chair, though I've done that. The special revulsion I feel goes back to childhood. The giant cockroaches that infested the projects one year—we called them water bugs—brought me to hysteria. How many times had I seen my mother take the whole place apart trying to locate the nest? The very thought of their proximity would keep me awake all night. And so when I realized that the psych lab would oblige me to handle rodents while I studied their reactions, I decided, a little perversely, to make the most of it. Undertaking a course of what psychologists call exposure therapy, I devised an experiment that required me not only to hold the rats but to implant electrodes in their brains.

It was going surprisingly well at first. I had steeled myself to picking the rats up by the tail and holding their furry bodies as I gave them a sedative injection. Once they were drugged, implanting the electrodes wasn't so bad. Tracking their behavior was no fun: it meant watching them continuously, without turning away in disgust. But I was doing it. It wasn't until the final weeks of the semester that everything went awry. I came into the lab one day to find all my rats milling around the same spot in the cage in an oddly intent way. I couldn't see what the attraction was, but the sight of their frenzied huddle was enough to stir the old revulsion: I certainly wasn't going to stick a hand in that cage. I found a stick and poked one of them off the pile. He turned to look at me, and in the gap that opened up, I saw the rat they were gnawing at, its abdomen already half devoured.

The grad student overseeing my efforts intercepted me as I ran out of the room screaming. As I tried to contain my hysterics, he explained that cannibalism is normal rat behavior, that it had evolved as a way to control disease in the population and, as such, was a widely recognized sign of plague. Somehow that didn't help. He suggested I calm down and come back tomorrow.

The next day my state of mind was no better: the trauma had done its damage. It was horrifying even to imagine handling a rat as I had been doing for months, and no less so to think I had botched a whole semester's work. Fortunately, my professor took a philosophical view when I explained why I was utterly incapable of seeing my project through. As a psychologist he credited the motive of trying to cure my phobia by means of this experiment, and as a teacher he could see I had been at it diligently from the start. My grade wouldn't suffer much because of this fiasco. "Your plan was perfectly suited to what the course was intended to teach," he allowed. "Not every experiment is a success. That's the nature of doing science." The nature of doing many things, I might add: success is its own reward, but failure is a great teacher too, and not to be feared.

☆

Part of my financial-aid package committed me to weekly hours in the work-study program. At the start of freshman year, I was assigned to food service at the commons, but a lingering case of mononucleosis took me off the cafeteria line. I needed a desk job where I couldn't cause an epidemic. I was eager, too, to explore something new. The food service job was standard student fare in a predictable environment. But when I saw a posting for a keypunch operator at the Computer Center, I was intrigued.

Computers were a brave new world when I started work there in 1972, and access to their powers was confined to cavernous campus centers. Judith Rowe, head of the center's social sciences division, was a pioneer; among the first to envision the potential of quantitative analysis in the social sciences, she saw that computers would be the key to realizing it. To advance that vision, she encouraged graduate students to use the computer in analyzing their research data, an effort she facilitated by hiring work-study students like me to do the data entry.

I'd taken a typing class in high school, figuring that I could always get a job that way if necessary. That was qualification enough to start, as no one beyond the programmers themselves had any computer skills. Under Judith's guidance I learned a bit about programming and became skilled at keypunching. Because the work was specialized, I earned double what I had been making in the cafeteria. There were other perks too: we could set our own hours and come as we were, in jeans and T-shirts. It was a student's dream job, and I kept it all four years at Princeton, working there ten or fifteen hours a week on top of other jobs that came and went.

Later, in my senior year, I was taking a break from writing my thesis to catch up on a couple of hours of keypunch work when an idea occurred to me: Why not enter the text of my thesis on the same types of punch cards that we were using for data analysis? That way, I could make changes as needed to individual cards without having to retype all the subsequent pages. Judith was intrigued. She thought it was a worthwhile experiment, and she assigned another operator to do the data entry for me. It's hard to be certain, but I might have submitted the very first word-processed senior thesis in Princeton's history, and I didn't even have to type it myself.

In my freshman year, however, I had cause to doubt that I would be able to write a senior thesis eventually. My very first midterm paper, for American history class, came back with a C, a grade I couldn't remember getting since the fourth grade. I was flattened, but even worse, I had no idea where I had gone wrong. I'd fallen in love with the subject—the Great Depression and Franklin D. Roosevelt's New Deal—pursuing it with everything I had. And the professor had been so inspiring that I wanted to impress her. Nancy Weiss was chair of the department, one of the first women in the whole country to hold such a post; later, as Nancy Malkiel, she would become the longest-serving dean of the college.

Professor Weiss told a familiar tale: although my paper was chock-full of information and even interesting ideas, there was no argumentative structure, no thesis that my litany of facts had been marshaled to support. "That's what analysis is—the framework of cause and effect," she said. Her point was a variation of what Miss Katz had been getting at, though now it was coming across more clearly and consequentially. Obviously, I was still regurgitating information. It was dawning on me that in all my classes, I was so concerned with absorbing the facts in the reading that I wasn't organizing them into a larger argument. By now, several people had pointed out where I needed to go, but none could show me the way. I began to despair of ever learning how to succeed at my assignments, when quite unexpectedly it occurred to me: I already knew how.

Running into Kenny Moy outside Firestone one day got me thinking about my days in Forensics Club. Suddenly I realized that what had made me a winner on his team was precisely what I needed to do in my papers. I would not have dreamed of opening my mouth in a debate without first mapping out a position, anticipating and addressing objections, considering how best to persuade my listeners. Seeing the task in the context of another I already performed well largely demystified the problem. In my next few papers I would start doing in prose what I had learned how to do in spoken words. But before I could do that really well, I'd have to face up to another obstacle: the general deficiency of my written English.

Whether it is a pregnant pause or even talking with her hands, a debater has many expressive tricks in her repertoire, some of which may cover a multitude of sins against the language. In writing, however, one's words stand naked on the page. Professor Weiss had minced none of her own informing me that my English was weak: my sentences were often fragments, my tenses erratic, and my grammar often just not grammatical. If I could have seen it myself, I would have fixed it, but what was wrong sounded right to me. It wasn't until the following year, when I took Peter Winn's course in contemporary Latin American history, that the roots of my problem were uncovered: my English was riddled with Spanish constructions and usage. I'd say "authority of dictatorship" instead of "dictatorial authority," or "tell it to him" instead of "tell him." Peter's corrections in red ink were an epiphany: I'd had no idea that I sounded so much like my mother! But my English wouldn't be as easy to fix as the lack of an argument in my essays. I bought some grammar handbooks and, as part of the same effort, a stack of vocabulary booklets. Over summer vacations spent working at Prospect Hospital, or later at the Department of Consumer Affairs in Spanish Harlem, I'd devote each day's lunch hour to grammar exercises and to learning ten new words, which I would later test out on Junior, trying to make them my own. Junior was unfazed by my semantic challenges. He was just happy to be out of my shadow in his final years at Cardinal Spellman.

I came to accept during my freshman year that many of the gaps in my knowledge and understanding were simply limits of class and cultural background, not lack of aptitude or application as I'd feared. That acceptance, though, didn't make me feel less self-conscious and unschooled in the company of classmates who'd had the benefit of much more worldly experience. Until I arrived at Princeton, I had no idea how circumscribed my life had been, confined to a community that was essentially a village in the shadow of a great metropolis with so much to offer, of which I'd tasted almost nothing. Once, I was trying to explain to my friend and later roommate Mary Cadette how out of place I sometimes felt.

"It must be like *Alice in Wonderland*," she said sympathetically.

"Alice who?"

She was kind enough to salvage the moment with a quick grace: "It's a wonderful book, Sonia, you must read it!" In fact, she would guide me thoughtfully toward a long list of classics she had read while I'd been perusing *Reader's Digest*. What did my mother know of *Huckleberry Finn* or *Pride and Prejudice*?

Later, at the Computer Center, I would enter data for a project that Judith Rowe described as a study of how people paid for college. My fingers froze on the keys as I read what I was typing: financial figures of the most well-off at Princeton. This was my first glimpse of trust funds; tax write-offs and loopholes; summer jobs at Daddy's firm that paid the equivalent of a year's tuition; incomes in the millions, disbursed a half million here, a few hundred thousand for that poor guy there. Between her own salary from Prospect Hospital and her survivors' benefits, which would end very soon, my mother's income was never more than five thousand dollars a year. Nothing could have clarified as starkly where I stood in relation to some of the people among whom I was now living and learning.

I never deluded myself that I could fill in everything I had missed growing up. Nor did I fail to appreciate that I'd had experiences of my own to prize or that I'd seen some aspects of life of which my classmates were sometimes naively unaware. Suffice it to say that Princeton made me feel that long after those summers spent first discovering the world's great books, I'd have to remain a student for life. It has been my pleasure to be one, actually, long after the virtue has ceased to be such a necessity.

Fourteen

Every week, like clockwork, a small, square envelope arrived in the mail, addressed in a familiar, scratchy hand. Inside the envelope was a paper napkin and inside that a dollar bill. Abuelita wasn't much of a correspondent. She might sign the napkin or not, but the loving gesture was reliable and steadfast. It meant a lot to know she was thinking of me, and a dollar was no small thing, for her or for me. Once in a rare while she would send a five-dollar bill, and I could see her smiling from seventy miles away.

Kevin came to visit with an equally reliable regularity. Driving down to Princeton from SUNY at Stony Brook every single weekend, he would make a detour through Co-op City to pick up a care package of fruits and juice from my mother. He would arrive around midnight frazzled and exhausted, still not accustomed to freeway driving, but as the weeks passed, he became more confident at the wheel.

When I asked my roommate, Dolores, if she would mind Kevin sleeping on our floor, she offered to spend weekends in a friend's room. I thought that was so generous of her, so graciously thoughtful. She meanwhile was thinking I was incorrigibly wild. She never let on, but later, after we'd gradually warmed to each other and become good friends, we'd have occasion to laugh about our first impressions of each other.

Actually, I wasn't wild at all: Kevin and I spent our wild weekends studying side by side. Stony Brook was a party scene, and he was glad of the chance to catch up on work. I offered many a time to come visit him there and save him the drive, but I don't think he wanted me to see just what a party scene it was. Only once did he accept, and that was on a holiday weekend when the campus was deserted. I could see why he preferred Princeton to the institutional, nondescript concrete of Stony Brook. He fell in love with the environment the same way that I had; later he would find his way back there for graduate school.

My mother came to visit me on campus once or twice each year. The first time, my cousin Charlie drove her and Junior down, along with Charlie's girlfriend. Kevin came too, of course. Nassau Inn, where many of my classmates' families would stay, was unimaginably expensive, so we had a slumber party. I gave Mami my bed and borrowed sleeping bags, mattresses, blankets, and pillows to make the rest of us comfortable on the floor. Charlie had a moment of profound shock in the bathroom, having forgotten that this was a girls' dorm. I sent him over to the male dorm next door, but their informal policy of sharing the showers with girlfriends was even more shocking to him. He's talked about it ever since.

When I came home from Princeton for a midterm break in my first year, Mami was panicking. She was in the final stretch of getting her nursing degree. The bilingual program at Hostos Community College included an English writing requirement. It wasn't as terrifying to her as the math, but it was onerous and she was struggling with it. She conceived the insane plan that I should write her paper for her.

"No way! That's cheating!" Facing dire threats that she would quit, I compromised. I agreed to look at what she had written and give her advice. We spent untold hours of my brief vacation at the kitchen table poring over her sentences. "There's no structure here, Mami. It wanders."

"I don't know, Sonia, I'm not good at embellishing."

"Forget about embellishing. What's the story you're trying to tell? What's your theme?"

"Ay, Sonia, please just write it for me!"

I didn't say it out loud, but I thought: Please, Mami, I don't have time for your insecurities. I have my own to deal with.

Her final exams were a torture worse than the English papers. Studying was not the problem. She had been doing that relentlessly for two years; she was used to it. But when exams loomed, the tension rose to a pitch higher than human ears could bear, the whips and chains came out, and the self-flagellation began in earnest. "I'm never going to pass," she moaned. I reassured her. She knew the material inside out. She had been doing these same procedures at Prospect Hospital for years.

"No, Sonia. I must have had some brain damage when I was small. Nothing stays in my memory."

"Don't be ridiculous! You're going to pass. Do you want to bet on it?"

"Yeah, I bet I'll fail."

We wagered a trip to Puerto Rico and shook hands on the stupidest wager I'd ever heard of: The winner would be the bigger loser. If she passed the exams, she would buy me a plane ticket. If she failed, I would pay for her trip.

I don't know if the bet was reverse psychology or a perverse good-luck charm, but it seemed to steady her resolve. In the end, of course, I won: my mother passed all five of her qualifying exams on the first try, which doesn't happen very often.

Late in the fall semester of my sophomore year, I sensed that something wasn't right. For two weeks in a row, no envelope had arrived in the mail. I was worried and phoned my mother: "Where's Abuelita? Why haven't I heard from her?"

There was a long silence before Mami finally spoke. A tone of blustering hesitation in her voice told me that I was the last to hear the news. No one had the courage to tell me. Abuelita was in the hospital, at Flower–Fifth Avenue. She had ovarian cancer. Like so many older women, she had stopped seeing a gynecologist long before. She thought—and she was sadly wrong, I want to stress—that routine checkups were pointless since she was past having children. And so the cancer was far advanced when they found it. I was ready to get on the next bus, but Mami said, "No, wait till you come for Christmas. Hopefully, she'll be home by then."

That was a few weeks away. I had no experience with cancer of any kind then, no point of reference, no way to guess at how serious it might be. All I knew was that winter had set in and the sky hung lower with each passing day.

By the time I got there, Abuelita was delirious and hallucinating. I spent the days at her side, just being there, studying while she slept. Aunts and uncles and cousins squeezed into her hospital room, and then at some point on Christmas Eve the crowd vanished. People were anxious because the oil embargo caused by the Arab-Israeli war meant hour-long lines at every gas station and they needed to fill up before the pumps closed for the holiday. Titi Gloria said, "Come, you'll get stuck here." My cousin Charlie and I looked at each other: no way were we leaving.

We decided to go get a Christmas tree for Abuelita; Charlie was the one who always decorated her apartment for the holidays, just as I had done our tree ever since Papi died. It started to snow as we walked down Lexington Avenue in the fading light. We'd gone all the way to Ninety-Sixth Street before finding a florist that was open. We picked out a small tabletop tree that was beautifully decorated and took turns carrying it back, our hands freezing. The snow was already sticking; it was that cold.

At her bedside, Charlie was trying to feed Abuelita a few spoonfuls of Jell-O, but she wouldn't take any. She kept asking for her clothes, as if she were going home. I was sitting in the chair by the door, and she looked right through me, talking to someone who wasn't there. "Angelina," she said. A chill went down my spine. I recognized the name: her sister, who'd passed away years ago. Charlie left the room for some reason, and then Abuelita said to me, *"Sonia, dame un cigarrillo."*

It was the first time she'd said my name since I'd arrived from Princeton. "Abuelita, this is a hospital," I said gently, hating to deny her. "You can't smoke in here."

She said it again, imperiously: "Sonia, give me a cigarette!" The voice of the matriarch. I found my purse, pulled out a cigarette, lit it. I held it to her lips. She took a puff and gave a little cough. Then, as I watched, the life left her face.

I gave her a hug. *"Bendición, Abuelita."* And then I yelled for the nurse. People came running, shooed me out of the room. It was just as well. I didn't go back in. I needed to be alone.

At the funeral, my sorrow flared into rage when I saw Nelson appear briefly, a spectral presence on the fringe of the mourners. I hadn't set eyes on him for three years, and now here he was, nodding in a doped-up daze. It was disrespectful of him to show up in that state, I fumed in silence. And it was desperately sad, sadder than I could bear just then. Nelson had gotten himself addicted to heroin while he was still in high school and then flunked out of half a dozen colleges while his father refused to accept the reality right before his eyes. His test scores were stellar, off the charts, so he'd get in the door easily enough, but he couldn't bring himself to show up for class or do the work. He slipped away from the funeral before we could say anything to each other, and I wouldn't see him again for several more years.

In the weeks that followed, I understood for the first time Abuelita's devastation when Papi died, how it had cut into her spirit. Her death did the same to me. A piece of me perilously close to my heart had been amputated. The sense of loss was startling, physically disorienting. It occurs to me that Flower–Fifth Avenue is the same hospital where I was born. "Full circle" is the phrase that pops into my mind, as if we were one person. *"Mercedes chiquita."* I can still hear her voice sometimes, all these years later. "Don't worry, *mi'jita*," she says, and I feel her protection.

Fifteen

I met Margarita Rosa a few weeks after arriving at Princeton, and we soon became fast friends. Coming from a poor neighborhood of Brooklyn and a traditionally conservative Puerto Rican family herself, Margarita understood instinctively the path I had traveled to Princeton. We rarely needed to talk about the incongruities of our being there, and so our rapport progressed quickly to more urgent matters.

"Three guys for every girl, and I can't get a date! What's wrong with this picture?"

"Don't take it personally," I'd say. "They didn't want to let women in the door, and now that we're here, they don't know what to do with us." Princeton had turned coed just three years before, and the presence of women on campus was still a thorn in the side of many old-school diehards.

"Not true, Sonia. If you're a blue-eyed blonde, they know

what to do with you. If you're black, there's at least a handful of brothers ready to stand up and say you're as beautiful as they are. But a *café-con-leche* Latina with a 'fro? That they don't know what to do with."

Margarita's tough luck with men mystified me. To my eyes, she was indeed attractive, petite, and lively, as well as being eloquent and passionate about making the world a better place. She was a junior when I was a freshman, and I could only hope to become like her.

"At least you don't have a pudgy nose," I offered.

"At least you've got Kevin," she returned.

We often studied at Firestone Library until closing time, when we would walk back to the dorms together. About once a week, before going home, we would stop off at the pub to continue the conversation over a glass of sangria and a slice of pizza. Margarita was pushing me to join Acción Puertorriqueña, the Latino student group that she was involved in, and I was pushing back. It was no reflection on the group; nor was I being standoffish. I just wasn't inclined to join anything until I'd gathered my bearings and felt more comfortable with my course load.

I've since come to recognize a personal tendency. In high school, I hadn't tried anything like student government or the Forensics Club until my second year, and it would be the same at Princeton and again at law school. The first year that I face the challenges of any new environment has always been a time of fevered insecurity, a reflexive terror that I'll fall flat on my face. In this self-imposed probationary period,

I work with compulsive intensity and single-mindedness until I gradually feel more confident. Some of the looming panic is no doubt congenital; I often see in my reactions something of my mother's irrational fear of being unequipped for nursing school. I have gone through this same kind of transition since becoming a judge, first on the federal district court, then on the appeals court, and finally on the Supreme Court.

Sure enough, I would join Acción Puertorriqueña during my sophomore year. I would bicycle out to the far edge of campus, where the architecture descended from Gothic Revival heights to the more human scale of colonial, and then on to the less-than-human industrial modern of graduate student housing. Just before the campus dissolved into suburban New Jersey, you reached the modest redbrick building of the Third World Center: headquarters and party central not just for Acción Puertorriqueña but for all the minority student groups on campus. I knew the area well: across the avenue were the Computer Center and Stevenson Hall, a relatively new dining facility that offered alternatives to the exclusive Princeton eating clubs. I'd embarrassed myself once in Stevenson asking for a glass of milk with my meal in the kosher canteen there, but after that I felt right at home. In fact, that part of campus became my neighborhood.

A space where one had a natural sense of belonging, a circle of friends who shared the same feeling of being a stranger in a strange land, who understood without need for explanation: it amounted to a subtle but necessary psychic refuge in an environment where an undercurrent of hostility often belied the idyllic surface. The *Daily Princetonian* routinely published letters to the editor lamenting the presence on campus of "affirmative action students," each one of whom had presumably displaced a far more deserving affluent white male and could rightly be expected to crash into the gutter built of her own unrealistic aspirations. There were vultures circling, ready to dive when we stumbled. The pressure to succeed was relentless, even if self-imposed out of fear and insecurity. For we all felt that if we did fail, we would be proving the critics right, and the doors that had opened just a crack to let us in would be slammed shut again.

It was because of this uneasy climate that so much of the work of Acción Puertorriqueña and other such groups focused on freshman admissions. In those early days of affirmative action—again, the practice was so new to Ivy League admissions that the first Latino students had yet to graduate when I arrived—many factors that complicate the cost-benefit analysis a generation later were at the time nonexistent.

Until we would raise kids of our own, no minority students had alumni for parents, and rare indeed were those who had not come from poor communities. The typical undergraduate had been guided to Princeton by relatives, by prep school guidance counselors, or else by teachers savvy about the system. Minority kids, however, had no one but their few immediate predecessors: the first to scale the ivy-covered wall against the odds, just one step ahead ourselves, we would hold the ladder steady for the next kid with more talent than opportunity. The blacks, Latinos, and Asians at

Princeton went back to their respective high schools, met with guidance counselors, and recruited promising students they knew personally. Then, every time a minority application landed in the pile of potential admissions, they'd reach out to make the applicant feel welcome or at least a little less intimidated.

This outreach was vital because disadvantaged students often had no idea that they stood a chance at a place like Princeton, assuming they'd even heard the name. In high school, I was vaguely aware that affirmative action existed, but I had no idea how or to what extent it worked in practical terms. When the two Hispanic students met me at the station in New Haven to show me around Yale, I was inclined to see their ethnicity as more a matter of pleasant coincidence than a programmatic effort. At most, I figured, they were being nice to one of their own kind, rather in the way Ken had encouraged me to consider Princeton and the other Ivy League colleges, not out of any political agenda. My innocence was the result of being unaware of just how few Latinas there would be in a place like Princeton, or for that matter that my being one could have figured so much in my admission.

One of Acción Puertorriqueña's most pressing objectives was to convince the administration to honor its commitment to increase the hiring of qualified Hispanics. There were almost sixty of us enrolled as students, a huge increase over just a few years ago, thanks mostly to the efforts of groups like ours. But there was not one Hispanic on the faculty or the administrative staff. It was hard, they said, to find qualified scholars, but could they not locate even one Latino janitor? You would never have known that Puerto Ricans made up 12 percent of the population of New Jersey. Quotas had not been declared illegal by the Supreme Court then, but we were not arguing in their favor. We were arguing only for some good-faith effort to correct historical imbalances.

It was not until we filed a formal complaint with the Department of Health, Education, and Welfare that we got President William Bowen's attention and a dialogue opened. Within a month, the Office for Civil Rights at the Department of Education had sent someone to meet with us in the provost's office. Before you knew it, Princeton had hired its very first Hispanic administrator—and not just any administrator: the assistant dean of student affairs, whose role was to advocate for students like us.

When I first joined Acción Puertorriqueña, the Mexican-Americans had their own separate group, the Chicano Organization of Princeton. Clearly, numbers as small as ours were better not divided, so we often joined forces on issues of mutual concern, and the two groups almost always partied together. There were a handful of nonaligned minority students—Filipinos, Native Americans, and other Latinos—so we at Acción Puertorriqueña invited them in, tacking "y Amigos" onto the end of our name. I liked the indiscriminate amiability of how that sounded, but even more the inclusiveness in practice. As much solace and strength as we gathered from group identity, it mattered greatly to have an open door. After all, the failure to include was why we had come together.

All of the different minority student groups at Princeton shared the Third World Center, and together they elected a governance board to run the facility. To assure balance, equal numbers of seats were allotted to African-American, Hispanic, and Asian students. In addition, there was an "open" section usually filled by African-Americans, by far the largest minority on campus. I took the risk of running outside the Hispanic category, becoming the first nonblack to win one of the open seats. I was proud of that victory, seeing it as a tribute to how well I listened and brokered compromises between factions.

For all the sense of accomplishment and the embrace I felt at the Third World Center, I had no wish to confine myself to a minority subculture and its concerns. The Latino community anchored me, but I didn't want it to isolate me from the full extent of what Princeton had to offer, including engagement with the larger community. I would warn any minority student today against the temptations of self-segregation: take support and comfort from your own group as you can, but don't hide within it.

My opportunity to venture out came with the chance to serve on the student-faculty Discipline Committee. The body typically dealt with the predictable lows of student behavior: stolen library books, dorm rule infractions, intoxicated rowdiness. Sometimes I wanted to cringe, as when a pair of our "amigos," Native Americans, had had a few too many and started tossing furniture out the window at the Third World Center. I shook my head in despair: drunken Indians? Talk about making it easy for the cranky alumni letter writers in the *Daily Princetonian*! A more serious incident involved a brilliant student wrongly accused of hacking into the university's computer system. Getting to the bottom of that one proved a challenge more technical than any other we would face, but I was able to draw on my experience at the Computer Center for clarity, in what was arguably my first judicial role.

There are few places in this country where institutional history overlaps the national narrative as self-consciously as it does at Princeton. The cannon in the center of the green saw action in the Revolutionary War. Among the über-alumni: James Madison, class of 1771, author of the Constitution. The Continental Congress of 1783 sat in Nassau Hall to receive news of the Treaty of Paris. Those self-assured people surrounding me, who had traveled the world confident of having an influential role in it one day, were no less certain of themselves as the rightful inheritors of this history. It was not something on which I could ever hope to have the same purchase. I needed a history in which I could anchor my own sense of self. I found it when I began to explore the history of Puerto Rico.

I had studied American, European, Soviet, and Chinese history and politics, but I knew next to nothing about the history of my own people. In the course offerings in Latin American history and politics, Puerto Rico was barely mentioned. Fortunately, it was possible for students to initiate courses.

Years before, I discovered, a Princeton student had put together a course on Puerto Rican history, and now, under the guidance of Professor Winn, I set out to revive it, bringing the syllabus up to date and recruiting the necessary quorum of students. I didn't make it easy on those who might be interested: my reading list was ambitious, to say the least.

The history that emerged from our reading was not a happy one. Under Spain, Puerto Rico suffered colonial neglect and the burden of policies designed to enrich distant parties at heavy cost to the island. Little effort was made to develop the natural resources or agriculture beyond what was needed to provision and mount the conquistadores on their way to Mexico and South America. Poor governance was compounded by bad luck—hurricanes and epidemics— as well as state-sponsored piracy by the British, French, and Dutch. For the Spanish settlers, as for the enslaved indigenous tribes and those from elsewhere in the Caribbean who took refuge on the island, it was a precarious existence that would not begin to improve until well into the nineteenth century. There was negligible civic life and minimal economic activity beyond smuggling. Any liberties the Spanish crown granted were often quickly revoked.

When Spain ceded Puerto Rico to the United States in 1898, along with Cuba and the Philippines as the spoils of the Spanish-American War, Puerto Ricans held an optimistic faith in American ideals of liberty, democracy, and justice. But that optimism would yield to a sense of betrayal for many. Governed without representation, exploited economically, some islanders came to feel they had merely exchanged one colonial master for another.

It was clear that the idea of Puerto Rico as the "rich port" was never anything but a fantasy. The island had always been poor. At the same time, it was tied to an old culture and several continents. One didn't have to romanticize the past or succumb to mythology to appreciate its thread in the fabric of history.

The classroom discussions were heated and often loud.

Again and again, the conversation returned to the island's political status. Did we want to remain a commonwealth, with some self-rule and a preferential trade relationship with the mainland? Half the class believed that was no better than being a colony of the United States, living as second-class citizens. But if we should aspire to statehood, the full rights of citizenship would come at the price of the full obligations, including a tax burden that, arguably, might have crippled our economy at the time. Some proposed, with passionate conviction, that full independence was the only way to preserve our culture and the proper dignity of self-determination. The economic repercussions of each position were as inscrutably complex as they were critical to the arguments.

When my mother made good on our wager of a plane ticket and I found myself in Puerto Rico for two weeks, I had my first chance to view the island through adult eyes and with an evolving new consciousness of my identity. Some things hadn't changed since childhood visits. We still made the ritual stop for a coconut on the road from the airport, but now the vendor would add a bit of rum to my libation from a bottle he kept out of sight. I still began the trip with a round of visits to every family member in order of seniority, still feasted on mangoes fresh off the tree. But instead of playing the Three Stooges, my cousins and I enjoyed dominoes, dancing, and the ubiquitous bottle of rum. The kindness of strangers was still striking: a flat tire fixed, cups of coffee offered while we waited.

The stunning natural beauty of the island, which I had barely registered as a child, made a deep impression on that trip as I played tourist. In the rain forest at El Yunque, waterfalls trick the eye, holding movement suspended in lacy veils. Wet stone gleams, fog tumbles from peaks to valleys, mists filter the forest in pale layers receding into mystery. On the beach at Luquillo, when the sun appears under clouds massed offshore and catches the coconut palms at a low angle, the leafy crowns explode like fireworks of silver light. At night there is liquid stardust swirling in the dark waters of the phosphorescent bay. Almost every evening there are sunsets of white gold where the sky meets the sea.

Another revelation of my adult trips to the island was

how much the political questions broached in my course, especially about the island's status, infused everyday life. You'd see party symbols everywhere, the straw hat for the faction supporting commonwealth, the palm tree for those supporting statehood, the green flag with the white cross for those who favored independence. Everyone pored over the newspapers, dissected the candidates' positions on economic development, education, health care, corruption . . . During one election season, in the plaza of Mayagüez—and in many other towns too, I'm sure—traffic jams proliferated as cars honking horns and flying one party's flags refused to give way to other cars honking horns and flying the other party's flags. It was chaos, but at least people cared. I learned that 85 percent of the island's population had gone to the polls in recent elections.

This manic enthusiasm that gripped the island in election years, and still does, was a marked contrast to the political despondency felt by Puerto Ricans on the mainland in those years. The summer that I won the bet with my mother, I worked as usual in the business office at Prospect Hospital before going to Puerto Rico. For a couple of weeks, however, Dr. Jacob B. Freedman, the main owner of the hospital, lent me out as part of his community outreach efforts to work as an intern on Herman Badillo's ultimately unsuccessful campaign for mayor of New York City. Badillo was our congressman, the first Puerto Rican ever elected to the House of Representatives. It was then I first saw how difficult it was to energize a community that felt marginal and voiceless in the larger discourse of a democracy.

Puerto Ricans in New York then felt their votes didn't count. And so why should they take the trouble even to register? Having experienced discrimination intimately, they knew they were seen as second-class citizens, as people who didn't belong, with no path to success in mainland society. Their chances of escaping from the underclass, from the vicious cycle of poverty, were no better than those of their similarly alienated black neighbors and probably worse for those who didn't speak English.

Puerto Ricans on the island, by contrast, didn't have full consciousness of being a minority because they'd never had to live as one. There were inequalities in their world, but no one's dignity suffered merely on account of his being Puerto Rican. Whether content with commonwealth status or aspiring to statehood, or even independence, they took it for granted that they were fully American: American citizens born to American parents on American territory. To be mistaken for foreigners—aliens, legal or otherwise—would have been a shock.

It was dawning on me that if the Puerto Rican community in New York ever hoped to escape poverty and recover its self-respect, there were lessons to be learned from the island. The two communities—islanders and those on the mainland—needed to work together for their mutual benefit.

☆

For the final paper in the Puerto Rican history course, Peter Winn suggested a marvelous project, a family oral history. It was a challenge befitting any serious student of history: going mano a mano with primary sources, my cassette recorder planted on the kitchen table. Not everyone warmed to it: "You're wasting your time! Nothing interesting ever happened to me." For some, it was a grudging surrender to interrogation, slow and halting; others, the natural storytellers, proved surprisingly eager and voluble.

I was amazed by how many of these stories I'd never heard before. People had left their past behind when they came to New York. Memories of hardship and extreme poverty were of no use starting a new life on the mainland. With so much to deal with in the present, who had the luxury of dwelling on the past?

My family's shifting fortunes followed the island's economic currents: coffee plantations sold off piecemeal until yesterday's landowners took to laboring in cane fields that belonged to someone else. Child labor and illiteracy were normal; girls were married at thirteen or fourteen. We moved from mountainside farms to small towns like San Germán, Lajas, Manatí, Arecibo, Barceloneta; and after a time, on to what were then the slums of Santurce in San Juan; from there the mainland beckoned, and we answered, boarding the venerable US Army Transport *George S. Simonds*, the army transport that carried so many Puerto Ricans to New York, until Pan Am offered the first cheap airfares and we rode *la guagua aérea*, the aerial bus, between mainland and island. We were not immigrants. We went freely back and forth. We became New Yorkers, but we did not lose our links to the island.

Of all the links, language remains strong, a code of the soul that unlocks for us the music and poetry, the history and literature of Spain and all of Latin America. But it is also a prison. Alfred talked about moving from Puerto Rico to the South Bronx in third grade. His experience was common: no help in the transition, no remedy for his deficiency but to be held back. After that, teachers just shrugged and passed him from one grade to the next, indifferent to whether he'd understood a word all year. The sharpest kids would eventually pick up the language on their own and come out only a few years behind. Still, Alfred said, "the white kids were always the most advanced. The black kids were behind them, and the Puerto Ricans were last."

My cousin Miriam was listening in on our recording session, nodding in recognition. At the time, she was studying for a degree in bilingual education at Hunter College, and today she is no less passionate about that calling with decades of teaching experience behind her. "I want to become the kind of teacher that I wish I'd had," she told me. She'd had it rough in the public schools, where the teachers knew so little of Latino culture they didn't realize that kids who looked down when scolded were doing so out of respect, as they'd been taught. Their gesture only invited a further scolding: "Look at me when I speak to you!"

I felt my own shiver of recognition too, remembering my

early misery as a C student at Blessed Sacrament, in terror of the black-bonneted nuns wielding rulers, a misery that didn't abate until after Papi died and Mami made an effort to speak English at home. It seems obvious now: the child who spends school days in a fog of semi-comprehension has no way to know that her problem is not that she is slow-witted. What if my father hadn't died, if I hadn't spent that sad summer reading, if my mother's English had been no better than my aunts'? Would I have made it to Princeton?

For the topic of my senior thesis I chose Luis Muñoz Marín—the island's first governor to be elected rather than appointed by a US president—whose efforts at industrialization brought Puerto Rico into the modern world. I was inspired by his work in marshaling the *jíbaros*, politically marginalized peasants, into a force that could win elections. Some part of me needed to believe that our community could give birth to leaders. I needed a beacon. Of course I knew better than to let such emotion surface in the language and logic of my thesis; that's not what historians do. But it kept me going through the long hours of work, and it counterbalanced the fact that Muñoz Marín's story had no happy ending, as initial success generated other economic challenges. How could this have happened? It was hard to imagine a more fruitful area for study.

One morning, a small headline in the local paper caught my eye. A Hispanic man who spoke no English had been on a flight that was diverted to Newark airport. No one there knew enough Spanish to explain to him where he was or what had happened, and in his frustration and confusion he made a scene. He was taken to Trenton Psychiatric Hospital and held there for days before a Spanish-speaking staff member showed up and helped him reach his family. This, I fumed, is not acceptable.

When I called the hospital and asked some questions, I found that there were a number of long-term patients who spoke no English and had only intermittent access to Spanish-speaking staff. I could imagine nothing crueler than the anguish of mental illness compounded by mundane confusion and being unable to communicate with one's keepers.

The Trenton Psychiatric Hospital was beyond any influence of Acción Puertorriqueña. There was no way we could pressure the administrators to hire more Hispanics as we had the university. So I resolved to take a different approach, organizing a volunteer program under which our members spent time at the hospital on a continuous rotation so that there was always someone who could interpret for the patients and intercede with the staff if necessary. We also ran bingo nights and sing-alongs, finding that some very uneasy minds were nonetheless able to dredge their memories for the comfort of old songs their parents had sung. And before heading home for Thanksgiving and Christmas, we threw holiday parties for the patients, recruiting our mothers and aunts to prepare the traditional foods that were too complicated to attempt in dorm kitchens.

The program in Trenton was my first real experience of direct community service, and I was surprised by how satisfying I found the work. Modest as the effort was, I could envision it working on a grand scale—service to millions. But the operations of major philanthropy being then beyond my imagination, government seemed the likely provider. And so it was that I began to think that public service was where I was likely to find the greatest professional satisfaction. Under a banner reading *"Feliz Navidad,"* we had set out the stacking chairs for the patients, and on the folding tables we'd arranged a bounty of *pasteles* and *arroz con gandules*. This was not an audience you could expect to settle down and listen attentively, but when Dolores strummed the strings of her guitar, the harsh fluorescent light seemed somehow to soften. We mustered some Spanish carols, Nuyorican *aguinaldos*. But it was when she turned to old Mexican favorites that Dolores's voice truly shone as she serenaded those broken souls on a silent winter night in New Jersey:

> *Dicen que por las noches*
> *no más se le iba en puro llorar . . .* *

---

* They say that all those nights
All he could do was cry . . .
(from *"Cucurrucucú Paloma,"* a popular Mexican song)

They say he survived the nights on tears alone, unable to eat . . . Dolores sings the Mexican ballad of a lover so bereft that after he dies, his soul, in the form of a dove, continues to visit the cottage of his beloved. Even my heart, as yet untouched by such passion, is captured, and I am transfixed as Dolores coos the song of the lonesome dove: *cucurrucucú* . . .

In the audience, an elderly woman is staring into space, her face as devoid of expression as ever. She is always the unresponsive one, who has not spoken a single word since we've been coming to Trenton. Tonight, even she is tapping her foot gently as Dolores sings.

Sixteen

Felice Shea was sitting at my desk, waiting for me to walk over to the commons with her for dinner. She was that very fair-skinned Irish type, blushing at the slightest discomfort, and I had gotten pretty good at reading her reactions. Seeing at this moment a virtual red tide, I asked her what was up.

"I really hope you don't think I was snooping, Sonia, but I couldn't help noticing that letter in your wastebasket . . ."

"It's just junk mail from some club. They want you to pay for membership, and then they want more money for some trinket engraved with your name. What a scam!"

Felice now looked more embarrassed than ever as she tried to explain that Phi Beta Kappa was totally legitimate. More than legitimate, in fact: an honor of such prestige that she insisted I had to accept the membership even if she had to pay for it. Felice was not only exceptionally kind and generous;

as the daughter of two college professors, she knew all the ins and outs of academia and had guided me through many such blind spots. After four years at Princeton, I thought I knew the terrain pretty well, but every once in a while, even as a senior, I'd hear about something that made me feel like a freshman. I wasn't going to take Felice's money, but I did take her advice.

Something similar had happened not long before. I was asleep when the phone rang; the voice on the other end said it was Adele Simmons, dean of student affairs, calling to congratulate me on having won the Pyne Prize. You'd have thought it was Publishers Clearing House from the excitement in her voice describing this honor I'd never heard of, obviously not paying attention to it in the *Daily Princetonian;* but inferring it was important from her tone, I found the presence of mind to express how astonished and grateful I was. It wasn't until after I hung up and dialed Felice's number that I got a full briefing on the Moses Taylor Pyne Honor Prize. It seemed I would have to give a speech at an alumni luncheon where the award was presented. Felice and I were already into a discussion of appropriate attire, and planning a shopping trip, when she let drop the most important detail: "It's the highest award that a graduating senior can receive."

I had not shopped for clothes seriously since the day I acquired my going-to-Princeton raincoat, which was now eligible for retirement. My complete wardrobe fit in one laundry bag, easy to carry home on the bus. It consisted of three pairs of dungarees, one pair of very 1970s plaid pants, and an assortment of interchangeable tops. When my summer job demanded a more professional look, I managed to avoid the problem by wearing a hospital uniform. Felice and her mother took me to Macy's and helped me pick out a gorgeous suit for fifty dollars. It was the most expensive outfit I'd ever worn, but to judge by how I felt wearing it, it was a good investment.

The gymnasium was transformed by tables dressed in white linen, flatware, and flowers. The crowd was vast—alumni, professors, and deans, all abuzz with greetings and congratulations, their hands extended, smiling broadly, glasses raised. A part of me still felt uncertainty—or was it disbelief?—about all this fanfare and how to take it, but there was no denying that whatever it meant, it felt great. I had worked hard, and the work paid off. I had not disappointed.

Among the recent graduates were those who, as women or as other minorities, had already altered that old image of a Princeton alumnus long cherished by some. There were friends who had graduated a year or two ahead of me, like Margarita Rosa, who came down from Harvard Law School for the occasion. Others were only names to me until that day. Nearly every living Hispanic who had ever graduated from Princeton showed up, overflowing with pride and camaraderie, for what amounted to a triumphant reunion. My family, of course, was there in force, Mami sitting with a dazed smile that burst into beams of happy recognition with each friend or acquaintance who came over to congratulate her. My own face was sore from all the grinning.

As I took to the podium to give my speech, stricken with the usual bout of nerves, I scanned the upturned faces of hundreds of strangers. With the exception of our small cluster of "Third World" friends and family, the audience was uniformly white. It was a fitting reminder of what I was doing up there. The Pyne Prize, often shared by two students, recognizes excellent scholarship but also leadership that provides "effective support of the best interests of Princeton University." My efforts on the Discipline Committee had been a significant factor in my award, but so had my work with Acción Puertorriqueña and the Third World Center, which Princeton recognized as a benefit not merely to the few dozen student members of those organizations but to the broader community as well. The dynamism of any diverse community depends not only on the diversity itself but on promoting a sense of belonging among those who formerly would have been considered and felt themselves outsiders. The greater purpose of these groups had been to foster a connection between the old Princeton and the new, a mutual acceptance without which the body as a whole could not thrive or evolve.

This was the work not of one person but of a community: "y Amigos." And in my speech I wanted to acknowledge that collaboration, as well as bow to those among the newest alumni, like Margarita Rosa, who, walking in shoes very much like my own, had cleared a path for me to follow in.

"The people I represent are diverse in their opinions, cultures, and experiences. However, we are united by a common bond. We are attempting to exist distinctly within the

176

rich Princeton tradition, without the tension of having our identities constantly challenged and without the frustrations of isolation. In different ways and in different styles, some loudly and others quietly, Princeton's minorities have created a milieu in which I could act and see the efforts accepted. In this way, today's award belongs to those with whom I have worked to make Princeton realize that it contains groups which are distinct and honorable in their own traditions.

"However, Princeton's acceptance of our existence and thoughts is only a first step. The challenge to both myself and Princeton is to go beyond a simple recognition. I hope today marks the beginning of a new era for all of us: a new era in which Princeton's traditions can be further enriched by being broadened to accommodate and harmonize with the beat of those of us who march to different drummers."

Looking out at that crowd, I imagined those who had not yet arrived, minority students who, in years to come, would make this multitude of faces, the view from where I now stood, a little more various. If they could have heard me, I would have confided in them: As you discover what strength you can draw from your community in this world from which it stands apart, look outward as well as inward. Build bridges instead of walls.

Spring eased into summer, exams and final papers were wrapped up, my thesis review completed. Graduation brought one last unfamiliar laurel when Peter Winn called me into his office to tell me that I would graduate summa cum laude. Once again, facing the pleasure with which this news was delivered, I didn't have the heart to inquire what it meant; for now it was enough that I should act very glad and honored. When I'd finally looked up the translation of the Latin phrase, the irony of my needing to do so was not lost on me. It was perhaps then that I made a measure of peace with my unease: the uncertainty I'd always felt at Princeton was something I'd never shake entirely. For all the As and honors that could be bestowed, there would still lurk such moments of estrangement to remind me that my being there was not typical but an exception.

I marched out of Princeton's Nassau Gate with my classmates in a final ritual of return to the real world, knowing that I was headed back to the Ivy League for law school at Yale in the fall. Meanwhile, a summer job doing research in the Office of Social Responsibility at the Equitable Life Assurance Society in Manhattan would provide my first glimpse inside corporate America. It was, to say the least, a letdown: I was shocked at how much time presumably productive people were capable of wasting. It was similar to what I'd observed the summer before, working in New York City's Department of Consumer Affairs, only stranger, perhaps, considering it was a business with the aim of making money.

Junior by then had graduated from Cardinal Spellman and completed the first year of a program at New York University that would lead to medical school. He hadn't grown up with dreams of becoming a doctor. His ambition at that stage of life was only to do something different from whatever I was doing, to find his own path out from under my shadow. Though our constant bickering had mellowed by then, and mutual respect prevailed, each of us was too involved in his or her own life to pay much attention to the other's. But in a bind we would always turn to each other first, and given the experience that we alone shared, not much would need to be said. Family was family.

The big event for ours that summer was the wedding. That Kevin and I would eventually marry had been a given ever since the day I introduced him to Abuelita. With hindsight I can see how unexamined that certainty was. My aunts had married at fourteen or fifteen, my cousins at eighteen. I had long mapped out that I was going to do things in the right order and finish my education first. But with the prospect of my beginning law school at Yale, and Kevin's own plans for grad school still up in the air, it seemed sensible that he should move to New Haven with me. In our world, that couldn't have happened without our getting married.

My mother and I had radically different views of what the wedding would be like. My vision was frugal, modest, and practical. Hers was extravagant. Her own wedding had consisted of a visit to city hall and dinner at Abuelita's. She had not walked down the aisle, and therefore I had to. We battled over every detail, and she wasn't above playing dirty. If I crossed someone's name off the list in an effort to trim the numbers, she'd find an opportunity for us to run into that person and mention, to my well-masked dismay, that the invitation was in the mail.

Once I recognized that this whole production had more to do with her needs than mine, I resigned myself to simply getting it done as painlessly as possible. I scoured the city for the cheapest ways to furnish the essential elements. The prices horrified me, each piece of the fairy tale seeming a bigger rip-off than the last.

"I'm not spending hundreds of dollars on a dress that I'll only wear once. I'm just not doing it!"

"So what are you going to wear, Sonia?"

How many times could we repeat that exchange? Elisa was my savior. She was an old friend and neighbor of my mother's from the Bronxdale Houses and also a seamstress. It had been a while since I'd gone back to the projects after our move to Co-op City, and I was stunned by how tiny and cramped the rooms seemed when we visited Elisa. I drew a diagram, a simple A-line dress. "That's all I want." I could see the horror rising in Mami's eyes like water in a sinking boat.

"It's too plain. You have to make it fancier!"

"It's my wedding! You've decided everything else!" I couldn't believe we were fighting so shamelessly in front of Elisa, but she handled it with a skill that hinted at plenty of prior mother-daughter experience.

"Sonia, we can keep it simple and still make it elegant with a little beadwork here and here . . ."

And so, with help from friends and family, gradually the

plans came together. Junior was still working as a sacristan at St. Patrick's, and it was one of the privileges allowed employees that they could arrange to have wedding Masses for family celebrated at the cathedral. Through his job selling insurance, Alfred had a client with a limousine rental service who gave him a spectacular discount on three antique Rolls-Royces.

Marguerite, who had remained a close friend since high school, was my maid of honor. She graciously volunteered to host the bridal shower, but it was not such a simple proposition given that we were all New Yorkers, among whom assumptions and traditions run deep and are as varied as the places we come from. Would it be tea sandwiches and punch for ladies only on a Sunday afternoon? Or rum and real food and dancing on a Saturday night, with the men of course invited too? Somewhere equidistant from Poland, Germany, Ireland, and Puerto Rico we negotiated a path.

"Sonia, what are we going to do about *los regalos*?" Mami looked seriously worried. The gifts she was concerned about were those rather risqué items traditionally given a bride, who is assumed to be innocent and in need of instruction about the wedding night. Along with these oddities, there are of course practical gifts: the toaster, the vacuum cleaner, and other household necessities. Typically, the women arrive early for the giving of the gifts; the men don't need to know about such things. Asking my aunts and cousins to abandon this custom was not an option. It would have been seen as disrespectful, and anyway they wouldn't have listened. The best we could do was contain the danger of Irish sensibilities being scandalized by Nuyorican humor: we would deploy a strategic seating arrangement and various other diversionary tactics as the boxes were passed around for inspection.

The Puerto Rican idea of a registry was for the bride's aunts to check in with her mother to see whether they could help to furnish anything needed for the wedding itself. Titi Gloria, for example, took me shopping for a gorgeous pair of silver shoes to match my dress. The traditions in a modest Irish family like Kevin's were not so different. At the wedding, people gave cash in substantial amounts. That was how a young couple could be expected to pay for the party, as it was their obligation to do, and also start a new life.

On the big day, I was woken and dragged out of bed by a gang of women bent on getting an early start at the beautification effort. They were yakking nonstop, also running my mother through her own preparations, just one step ahead of mine.

"Celina, get out of the shower now!"

"You want the hair first or the makeup first?"

"Ay! Who took the iron?"

I felt like a mannequin passed from hand to hand, until the very end, when, with the cars already downstairs, their engines idling, I finally got a word in edgewise. We had forgotten one very important thing: I needed to eat something and have a shot of insulin. My mother froze in panic: whatever she had in the kitchen had disappeared in the comings and goings. So my cousin Tony ran to the diner across the street to get a turkey sandwich. I gave myself the shot and devoured the sandwich with a towel for a bib as the roomful of women screamed at me not to get mustard on the dress. With that, we were off.

At the church, Kevin was waiting, dressed in a rented but very fashionable beige tuxedo, beaming proudly. Marguerite showed me the sugar cubes she'd tucked into her bouquet, assuring me that the maid of honor would be sticking very close by in case the bride suffered any drops in blood glucose. I was especially thrilled to see my cousin Milly arriving with her husband, Jim, and her mother, Elena. They were yet another family of Mami's brother Mayo, and when they had first arrived from Puerto Rico, before I was born, they had come to live with Mami and Papi. I rarely saw them anymore, because they lived upstate, but they were very dear to me. It was Milly, a champion at dominoes, who finally taught me to play. With them beside me, my wedding felt like one of those parties from my childhood that I missed so much.

And so it would be: after the ceremony in the Lady Chapel, we danced into the wee hours at a wedding hall in Queens, along with a dozen other nuptial parties in neighboring rooms. We ended the night by tossing frugality to the wind and splurging on a room at the Hotel St. Moritz overlooking Central Park. I was happy to sign the register as Sonia Sotomayor de Noonan. Room service was closed by the time we checked in, and I was starving; the banquet fare had left much to be desired. Kevin walked several blocks in the rain on a chivalrous quest for a greasy hamburger with cold fries.

All told, having a real wedding wasn't as bad as I'd feared, although it didn't increase my taste for such extravagance. I still tell all my cousins—and every bride-to-be I know—skip the pageant and take the money instead. Nobody listens.

Me, age one, between Papi
and Mami

First birthday. The photo
was given to Abuelita as
a memento years later
when it was inscribed
"For Grandma, from your
granddaughter who never
forgets you. Sonia."

Para abuelita
de tu nieta que
no te olvida
Sonia

6/25/55

Celina in the Women's Army
Corps, age nineteen

Juli as a young man, soon after
arriving in New York

With Junior on his first birthday

Birthday girl with *(left to right)* my godmother, Carmine; mother, Celina; and maternal aunt Aurora

Celina *(center)* was the Jackie O of Bronxdale, but Carmen *(right)* was a beauty, too. Abuelita is second from top left, flanked by her sisters. Gloria is behind Carmen, and in the front-row peanut gallery, from left, are Junior, Nelson, me, Eddie, and Miriam.

At Blessed Sacrament, I first discovered love of learning and a lust for gold stars. *(left)*

Senior year at Cardinal Spellman High School *(right)*

SONIA MARIA SOTOMAYOR

I am not a champion of lost causes, but of causes
not yet won.
— Norman Thomas

My Princeton experience has been the people I've met.
To them, for their lessons of life, I remain
eternally indebted and appreciative.
To them and to that extra-special person in my life

Thank You — For all that I am and am not.
The sum total of my life here, has been made-up
of little parts from all of you.

In the Princeton yearbook, class of 1976

Beside one of the bronze tigers
outside Nassau Hall

In the kitchen with Titi Aurora and Mami on a visit home from Yale *(left)*

I whip up some homemade Chinese food for the gang at Yale. *(right)*

High school sweethearts just after the wedding in the Lady Chapel
at St. Patrick's Cathedral. Mami's friend Elisa helped design the dress,
and Kevin rented the tuxedo. *(left)*

Discovering the grandeur of America's wide-open spaces for the first
time, while struggling to figure out a career plan *(right)*

Sonia Sotomayor, Assistant District Attorney, representing the people of the County of New York

... and the badge to prove it

Partners and associates of Pavia & Harcourt gathered to celebrate a wedding of one of their own soon after I became a judge. David Botwinik is at bottom left and George Pavia is beside him.

My Yale mentor, now Circuit Court Judge, José Cabranes administered the oath of office at my induction to the U.S. District Court for the Southern District of New York. *(Inset)* With Robert M. Morgenthau ("The Boss") on the day I was sworn in.

The annual courthouse follies: After much rehearsal, I make a serviceable singing hobo alongside U.S. District Court Judges Charles S. Haight, Jr., and Jed S. Rakoff.

At the White House: Mami, Kiley, Conner, and Corey as
President Obama announces my nomination to the Supreme Court

Justices of the Supreme Court of the United States are required to
take multiple oaths. Here I take the Judicial Oath, administered
by Chief Justice Roberts in the Justices' conference room, with my
mother holding the Bible and Junior looking on.

Seventeen

If our decision to get married was essentially unexamined—it was what couples like us were expected to do—we were hardly more reflective about the marriage once inside it. We simply set about playing house. Like me, Kevin had been young when he lost his father. Neither of us had observed particularly inspiring models of married life, TV sitcoms providing what baseline we had.

Kevin's own plans were still uncertain. He was applying to medical schools while also contemplating a research track in science. Law appealed to him too; we had taken the LSAT together, he getting the higher score. He was intellectually equipped for any path he might have chosen, but the gears hadn't yet meshed to drive him forward. So in the meantime, he took a job as a laboratory assistant in the biology department, and I picked up one in the mimeograph room of the law school. A full scholarship covered my tuition, so all we needed was money to live on.

We scoured New Haven for something affordable in an unthreatening neighborhood, finally finding a small apartment in what was once a boardinghouse on Whitney Avenue, a mile from campus. Our landlord betrayed a not very high opinion of lawyers, so I let Kevin do the talking. Home was a living room with a built-in storage chest that doubled as a couch; there was a real bedroom, separate from the living room, and a tiny cubbyhole of a kitchen. We loved that place and would keep it for the three years, 1976 to 1979, I was at Yale. Though furnished entirely with hand-me-downs, it never lost the glow of a first home, the sweet mix of nesting and independence.

Kevin decided that we needed a dog to complete our nuclear family, and Star was the much-loved addition. He was a tiny, camel-colored greyhound mutt with steel springs for legs and a passion for chewing. The very first sacrifice to his toothy enthusiasm was my wedding shoes, that pair of gorgeous silver sandals that Titi Gloria had spent an unthinkable fortune on. Well, they were wretchedly uncomfortable the one night I wore them, anyway.

The housework was a team effort. I handed Kevin my paychecks, and he paid the bills. I dusted and made the bed; Kevin mopped the floors. He washed the clothes; I ironed them. I did most of the shopping and cooking; he did the dishes. I learned how to boil an egg, and much more, from the *Joy of Cooking.* When in doubt, I phoned Mrs. Gudewicz, Marguerite's mother. One time I found turkey drumsticks on sale for pennies a pound, and she helped me wrangle them long-distance. Every few months, Marguerite and her boyfriend and future husband, Tom, would come for a weekend visit, always with a care package of quality meat we couldn't have afforded. Marguerite's mother was a second mother to me, and nothing says "we believe in you" like a New York sirloin.

Yale Law School was and is uniquely small among the top law schools in the country. There were only about 180 in our class. The numbers reflect not only highly selective admissions but also a commitment to fostering a supportive environment on a human scale. Not surprisingly, I found myself surrounded by the most brilliant, dazzlingly articulate, and hard-charging people I'd ever met. Many were entering the field having already established stellar reputations doing something else. There were PhDs in philosophy, economics, math, and physics. We had writers, a doctor, a film critic, and an opera singer, not to mention several Rhodes scholars in our class. It would have been even more daunting if we could have known at the time that the class of 1979 would go on to extraordinary success even by the school's extraordinary standards: so many members are now deans and professors at top law schools, federal and state judges, or otherwise in the highest echelons of government or practice. I'm told that this rarefied company made everyone feel as insecure as I felt, but that would be difficult to verify.

No one wanted to be seen trying too hard, and all affected a coolly casual demeanor. But behind closed doors they were working like maniacs, and I was no exception. I read the cases scrupulously and would never have dreamed of walking into class unprepared. But that wasn't enough to banish the threat of being humiliated at any time. Instruction proceeded by a process of interrogation, with professors sometimes eliciting an inadequate answer as an opportunity to dig deeper and lay fully bare the flawed understanding that had produced it. Even a correct answer could lead to further probing that might leave you looking for a hole to crawl into.

I could see there was a method to this torment. We were being conditioned to think on our feet and immunized against the emotional rough-and-tumble of an adversarial profession. Professors at Yale did not look down on us: they assumed that everyone there was smart and in many ways related to us as peers. But often I felt as if I were floundering. It wasn't merely the intense circumstantial pressure. Listening to class discussions, I could follow the reasoning, but I couldn't anticipate where it was headed. For all Princeton had taught me about academic argumentation, law school seemed to operate on a plane of its own. If history involved more than memorizing names and dates, the practice of law was even more removed from merely learning a body of rules and statutes, as I had naively assumed it would be. Instead, becoming a lawyer required mastery of a new way of thinking, and not one that followed obviously from other disciplines.

It may seem unlikely, but even among my ultra-high-wattage classmates, and with minimal time to spare for social life or extracurriculars, I did not feel isolated at Yale. Partly, this was because first-year law students were divided into small groups for some classes. In this way, the intense pressure we all felt became a bonding experience, with competitive antagonism channeled outside the group while within it we made some friends for life.

There was also something of a sisterhood in my class. Although the law school had been admitting women since 1918, they were still a minority. In our class of 180, there were only 41 of us, and that was a significant increase over previous years. Naturally, we felt connected and especially supportive of one another.

My very closest friends, however, were of a different stripe.

Felix Lopez, a Puerto Rican orphan from the tenements and projects of East Harlem, was a high school dropout who'd been clever enough to let himself get caught in a minor act of controlled arson so that he could enter the safe haven of a home for juvenile delinquents. From there, via Vietnam and the GI Bill, he would graduate at the top of his class at the University of Michigan. Early struggles wouldn't prevent

Felix, a teddy bear with a huge heart, from committing himself to alleviating the suffering of others. If he hasn't yet saved the world, he's not done trying.

Born a member of the Mohawk nation, Drew Ryce, with his street Spanish, could have passed for Latino, especially after he'd cut off his braids. He recounted tales of surviving a childhood on the streets of Chicago so close to hell that its fires burnished his accounts of that time with a sometimes unbelievable glow, or of how Yale had poached him from Harvard. He had a mind like an IBM mainframe, only much less predictable. He and Kevin would become very close, spending long hours talking music and old movies.

A Chicano from small-town New Mexico, Rudy Aragon spent six years in the air force as an intelligence officer, after which he had a very clear objective for his career in law: he was aiming for the top of a major law firm. George Keys, who had known Rudy since their US Air Force Academy days, was similarly hell-bent on corporate success, determined to attain what had been denied his father as a black man living in the segregated southern town that was this nation's capital.

These compadres, whose concern and intelligence I could always count on, were the four older brothers I'd never had. Each remained acutely aware of the parallel universe, the other America, from which he had been beamed into New Haven. Each was worldly-wise beyond any experience of mine. They all called me "kid." And that's how I felt around them.

They became the center of my extracurricular life, what

time for it we could spare. With Rudy, I co-chaired LANA, Yale's Latino, Asian, and Native American student association. The focus was on recruitment and other issues like those I'd dealt with at Princeton. It was sometimes surprising how the support of their own kind, which had been so essential to my survival at Princeton and which in a smaller way I'd re-created among my law school friends, was not such a priority among some of the minority students at Yale. Here I found more Latinos and members of other groups who seemed determined to assimilate as quickly and thoroughly as possible, bearing any attendant challenges and psychic costs in private. I could understand the impulse, but it was never a choice I could have made myself.

Drew got me into more mainstream activity at the Graduate and Professional Student Center, better known as the GPSC—or "Gypsy." Essentially, it was a bar for grad students—the cheapest drinks in New Haven—and as vice-president of operations, he hired me to work the door, taking tickets and checking IDs. I would have preferred to work behind the bar, which paid better, but I was a more than adequate bouncer. Nobody could talk their way past me, and I ejected many a townie trying to climb in through the window to avoid the cover charge. My instincts only failed me once: A group of girls wanted to have a look around inside before paying the cover, to see if they really wanted to stay. Not having been born yesterday, I told them nice try and was about to send them on their way, when Drew appeared. Getting worked up when he caught wind of the situation, he wound up apologizing to the ladies and insisting I let them in for free. The bar, he told me, was full of desperate guys with no one to dance with—a very bad situation for liquor sales.

"It's not right, Drew, the guys are paying, why should the women get in free? Can't you see that's sex discrimination?"

"Not everything is a civil rights case, Sonia!" he yelled. "I've got a band to pay and nobody's drinking." We argued some more, until finally he solved the problem by promoting me to bartender and putting someone else on the door.

With such a colorful crew, alliances could shift and tensions flare from time to time, but the gravitational pull of adoptive family always held. I invited my compadres to Co-op City to meet my mother and then for many a holiday dinner.

It was at Yale that I met the first person I can describe as a true mentor. I had long known the good of seeking out the guidance of teachers, from Miss Katz to Nancy Weiss and Peter Winn at Princeton. And I had an even older understanding of how much friends and classmates could teach me. But I had not yet discovered the benefit of sustained dialogue with someone who epitomized the kind of achievement I aspired to, and much beyond that.

I first met José Cabranes through a Princeton friend who'd worked with me in Acción Puertorriqueña. Charlie Hey-Maestre had been a year behind me, and when I was in my first year at Yale, he was writing his senior thesis, which dealt with issues around US citizenship for Puerto Ricans. He had come to Yale to consult José Cabranes, who was an expert on the topic. I had offered Charlie our couch for the night, and we stayed up late talking. "So who is this Cabranes guy?" I asked. Charlie explained: José Cabranes had served as special counsel to the governor of Puerto Rico and head of the commonwealth's Washington office, and he was now Yale's general counsel, the first ever named to that position. Earlier, he had been a founder of the Puerto Rican Legal Defense and Education Fund and a professor at Rutgers University. He was a trailblazer and a hero to many for his work promoting civil rights for Hispanics.

Charlie insisted that I come along to the lunch meeting he had arranged. José Cabranes was gracious, warm, and brilliant. He spent the first half hour addressing Charlie's questions and then gradually drew me into the conversation. We talked about the relationship between the mainland and the island and how it affected Puerto Ricans' view of the world, our self-image, and the scope of our future.

It had been three hours when José looked at his watch and said he needed to get back to work. Charlie and I thanked him and said our good-byes. As we were about to leave, José turned to me and said, "What are you doing this summer? Come work for me." I had just arrived at Yale and certainly hadn't thought that far ahead. But I didn't hesitate a moment before accepting, nor did I wait for summer before starting work for him.

My job involved research for the book he was writing on

the legislative history of US citizenship for Puerto Ricans, as well as minor assistance with the day-to-day legal work of the university. But what I learned came from having a front-row seat, observing his conduct of meetings or simply the traffic of people, issues, and ideas through his office. In the hothouse of very bright people that Yale was, he was one of the brightest, with an intimate knowledge of the law, a passion for history, and the skill to engage with warmth and depth whomever he encountered.

Until I met José Cabranes, I could not have imagined him. José maintained community relations in his pro bono volunteer work as the very model of a citizen-lawyer, but he could maneuver with equal skill and self-assurance in the most rarefied corridors of power. And yet he remained infinitely generous with his knowledge, time, and influence, especially with young people. He would take Felix under his wing too, and offer Drew guidance on the confusing thickets of Indian tribal law, a different manifestation of the American empire. We tried mightily to impress him. If he doubted some of the ideas we presented to him, like so many dead mice offered up by eager kittens, he always tempered his skepticism with good humor.

A role model in the flesh provides more than an inspiration; his or her very existence is confirmation of possibilities one may have every reason to doubt, saying, "Yes, someone like me can do this." By the time I got to Yale, I had met a few successful lawyers, usually in their role as professors. José, the first I had the chance to observe up close, not only transcended the academic role but also managed to uphold his identity as a Puerto Rican, serving vigorously in both worlds.

I still consider José's advice carefully—indeed, I've sought it at every crossroads in my career—though I'm more likely to translate it into my own terms than to take it up directly. José has often spoken of what an unusual protégée I've been: how I often confer with him, only then to do exactly as I please. He's only half joking.

In the absence of grades and class rank, the only clear mark of standing at Yale Law School is to get on the *Yale Law Journal*. The most straightforward way to do that is to write a piece and have it accepted for publication. It's called a "note," but it's really a very thorough paper.

"Bring me a proposal," said Bill Eskridge, who was the notes and topics editor. Bill has since returned to Yale as a respected professor specializing in statutory interpretation, though in my memory his lanky form, forever in plaid shirt and jeans, is of a piece with the journal's stifling, dust-caked offices at the top of the Sterling building. He laid out the criteria: the note had to be original, significant, and logically cogent. I had to find some unresolved legal problem—one tightly focused but of real consequence—and then solve it. It sounds straightforward until you consider that countless students have ascended this temple to propose a topic and been rebuffed.

At Princeton, I had pondered the question of Puerto Rican

citizenship historically, politically, and economically, but in doing research for José Cabranes's book, I had started to see it in legal terms. If you look closely at what the islanders had been granted as against what other US citizens enjoy by birth or naturalization, issues emerge that no one wants to grapple with. Could, for instance, the US citizenship of Puerto Ricans living on the mainland be revoked were they to return to the island in the case of independence? If I could find one legal knot to untangle, it might avail not only a good topic for a note but something useful for Puerto Rico.

The island couldn't afford statehood or independence, many people reasoned at the time. But having studied seabed rights, treaties, and offshore territorial sovereignty in admiralty class, I could see a wealth of potential for the island underwater. Might the unexploited mineral and oil resources be tapped to fund development? After all, the island's poverty had always been ascribed to the dearth of natural resources. Control of those neglected rights would be vital to local prosperity, whatever the island's future, be it commonwealth, statehood, or independence. Many have since argued, however, that the economic impact of the seabed rights would be negligible, and in fact thirty years later little of their promise has been realized.

I was in the ballpark. Now I had only to narrow the topic to a single legal question I could answer. I focused on statehood for purposes of the note because that was where precedent was clearest. I combed the old case law cases relating to the so-called equal footing doctrine, which gives new states joining the Union the same constitutional rights enjoyed by existing states, even while ceding to the federal government other powers enumerated in the Constitution. There were among the precedents a variety of obstacles, strange particulars of what some states had been permitted or denied. In the end, I couldn't establish affirmatively that Puerto Rico was entitled to its seabed rights in all circumstances, but I could prove that retaining them would not violate the doctrine of equal footing in the event of statehood. It was one small step, a tiny clearing in the jungle that has grown around the status question, but I thought it unassailable.

Bill Eskridge liked the idea. Fortunately, the other members of the journal did too, despite their preference that notes address themselves to current case law. After seemingly endless rounds of drafts and revision, "Statehood and the Equal Footing Doctrine: The Case for Puerto Rican Seabed Rights" was published.

One day, we were having a perfectly civil exchange when out of the blue Rudy interrupted me: "You know what I love about you, Sonia? You argue just like a guy." Kevin, stretched out on the couch, snorted a gulp of his soda, choking down a laugh.

"What is that supposed to mean, Rudy?"

Suddenly I was seething, and they knew it. Felix asserted his calming influence: "It's a good thing, Sonia, he means it as a compliment." I had heard compliments like that before.

Rudy forged on, explaining: I didn't hedge every statement with disclaimers, apologies, and self-doubts. He did his impression of how women raised their hands in class. "'Excuse me, Professor, I'm sorry, this might not be important, but you may want to consider the possibility . . . ' Not you, Sonia," he said. "When you ask to be called on, you just state your case plain and defy anyone to prove you wrong."

Rudy was right in that sense: I have always argued like a man, more noticeably in the context of those days, when an apologetic and tentative manner of speech was the norm among women. I don't know where I learned this style, but it has served me well, especially in the years when most of the people I was arguing with were men.

Where Rudy was wrong, however, was in suggesting that I had ever volunteered to speak in class. Having suffered the repetitive trauma of getting grilled, I was well into my third year before I'd ever raised my hand. But when I did, Rudy would be there to see it. It happened in Clark's class on trusts and estates; he was teaching the common-law rule against perpetuities, which limits how far into the future a will can control a line of inheritance. Professor Elias Clark was charting a hypothetical family tree on the blackboard, a sequence of births and deaths, when it occurred to me that the fate of this inheritance was essentially a math problem. Moreover, I could see a mistake in his calculation. I raised my hand, he called on me, and I pointed out the error. He turned and stared at the blackboard for several very long, silent minutes. Finally, he turned around. "She's absolutely right," he said.

"I've made a mistake." He explained to the class what I'd caught and put up another example, only to make a similar mistake. When I raised my hand this time, he paused more briefly before turning around and saying, "Why don't you come up and teach this part?"

I got a slap on the back from Rudy after class. But an even bigger confidence breakthrough was shortly to come, with my participation in the mock trials for the Barristers' Union competition. Perhaps the courtroom playacting somehow liberated my inner Perry Mason. Somehow or other, in this setting I felt for the first time I could actually be a lawyer.

As it happened, in one trial, Drew was my client, the defendant in a he-said/she-said rape case. We rehearsed the argument in great detail, but in the moment when I stood before the jury, people recruited from the community through an ad in the local paper, the analytic preparation receded into the background, and some other instinct came forward. I found my eyes automatically scanning their faces, trying to read them: Are they following me? Do I need to push harder or to pull back? There was a sweet spot where I was able to meet them halfway. Most of them, anyway.

In the jury box, one middle-aged man kept shaking his head ever so slightly and pursing his lips, again and again. But the subtle signals of antipathy didn't track my remarks; they were out of sync, as if he were responding to some other stimulus rather than what I was saying. We were encouraged to approach the jury members afterward for feedback on our performance. As people were milling around at the end of the session, I approached him and said, "I have a feeling I rubbed you the wrong way. Can you tell me why?"

He seemed startled, then shook his head. "It's nothing you did."

I told him that I was trying to learn. That was the purpose of the exercise. Whether it was something I was doing or not doing, I wished he would let me know so that I could adjust my approach in the future.

He shut down. "It's my own thing," he said. "I can't help you." But I continued to press him politely. Finally, he blurted it out. "Look, nothing personal. I just don't like brassy Jewish women." That took me by surprise. I froze as my mind raced through the things I could possibly say to this man, when the right response occurred to me.

I looked at him. "You're right," I said. "I can't do anything about that." And I walked away.

My second summer at Yale, I landed a job as a summer associate at Paul, Weiss, Rifkind, Wharton & Garrison, one of the very top law firms in Manhattan. I was working under men known as giants in courtroom work, and I was given a variety of assignments, the most challenging of which was a contribution to a brief being prepared for a huge antitrust case—an auspicious opportunity if ever there was one. But when I sat down to write, my arguments seemed continually wide of the mark. True, antitrust was not an area of the law I'd studied, and I had no background in business to speak of. But I couldn't figure out why I was failing to articulate a persuasive argument on the client's behalf, despite racking my brains on the long daily commute between New Haven and New York. I finally handed in my effort to a young associate one notch up the totem pole. Only when I saw what he eventually wrote himself and passed up to the next level did I fully realize how poor a job I had done. I obviously wasn't thinking like a lawyer yet. If this was what it meant to work in a prestigious law firm, I clearly was not ready.

The sense of failure was confirmed when I concluded my stint as a summer associate without receiving a job offer. I had never heard of such a thing happening at Yale Law School, and though I've learned since it was not so uncommon, of course no one advertised it. But anyway, in my own eyes I had officially blown it. I had worked hard—I always had and still do—but somehow that wasn't enough. And it was difficult not to conclude that I was simply not in the same league as my classmates who were pulling in job offers from firms just like this one. For this pain of failure—the first real failure since having enrolled in law school—I had only myself to blame, and knowing that, I was profoundly shaken.

The way forward was daunting if obvious. I needed to figure out what I was doing wrong and fix it. At the very least I had to learn this area of law, and so I signed up for Professor Ralph Winter's class on antitrust as well as one called Commercial Transactions. The trickier part would be mastering the skill that was at the heart of being a lawyer, my deficiency in which had been exposed: how to write a brief, not as some classroom exercise aspiring to an objective analysis of the case law, but as a piece of persuasive advocacy, advancing the interests of my client. In both kinds of remedial efforts, I would do what I'd always done: break the challenge down into smaller challenges, which I could get on with in my methodical fashion. And certainly I would need to prove myself at another kind of work in the legal profession before I could even consider joining a large commercial firm. In the meantime, the unfamiliar taste of utter failure from that summer would stay in my mouth. The memory of this trauma, which I was determined not to repeat, would overhang my every career choice until I became a judge.

One obvious good did come of my ordeal at Paul, Weiss: I made more money that summer than I had ever seen before. Now Kevin and I could actually afford a honeymoon, and a change of scene seemed in order as I licked my wounds and considered the way forward. Soon dreams of America were unfolding across our living room floor as we planned to cross the continent and head west.

For years I had studied American history, law, and society, but I had barely scratched the surface of the great geographical reality. The natural wonders I recognized only from childhood picture books and the plates of our *Britannica*, but it was something else altogether to watch the vast stretches of forest and plain unfurl for hours along the highway, or to feel dwarfed by the immensity of the sky. As we headed south out of Denver, the Rocky Mountains lay to the west like bones of the continent exposed to the afternoon light. As the road ran straight and flat, my mind rambled along its own bumpy, winding course. Two-thirds of the way through law school, and everyone around me was considering job offers. I needed to figure something out.

Most of my classmates were aiming in the direction of prestigious midtown law firms, including Rudy, whose objective couldn't have been more unvarnished: make big bucks. If the shortest path to that goal was to defend corporations, then so be it. He could always pursue labors of love by doing pro bono work on the side. My own ambitions were not as susceptible to the same inducements, but I did recognize a greater good in Rudy's approach. Until minorities learned how to navigate at those altitudes of the legal system, their communities would lag the rest of the country. If our experience as a group was ever to advance beyond disadvantage and grievance, we needed to move with ease where money and power move.

My ruminations continued through the days of driving, as if the white line in the road were an arrow pointing toward the future. José Cabranes had advised me to keep my sights on a major law firm in the long term, saying it was a good platform from which to launch into government or any other direction, but that first of all I should clerk. I had heard classmates mention clerking and I knew it was prestigious, but José had to explain to me that it meant working, essentially as a researcher, for a judge. Though I knew he wanted the best for me, clerking sounded tediously academic. How much longer could I live in the library? Much later I would realize my naïveté. Especially working with my own clerks, I've come to appreciate how clerking for a judge can be the most vital mentoring relationship open to a young lawyer. Part of me still regrets not having taken José's advice at face value.

I had not forgotten my childhood dream of becoming a judge, but if law school had taught me anything, it was what pure fantasy that dream would have to remain. Even at Yale, there was no such thing as a "judge track" to prepare you specifically for the rigors of those heights of the legal profession. The relative scarcity of women on the bench and the practical nonexistence of Latinas also gave me reason to keep this idea in the drawer with other idle wishes, any expression of which would have marked me as delusional.

At the all-star break in 1978, the Yankees lagged a dozen or so games behind the Red Sox, and yet there was no question but that I'd be betting on them to win the American League East. My hometown loyalties run deeper than any season's ups and downs, and while I'll root for the underdog in many other arenas, when it comes to baseball, the Yankees' knack for setting aside the day's personal dramas to get out there and win always impresses me. Felix, as a New Yorker, was with me, of course, and Drew was shrewdly calculating the odds. But Rudy and George were backing the Red Sox out of sheer contrariness, and so I arranged that when the Yankees won the pennant, those guys would buy me dinner at the best restaurant in New Haven.

It was the top of the seventh in the final, tie-breaking game. The Yankees had two men on when Bucky Dent, a shortstop with no hitting power in his history, came up to bat. The bat cracks, like a sign from heaven. He takes a new bat, and when it kisses the ball, a hand reaches down from the sky and lifts it out of the park. There's an eerie silence over Boston as Bucky Dent crosses home plate. All hell broke loose. Rudy and George were screaming in agony, Felix was crowing like the sun just rose, I was sitting there shaking my head, saying over and over, "They did it! They pulled it out again!"

My winner's dinner would have to wait till another night, however, even if we hadn't already felt stuffed to bursting on Felix's feast of *picadillo* with rice and black beans—the best I'd had since Papi died. Though nothing would have made me happier than to stay right there, basking in the glow of victory and friendship, I had to pull myself together for a recruiting dinner that same night. The host was Shaw, Pittman, Potts & Trowbridge, a well-respected, small Washington firm that did varied corporate and international work. Scott Rafferty, who had graduated summa cum laude alongside me at Princeton before also coming to Yale, had worked there as a summer associate and loved the experience. He enthusiastically encouraged me to attend the dinner.

There were eight or ten of us at a large table, and I happened to be seated facing the partner who was steering the event. Scott made introductions, circling the table with a few words about each of us. "Sonia's Puerto Rican and from the South Bronx in New York. She was at Princeton before she came to Yale." Very few words, as it happened, but as students we didn't have long résumés.

As soon as the introductions were over, and before another word was spoken, the partner facing me asked whether I believed in affirmative action. "Yes," I said, somewhat guarded but hardly imagining what my answer would unleash.

"Do Princeton and Yale have affirmative action programs?" Yes, of course they do, I told him, at which the challenge only escalated: "Do you believe law firms should practice affirmative action? Don't you think it's a disservice to minorities, hiring them without the necessary credentials, knowing you'll have to fire them a few years later?"

I was stunned, as much by the bald rudeness of the interrogation as by its implications. I'd heard nothing of the kind so blatant since the school nurse caught me off guard at Cardinal Spellman. "I think that even someone who got into an institution through affirmative action could prove they were qualified by what they accomplished there."

He looked at me skeptically. "But that's the problem with affirmative action. You have to wait to see if people are qualified or not. Do you think you would have been admitted to Yale Law School if you were not Puerto Rican?"

"It probably didn't hurt," I said. "But I imagine that graduating summa cum laude and Phi Beta Kappa from Princeton had something to do with it too."

"Well, do you consider yourself culturally deprived?"

Shall I talk about my ancestors, the heritage of Spain? About having two languages, two ways of seeing the world? Is there only one culture that counts? I didn't even know where to begin answering that one. And an awkward silence descended upon us, before spreading like a stain to the other end of the table, where Scott was seated. Sensing the discomfort, he deftly jumped in with a new topic. My adrenaline ebbed slowly, and I did what I could to get through the rest of the dinner without making others more uncomfortable. Afterward, Scott came to me to express outrage and apologize.

"It was horrible," I admitted. "So insulting."

"It was completely out-of-bounds," he said, adding he intended to complain about it the next day. But I asked him to wait. I needed to figure out what to do.

In the cafeteria the next morning, Scott had already found Rudy, Felix, and George. The forces were marshaled, the coffee flowing.

"I would have punched him out," Rudy announced, rarely one not to verbalize a thought.

"This guy was a lot bigger than me; I don't think I could have taken him," I said.

But when we got more serious about considering a proper response, I decided to go ahead with the formal recruiting interview scheduled later that same day, at which I could engage the partner from Shaw, Pittman in a more private setting.

With my résumé in front of him, he seemed to think we

were on a cordial footing. Before I knew it, he was encouraging me to come to Washington for the next step in the hiring process. That was when I called him on what he had said at the dinner.

"That was really insulting. You presumed that I was unqualified before you had seen my résumé or taken the trouble to learn anything about me."

He seemed to be waving it off as just a conversational gambit, albeit on a sensitive topic, and he expressed admiration at how I had stood my ground.

"You didn't seem terribly upset. You didn't make a scene. You were perfectly civil."

Now I really couldn't believe my ears. What was he expecting, Hysterical Puerto Rican Syndrome?

"That was the Latina in me," I said. "We're taught to be polite." If we were going to rely on stereotypes, at least they should be accurate. I further explained that it wasn't in my nature to cause everyone at the table discomfort because of how I felt about his behavior. But neither was I simply going to accept being treated so unfairly. I've long known how to control my anger, but that doesn't mean I don't feel it.

After the interview I talked through my options with the gang. I decided to address a formal complaint to the firm through the university's career office and challenge Shaw, Pittman's right to recruit on campus in light of that partner's disregard for Yale's antidiscrimination policy.

"You're going to need counsel, Sonia," Rudy said. "You're going to need one tough lawyer."

"You're hired," I said. "Pro bono, I assume."

"I think 'jailhouse lawyer' is the correct term," said Felix. Bluster aside, Rudy was the one who came to meetings with the dean and to the ensuing formal hearings of a student-faculty tribunal.

News of the incident flared across campus and divided the school into camps—those who thought I had made too much of some offhand comments, jeopardizing Yale's relationship with an important employer of its graduates, and those who were solidly in support of my action. The latter view spread far beyond New Haven as word reached one minority student group after another across the country. Letters and news clippings describing similar affronts elsewhere started to arrive. Clearly, I had opened a bigger can of worms than I'd intended. For while I was pleased that this type of offensive behavior was being brought to light, I had no wish for personal notoriety, as a symbol or anything else. I still wanted a career in law, not a place on every firm's blacklist.

The university, clearly uncomfortable with the attention the complaint was drawing, was eager to reach a settlement. The student-faculty tribunal impaneled to investigate the complaint negotiated a full apology from Shaw, Pittman. They were not barred from recruiting, but the firm and the offending partner did voluntarily keep a low profile at Yale for a time.

Throughout, I marveled at the courage that Scott Rafferty had shown in taking my side without hesitation. It meant giving up a plum job that he had been looking forward to. He had been very happy at Shaw, Pittman as a summer associate, but he was not eager to join a firm where a partner would behave in that way. That disillusionment did nothing to advance the start of his career, but it signaled a measure of integrity that would remain evident over a distinguished professional life in public service.

When the anger, the upset, and the agitation had passed, a certainty remained: I had no need to apologize that the look-wider, search-more affirmative action that Princeton and Yale practiced had opened doors for me. That was its purpose: to create the conditions whereby students from disadvantaged backgrounds could be brought to the starting line of a race many were unaware was even being run. I had been admitted to the Ivy League through a special door, and I had more ground than most to make up before I was competing with my classmates on an equal footing. But I worked relentlessly to reach that point, and distinctions such as the Pyne Prize, Phi Beta Kappa, summa cum laude, and a spot on the *Yale Law Journal* were not given out like so many pats on the back to encourage mediocre students. These were achievements as real as those of anyone around me.

My brother's story was similar. Junior stumbled into a program that put minority kids on a fast track to medical school, essentially free of cost. He wasn't inspired by childhood dreams of becoming a doctor; he had never considered the possibility. But once he started, he found that he loved what he was doing, loved the process of learning itself, and had excellent study habits compared with most kids in the program, 45 percent of whom would drop out. Affirmative action may have gotten him into medical school, but it was his own self-discipline, intelligence, and hard work that saw him through, where others like him had failed.

Much has changed in the thinking about affirmative action since those early days when it opened doors in my life and Junior's. But one thing has not changed: to doubt the worth of minority students' achievement when they succeed is really only to present another face of the prejudice that would deny them a chance even to try. It is the same prejudice that insists all those destined for success must be cast from the same mold as those who have succeeded before them, a view that experience has already proven a fallacy.

When my note for the *Yale Law Journal* was finally laid out and pasted up, typeset, proofed, printed, collated, and bound—in short, when it was a physical reality ready to go forth into the world—the editors took the unusual step of sending out a press release announcing it. It was an indication of their belief that my work had practical import beyond the limits of academia: that my argument might even have some influence on the outcome of the status question.

Meanwhile, acceptance of the note had come with an obligation to work on the journal in other capacities, such as checking citations. The teamwork of the job was wonderfully rewarding, and out of that camaraderie, as from my small group, would come some lifelong friendships. I so enjoyed the work that I volunteered to serve also as managing editor of another student-run journal, *Yale Studies in World Public Order*. After editing a couple of lengthy articles by alumni working in the field, I noticed myself feeling intellectually comfortable in a way that I could not imagine when I first arrived at Yale. That, together with the enthusiastic reception of my note among those working on Puerto Rican status issues, provided a feeling of real-world validation that was moving and meaningful in ways student honors could not rival.

Maybe, I thought, I am ready to go out there.

Eighteen

Yale was one of the very first law schools in the country to admit women, and yet every point in the building seemed to be separated by miles of corridor from the nearest women's restroom. On a typical trek, of an early evening, taking a study break from the library, I passed the open door of a conference room. At the back, I spotted a bonanza—a table of cheese and crackers and cheap wine, the kind of arrangement that passes for hospitality in university budgets and a free meal in the financially strapped lives of graduate students. The makeshift sign on the door read, "Public Service Career Paths." A panel of public-interest lawyers were pitching alternatives to private practice to a thin scattering of third-years. Just then, the moderator was introducing the final speaker, a district attorney from New York whose name I didn't recognize. He seemed none too comfortable at the podium and promised to be brief. I decided it was worth sticking around until he finished so I could make for the cheddar cubes.

My ears perked up when I heard him say that he had a couple hundred assistants who all tried cases. "Within your first year on the job," he said, "you'll be going to trial, with full responsibility for how you develop and present your own cases. You'll have more responsibility than you would have at any other job coming out of law school. At your age now, you'll be doing more in a courtroom than most lawyers do in a lifetime." I liked what I was hearing.

When the presentation was over and we descended on the food, I found myself in line next to the New York district attorney, Robert M. Morgenthau, a legend unbeknownst to me. His halting, raspy voice was no different talking face-to-face. This was not a man who relished chitchat. But being capable of talking up anybody, I proceeded to ask him to tell me a bit about his background, what he'd liked about each of his jobs. Maybe he was used to talking to ignorant students; he didn't betray any hint of annoyance. He asked me what my plans were—not sure, maybe a small firm, still exploring—and then he said, "Why don't you come by and see me? I have some openings in my schedule tomorrow."

Sure enough, the next morning at the Career Office, there were still interview slots open: among Yalies, the DA's Office was not the most sought-after place to work. But I was surprised to find my name already penciled in. In fact, Bob Morgenthau had come by, pulled my résumé, and already placed a call to José Cabranes, whom he knew well from their work

214

together on the Puerto Rican Legal Defense and Education Fund. The interview was actually enjoyable and ran a half hour longer than scheduled. At the end he invited me to visit his office in New York.

"You're interviewing *where?*" said Rudy, aghast. Even José, who had given me a glowing recommendation, seemed disappointed that I found the DA's Office more interesting than a clerkship. "Do you have any idea what they pay?" Rudy demanded. I did, but I had never seen money as the definitive or absolute measure of success. Sure, I wouldn't make much compared with an associate at a major firm. But my starting salary would still be more than what my mother had ever made as a nurse, which to Titi Aurora, who worked as a seamstress, had always seemed lavish.

In the end, as I usually do, I trusted my instincts, although I was a bit surprised where they were leading me. I knew I wasn't ready for a big firm, but apart from applying for a job at the State Department, I had not devoted much thought or effort to public-interest options. Nor was I encouraged to: unlike today, there were few pro bono volunteer law clinics at Yale then.

Nineteen

At the New York District Attorney's Office, "duckling" is the term of art for a rookie assistant DA, and in the mouth of a senior prosecutor it expresses gallows humor more than endearment. Forty of us tender, fuzzy types were about to be crunched in the jaws of a huge, complex, and fast-moving machine. Guidance of senior colleagues would add seasoning over time, but meanwhile we would need every scrap of what scant training would be provided during our first few weeks. I wasn't the only one among us with minimal background in criminal law—just the required basic course at Yale and the mock trials. But even if I had devoted all my studies to the finer points of the field, there remained essential lessons inaccessible in the classroom or from books and acquired only through the fiery baptism of the courtroom. I was about to get that baptism.

New York City in 1979 had been struck by a crime wave of tsunamic proportions. Mayor Ed Koch had been elected two years before on a promise to restore order after a summer of widespread looting, vandalism, and arson triggered by a ten-day blackout. If the immediate threat to public safety had lifted after the lights and air conditioning came back on, New Yorkers still had reason to live in a state of diffuse chronic fear. The city's fiscal troubles summed a decade of economic doldrums nationwide, and severe budget cuts were preventing the DA's Office, as well as the police department, from adding enough staff to cope with an avalanche of criminal cases. To make matters worse, rising tensions brought a rising number of police brutality complaints.

Most of the new ADAs were assigned immediately to one of six trial bureaus, each with up to fifty prosecutors of varying levels of experience, along with support staff. We would cut our teeth on misdemeanors: petty thefts, minor assaults, prostitution, shoplifting, trespass, disorderly conduct, graffiti . . . Later we would be promoted to felonies, and we might move to one of the bureaus that investigate fraud, racketeering, public corruption, sex crimes, or other specialized crimes. There was no choice in the matter, we were told. Soldiers go where they're assigned. Ducklings, too, apparently.

First we had to get to know the procedural maze. If a defendant is arraigned on an unsworn complaint, how many days do you have to fix it? Failing that, how do you handle a preliminary probable cause hearing? We also went out on patrols to get a sense of how cops do their job, the routines and the issues we needed to be sensitive to. Every sixth day we were in the complaint room for a nine-hour shift, interviewing arresting officers and witnesses to draw up the initial charges on each case. Every street arrest in the city funneled into the system through this room, which was not unlike a hospital ER on a rough night. It looked like chaos, but there were order and discipline under the surface, and that combination appealed to me. So did the pressure to improvise, the comfort of clear rules, and the inspiration of a higher good.

The office of Bob Morgenthau, the Boss, was a model of efficiency. But the city was strapped for cash. My first office was an anteroom, actually more of a doorway, into which a desk had somehow been implanted. Eventually, turnover would deposit me in slightly more commodious shared space, though my desk still blocked the entrance, behind which door was wedged an old couch, horsehair poking out of cracked leather. Papers were piled everywhere, stacks of files, boxes of evidence, somebody's lunch. In the summer the air conditioning failed constantly and sweat soaked through my suit, while in winter the same rooms became drafty caverns in which I might need to keep my coat and gloves on all day. The lights were dim, the electrical cords were frayed, and the plumbing leaked—sometimes into the courtrooms.

Of all the resources in short supply, time was the shortest, and mine perhaps more than most. Kevin had been accepted into the graduate program in biochemistry at Princeton, so we had moved there from New Haven. After our cozy nest on Whitney Avenue, we found ourselves living near campus in graduate student housing that had been built during and after World War II to shelter the families of returning soldiers. I was commuting by train between Princeton and Manhattan, sometimes up to two hours each way. I left home at dawn and rarely got back before nine. Kevin cooked and we'd share a late dinner every night, though I was routinely dead on my feet until the weekend brought a brief respite. I made it through the workweek on cans of Tab and my own adrenaline.

If the long hours were straining our marriage, I was too preoccupied to notice. What I did see, in the small corner of my awareness not cluttered with cases, procedures, and the minutiae of criminal law, was Kevin finally doing work that excited him and earning recognition for it. He was thrilled to be at Princeton again, this time on his own account, and he was making new friends. He was thriving at his own thing, just as I was at mine.

In the practice hearings that were part of our training, I was cast in the role of the defense attorney. Somehow by pure instinct I realized that a witness had implied vaguely that she had seen something, though she avoided stating it outright. On cross-examination, I asked an apparently tangential question that led her to describe the precise conditions that would have made a direct line of sight impossible for her. The senior assistant DA leading the exercise came up to me afterward. "I've been doing this training for years. You're the first person who ever spotted a hole like that in a witness's story and then pried it open." It was fortunate that thinking on my feet in such a situation came naturally to me, because I was the first of the ducklings to have a case assignment come to trial. It happened faster than I'd thought possible, just weeks after I'd started in August. None of us had expected to enter a real courtroom before the new year.

The defendant was a young black man who'd been charged with disorderly conduct for getting involved in a street fight. He was a college student, a pretty good one too, and from a solid family; at arraignment he pleaded not guilty. His counsel was Carole Abramowitz, a seasoned Legal Aid attorney, who had defended felony cases for years. I don't know why she was handling a misdemeanor that day, but she was determined to get the case thrown out, knowing full well that any plea to the least of charges could destroy a black kid's future. That was all I knew about the case, and I was learning it on the spot as the defense attorney and I stood before Judge Joan Carey in the first conference. Normally, I would have written up the complaint myself and interviewed the arresting officer, but this case had been reassigned after the departure of my predecessor, one file in a big stack of them that had been dumped on my desk and that I hadn't so much as opened yet.

"We're ready to go to trial," said Carole Abramowitz.

"We'll start Monday," said Judge Carey.

"But, but, but, but . . . ," I stammered. It was then Friday. I needed some time to prepare. I needed to find the witnesses. This was a real trial!

Judge Carey looked at me without pity. She complained that we weren't getting dispositions fast enough. "You'll start the wah-deer on Monday or I'll dismiss the case."

At least that's what I heard. I ran upstairs to Katie Law, adviser for the ducklings in our trial bureau. Katie was a Harvard graduate who had returned to law school after raising three daughters and getting a divorce. A southern belle from a wealthy family, she certainly didn't need to be in the trenches at the DA's Office, but she was passionate about community service. And she was infinitely patient with beginners.

"Katie, what does 'wah-deer' mean?"

She shook her head in despair. "They're sending babes into the wolves' den." It wasn't my fault, she assured me: not everything could be covered in our two-week training course. Katie spent the remainder of the afternoon explaining the voir dire process and jury selection, the strategies for making the most of this chance not just to disqualify unfavorable jurors but to establish a rapport with those selected. Public awareness of voir dire is much greater these days thanks to media coverage of high-profile trials, to say nothing of television court dramas, and the science of juror selection that has spawned an industry of consultants. But when I joined the DA's Office, it was all rather arcane stuff, especially since New York State is one of the few jurisdictions where lawyers can get involved in the process, which in many states, as in the federal system, is handled by judges.

I wish I could say that my first real trial was a triumph of spirit over experience, but in fact Carole Abramowitz mopped the floor with me, and then bad luck wrung me out. The courtroom was a repurposed office with a few rows of rickety wooden folding chairs serving as a jury box and gallery, and the bench was of painted plywood. In the middle of my summation, everyone's attention suddenly turned elsewhere: the defendant's grandfather clutching his chest in a sweat, the old man's daughter panicking beside him. The judge called a recess; the paramedics came trooping in. And by the time it was clear that the poor man was all right, an hour of confusion had intervened before I could continue my remarks. The jury took less time than that to find the boy not guilty.

If anything redeemed that day, it came in the swell of pride I felt when I first introduced myself to the jury—"I am Sonia Sotomayor de Noonan, and I represent the people of the County of New York"—a moment of grace that would repeat, and ground me, at the opening of every subsequent trial I prosecuted.

If my first trial was a cartoon of chaos, my second was a mess of a very different kind. A man had got into an argument with his wife while riding the subway. He chased her screaming off the train, before beating her and then kicking her in the face when she fell to the station platform. A Good Samaritan rushed to intervene, striking the husband with an umbrella, whereupon the defendant punched the Good Samaritan in the face, leaving him with a black eye. As often happens in cases of domestic violence, the wife was unwilling to testify against her husband, but a righteous and determined young prosecutor was not going to let that stand in her way. I subpoenaed the defendant's wife.

But on the day of the trial, the wife didn't show. She had a fair excuse; she was in the hospital. But then it became clear that she had scheduled an elective procedure on that day to avoid coming to court.

Even without the wife's testimony, however, we got a conviction. The defense attorney was Dawn Cardi, a rookie from the Legal Aid Society in her very first trial. She fumbled as badly as I had in my own maiden voyage, and this time by comparison I seemed like an old hand—pity the poor judge and jury with the likes of us two presenting! There were moments during cross-examination when Dawn seemed to be working for the other side, as when she got the Good Samaritan to repeat his story. Fortunately, there were no heart attacks, but Dawn did suffer the distraction of admission to the bar: while the jury was out for deliberations, she had to run out to attend her swearing-in ceremony. When she had raced back, the jury returned the guilty verdict. But any pleasure I might have derived from my first conviction vanished when we reconvened for sentencing.

"Ms. Cardi, I'm disposed to send your client to jail for a year," the judge said. The color drained from Dawn's face, and she began to tremble. I, too, was thunderstruck in that moment, realizing the terrible thing I'd accomplished.

"You can't do that!" Dawn sputtered. "He has a job. His family depends on him for support. He's never had an arrest before in his life. This will destroy him. You can't put this man in jail!" As Dawn's nervous verbal torrent flowed on, I was thinking about the length this man's wife had gone to not to be there. And a part of me would have preferred not to have been there either. I have always believed that individuals are ultimately responsible for their own actions, and I have no tolerance for spousal abuse. But I also understood that the defendant would not be the only one bearing the hardship of his punishment. Jail might be a justifiable punishment, and the only absolute insurance against his striking his wife, but it would exact a high price on his whole family.

Dawn trailed off, and the judge looked to me. "I think Ms. Cardi is right," I heard myself saying, without premeditation, and feigning a self-assurance I wasn't feeling inside. I acknowledged that putting him in jail would have significant negative consequences for his family. I said that I would be satisfied with probation if Dawn could get him into a treatment program for domestic abuse that required regular attendance and that also checked in on his wife regularly. For a man in his thirties with no prior arrests, I thought that treatment and the imminent threat of jail would be sufficient protection for his wife.

"Find the program," the judge said to Dawn. And we both breathed a sigh of relief.

Dawn thanked me afterward. She was stunned by my concession, which seemed especially strange for a beginner, given that a prosecutor's career is built on a reputation for toughness and winning stiff sentences. I was having my own doubts by the time I reported my actions to John Fried, my bureau chief. John heard me out and responded in his typically thoughtful and deliberate way. He noted that he might have done differently himself, since the assault on the Good Samaritan suggested a danger to society, but he acknowledged my reasoning: "You did what you thought was right." The freedom to exercise my judgment without fear of being disciplined promoted a confidence that helped me grow into the job more quickly.

Dawn and I would cross paths often, as her section at the Legal Aid Society was assigned to my trial bureau. Despite the unofficial rule against fraternization between prosecutors and defense attorneys, we became friends, and as we did, our conversations often edged into bigger themes. We often started at opposite poles of an argument, recognizing that our views were conditioned by personality differences. Dawn was a born public defender, her support of the underdog grounded in a native distrust of authority. I was by nature more the prosecutor, a creature of rules. If the system is broken, my inclination is to fix it rather than to fight it. I have faith in the process of the law, and if it is carried out fairly, I can live with the results, whatever they may be. This may sound naively idealistic, but there is a place for idealism in the practice of the law. It is what makes many of us enter the profession in the first place; it is certainly what drives some of us lawyers to become judges.

Dawn came to me in distress over another case we shared. "You've got to help me," she pleaded. It was a sad story: Her client had lived his entire life in institutions, foster care followed by twenty years in prison for killing a man in a fight. Then, released on lifetime parole, he had been given no support but a bus token. Without life skills, unable to find a job, he survived by selling copper pipes that he stripped from a derelict building, not fully aware that this was theft. The terms of his parole were such that a single violation, even a plea to a reduced charge of disorderly conduct, would have sent him back to state prison. There was something about this man that made Dawn trust him. All things considered, he wasn't doing so badly. He hadn't been dealing drugs; he hadn't robbed anyone. He wouldn't have been stealing pipes if he'd had any help finding a job. He had even met a girl and was in love . . . Dawn talked me into accepting an ACD, an adjournment in contemplation of dismissal, and she got him into a job program. If he stayed out of trouble for six months, the charge would be dismissed.

One day, two years later, he would be waiting for me outside the courtroom. He introduced himself, shook my hand. "You don't remember me," he said. "I'm the guy who was stealing the pipes." He had found a job and been promoted to supervisor. He had also married his girlfriend. By now, they had one child and were expecting another.

The quality of mercy: "It blesseth him that gives and him that takes."

The occasional merciful impulse notwithstanding, I was racking up convictions. Whatever my insecurities—and I had plenty (still do)—I was also fiercely competitive (still am). I became addicted to the thrill of verbal sparring at trial, the exhilaration of having to reinvent strategy on the spot, not knowing whether it would work, under the specter of a judge who at any moment might catch me out with a question. Fearing such humiliation, I prepared compulsively, the way I had in law school, and my reward was the chance to go out and risk it all again the next day. That I could never be sure of myself while doing it was a big reason I loved my work as a trial lawyer.

Notching up top-count prosecutions—convictions for the most serious charges—while giving up little ground in plea bargains became the adult equivalent of collecting gold stars in fifth grade. I liked the particular challenge of taking cases to trial with unsympathetic victims and unreliable witnesses, like the drug addict whose methadone was stolen by another addict, or the elderly couple with fifty felonies between them who were robbed by their young protégé, a grifter in training; or cases that were hopelessly circumstantial, like the jeweler whose half-million-dollar pouch of gems went missing after a family of Gypsies swept through his store—who could be sure the jewels even existed, until I managed to get them returned? I won quite a few of those.

Still, I wasn't willing to prosecute a case that I simply didn't believe in. I was especially lucky, therefore, to have a mentor in John Fried, who embodied just that kind of measured attitude.

John's essential fairness was of a piece with the idealistic standards that Bob Morgenthau set for the DA's Office. Nevertheless, it often felt as if we were swimming upstream against muddy currents with the right answer not clearly in view. With each prosecutor handling around a hundred cases at a time, expediency and rough justice were the order of the day. We fudged, we made do with the tools at hand, we performed triage in the trenches, but we still made an effort to do it with integrity.

Maybe my prosecuting misdemeanors with a ferocity usually reserved for felonies looked to some like real fire in the belly. In reality, it was still more like butterflies and the unremitting fear of leaving anything to chance that made me prepare and argue so intensively. But for whatever reason, I was among the first in our duckling group to be moved up to more serious crimes. By the time I switched to felonies, John Fried had moved up too and was replaced as bureau chief by Warren Murray. Warren had a very different style: extremely soft-spoken but a 100 percent hard-as-nails prosecutor. I worried about how I would fare under him.

I was given a handful of low-level felony cases and a few others that were being retried. One of those cases involved a purse snatching. The defense attorney alerted me that it was flimsy, and I was dismayed to see that the facts were indeed thin to the point of being nonexistent. The young defendant had a clean record. His teachers had described him as quiet, polite, well-behaved, but developmentally slow. He'd never missed a day of school. I interviewed the victim, an elderly woman. She hadn't seen the thief's face as he ran up from behind her, heading in the general direction of the subway entrance. The police grabbed a confused kid they found sitting downstairs on the platform bench, waiting for his train home from school. The woman identified him by the dark jacket he was wearing, like that of the thief, though she couldn't say what color it was. The purse was never found.

I wrote up a description of the evidence and took it to Warren. "You're right," he said. "It's weak. But we have the indictment, and it's our job to prosecute. Let the jury do theirs; they'll acquit him." I went back to my desk and pondered how to argue this to a jury. I went home to Princeton that night and thought about it some more.

By the time I marched into Warren's office in the morning, I was full of righteous indignation, fiery but totally in control. "I'm not trying this case. I can't lie to a jury. If you think you can go into that courtroom and argue that this is grounds to convict, then you'll have to do it yourself." I threw the file on his desk and walked out.

He came running after me. "Look, I just needed to make sure that you were sure."

"Why didn't you just ask?"

"Sometimes I figure I have to play devil's advocate."

I could have done without the drama. The office declined to prosecute the case.

The first time I found myself before Judge Harold Rothwax, he was in a full-throttle tantrum over the many delays that had dragged out a case before I'd caught it on reassignment. "And now, obviously," he shouted, "you're going to tell me that you're new and need a month to prepare!" I promised him that if he gave me fifteen minutes to confirm the availability of the witness, I'd be ready for trial the following week. That endeared me to him permanently. With plenty of misdemeanor trials under my belt, I had enough confidence—or the bravado of ignorance—to trust my performance under pressure. If nothing else, I knew my own standards of preparation. And sure enough, I would never once suffer the shame of his sarcastic warnings about "avoiding the dangers of over-preparation" dished out to so many other attorneys. I would, however, one time get a compliment of sorts out of him when, reading one of my motion papers, he allowed, "Misspellings are supposed to be a sign of genius. You must have plenty of it."

Judge Rothwax dealt with all felony pretrial motions for my trial bureau. He was painfully exacting and infamously unforgiving of lawyers who wasted his time, on one occasion sending defense counsel to jail for ten days for preventing the start of a trial. He was known as the Prince of Darkness, Dr. Doom, and Yahweh, among other epithets, particularly for striking terror in the heart of defendants whenever one with a weak case would decline his offer of a plea. His notorious stock line to defense counsel: "Your client has the constitutional right to go to prison for the maximum time allowable."

But it wasn't just fire and brimstone. Behind the infernal humor, a formidable clarity of mind and a keen legal acumen kept the docket moving with astonishing efficiency. A good judge must possess management skills as well as a deep understanding of the law. And there is no overstating the value of being able to keep all the facts of a case in your head. He might spend two minutes at a conference on a routine case, more on especially complicated ones, but two months later he would remember every detail.

Though I differed with some of Judge Rothwax's views of procedure, and didn't have much use for his hammy Prince of Darkness persona, the integrity and rigor of his thinking, his passion for the law, and the efficiency of his courtroom won my admiration. And he, in turn, offered me kind encouragement, even inviting Kevin and me to his home. As with José Cabranes, the deepest respect could not make me into a good enough protégée to take all his advice. Nevertheless, during those years at the DA's Office, a long-nurtured dream finally found a living example in Harold Rothwax's black-robed presence, the first embodiment of an ideal I would be able to observe up close.

Not long after I moved to felonies, I prosecuted the same defendant in two trials back-to-back. It was two different crimes; hence the two trials: the accused had jumped bail on an older charge of burglary, the outstanding warrant discovered when he was caught for a subsequent robbery. My cases were solid, but matched against a very experienced defense attorney from Legal Aid, I lost them both. It was a hard blow to my ego, but what was even worse, I couldn't figure out where I had gone wrong.

"Okay. Tell me what you did," Warren said in his usual tones, still the quietest voice I've ever strained to hear. I walked him through my presentation of both cases. He identified the problem instantly: I was appealing to logic, not morality, and in effect letting the jury off the hook. Since it is painful to most jurors to vote "guilty" and send a human being to jail, you couldn't simply reason with them to do it; you had to make them feel the necessity. "They have to believe that they have a moral responsibility to convict," Warren said. Even the most perfectly logical argument, absent passion, would make the choice seem like one of personal discretion rather than solemn duty.

Communicating your own moral certainty didn't necessarily mean chewing the scenery. But as when I had described the Kitty Genovese murder in forensics competition, the difference between winning and losing came down to the appeal by emotion rather than fact alone. It was something Abuelita could have told me without ever having gone to law school. And it was something I apparently knew in high school, if only intuitively, before the awareness was pushed aside by years of learning to reason dispassionately at Princeton and Yale.

Granting myself permission to use my innate skills of the heart, accepting that emotion was perfectly valid in the art of persuasion, amounted to nothing less than a breakthrough. Warren would teach me much else in the way of trial skills, as had John Fried, Katie Law, and others at the DA's Office. But that was the single most powerful lesson I would learn. It changed my entire approach to jurors, from the voir dire to the structure of my summations, and the results spoke for themselves: I never lost a case again. I had hung juries a couple of times, and once or twice a conviction on fewer than all counts of the indictment, but never an acquittal.

Leveraging emotional intelligence in the courtroom, as in life, depends on being attentive; the key is always to watch and listen. You don't need to take notes with the court reporter getting down every word. Lower your eyes to your pad, and you're bound to miss that hint of a doubt that flits across the witness's face. Scribble instead of listening, and you won't notice the split second of hesitation in which a witness hedges a choice of words, avoiding the ones that would flow naturally in favor of the ones whose truth he or she is more certain of.

Such attentiveness also figures in upholding one of a litigator's paramount responsibilities: not to bore the jury. If you are palpably present in the moment, continuously mindful of and responsive to your listeners, they will follow where you lead. If, however, you are reading from a script, droning on as though they weren't there, soon enough they won't be, irrespective of how unassailable your argument is.

The state's case is a narrative: the story of a crime. The defense has only to cast doubts on the coherence of that

story. The "why" elements of the story must make sense—
what would have motivated this person to hurt that person—
before you can engage the jurors' empathy, put them in the
shoes of the accused or the victim, as needed: make them feel
the cold blade held against their necks, or the pang of un-
appreciated devotion that might drive someone to steal from
a former employer. It is the particulars that make a story real.
In examining witnesses, I learned to ask general questions so
as to elicit details with powerful sensory associations: the col-
ors, the sounds, the smells, that lodge an image in the mind
and put the listener in the burning house.

Of course, narratives can be slippery. Katie was the one
who taught me what to do when, through no fault of your
own, the story unfolding suddenly changes, throwing your
case into unexpected chaos. In that eventuality, everything
depends on the power to improvise, the dexterity to change
tack as if doing so were part of your strategy all along. If a
witness alters his testimony without warning, the savvy prosecutor simply de-emphasizes the testimony and stresses the
cumulative weight of circumstantial evidence. Devising the
case is always a two-step process: build the strategy out of
reason and logic; then throw yourself into it, heart and soul.
But if you have to revise the plan, suspend feeling and revert
to logic until you can think of something you can sell with
passion.

Other lessons I would figure out for myself, often contrary
to conventional wisdom. Some prosecutors, for instance,
would look for legitimate reasons to eliminate black and His-

panic juror candidates in the voir dire, the assumption being that minorities are biased in favor of defendants. But to me that made sense only if you saw all people of color as potential perpetrators and believed, even more implausibly, that they all saw one another that way too. It was obvious to me that any black or Latino who held a job, or went to school, or stayed home to care for an elderly parent was likely as law-abiding as anyone in my own family and, if anything, far likelier to be the victim of a crime than to commit one. The notion that such a person would, on the basis of racial or ethnic solidarity, let anyone walk who might pose a danger to the community would have seemed laughable where I came from. And so I packed my juries with the kinds of people I'd grown up among; the results, again, spoke for themselves.

As I've said, the DA's Office was not the job that most Yale Law School graduates dreamed of, but it did furnish me with the basis for an eventual judicial temperament in ways that Yale could not. It also gave me the confidence that came of recognizing my personal background as something better than a disadvantage to be overcome.

Twenty

In the spring of 1980, seven months into my first year at the DA's Office, Bob Morgenthau encouraged me to join the board of an organization he had helped to found and had served for the better part of a decade. "They're on a campaign to recruit young talent, and I have given them your name," he said. In those days, few ADAs gave much time to pro bono work, or had much time to give. I already felt the combination of the daily commute and my caseload was testing my limits, but it's always hard to refuse the boss's invitations, and this was especially true of the Boss, who would become such a patron of my career. Besides, I was no stranger to the organization in question: the Puerto Rican Legal Defense and Education Fund (now LatinoJustice). I had applied for a summer internship there while I was at Yale. During the interview, they asked about my career goals. I allowed that I hadn't settled on a short-term plan, but I did know that in twenty years I wanted to be a federal district court judge. The interviewer raised an eyebrow, causing me to conclude that in the future it would be better to keep my fantasies to myself. I didn't get the job, but I remained interested in the group's mission.

The Fund, otherwise known by the acronym PRLDEF ("Pearl-def"), was founded in 1972 by a group of young Puerto Rican lawyers who drew inspiration from the NAACP's Legal Defense and Educational Fund and wanted to use their legal skills to challenge systemic discrimination against the Hispanic community. By the time I joined, PRLDEF was solidly established and had won significant reforms, its landmark *ASPIRA* suit against New York City's Board of Education proving as vital to Hispanics as *Brown v. Board of Education* had been to blacks. Until the *ASPIRA* case, Puerto Rican kids coming from the island, where Spanish was used in public schools, or from families like mine that spoke little English, entered the New York City public school system with no help at all making the language transition. These kids routinely floundered and, though otherwise perfectly capable, would often find themselves in classes for the intellectually disabled. They naturally dropped out in staggering numbers, turning an imagined handicap into a real one, a temporary need for remedial help into a lifetime of minimal employment and poverty. The *ASPIRA* consent decree won by PRLDEF in 1974 established the right of students with limited English to receive bilingual education in New York City's public schools. The very next year, my cousin Miriam would enter

237

college, eventually to graduate as one among the first wave of young teachers to earn a degree in bilingual education.

At PRLDEF I worked on the litigation committee, which hired the staff lawyers and set strategy for the types of cases we would take on. I also served on the education committee, which arranged internships and found mentors for minorities, as well as developing LSAT preparation materials to help more Latinos become law students. Beyond what I was learning from all the potential role models around me, these activities gave me a grounding in the nature of organizations and how competing interests within them had to be balanced: in a word, politics. The staffing work in particular threw me square into the problem of allocating limited resources. There were those with visions of taking on ever bigger cases and more areas of advocacy, my own preference as always being for smaller, more careful steps. Sometimes personalities clashed, especially given the presence of so many lawyers who had succeeded as aggressive litigators in large corporate settings and who were now maneuvering in the close quarters of a small nonprofit where everyone involved had a deep emotional investment. Occasionally, such conflicts can tear the very fabric of an institution if they aren't handled wisely.

Learning how to balance the needs of individuals with the no-less-real needs of an institution was an important lesson. It's fine to be on the side of the little guy, but he, too, will ultimately suffer if the health and concerns of the greater body he belongs to are neglected. That point would be driven home a year later, when my mother phoned in tears to tell me that she had lost her job. She, along with the entire staff of Prospect Hospital, had been locked out when it closed without warning. The sudden bankruptcy eliminated dozens of jobs, shattered a close-knit family that had shared their workdays for decades, put homes at risk, and destroyed an institution that had revitalized an entire neighborhood. My heart inclined to those who were locked out of their livelihood, but my head was calculating: What concessions, what better choices, might have preserved the institution and avoided this sad loss for all sides? Seeing Prospect Hospital disappear, I appreciated all the more the fine balance, the hard reckoning, and the personal sacrifices that ultimately kept PRLDEF intact through difficult times.

PRLDEF was my first real experience of pro bono work and the honorable role of a "citizen-lawyer." I would continue serving there for twelve years, long after I'd left the DA's Office and right up to becoming a judge. To use my education to help others was so gratifying that despite having no time to call my own, I would get involved with other groups as well over those years.

I particularly welcomed any chance to work on issues such as economic development and education that were crucial to the community in which I was raised. I not only cared deeply about those people but also understood their needs from firsthand experience. As I made my way in the world, however, I was seeing more and more that no group is an island. Even the most cohesive (or the most marginalized) consists of overlapping circles of belonging, just as every individual's identity is constituted of many elements. To do good ultimately meant seeing any particular interests in a larger civic context, a broader sense of community. The specific needs of people like those I grew up with would always tug at my heart, but increasingly the call to serve was beckoning me beyond the confines of where I'd come from.

It was somewhat in that spirit that I joined New York City's Campaign Finance Board, a relatively new organization founded in the wake of scandals that shook New York State in the mid-1980s, when certain vast campaign contributions, undoubtedly corrupting but some perfectly legal, were exposed. The need for oversight in the financing of the electoral process was dramatic, not only to guard against graft, but to ensure access for candidates who would be excluded if money alone determined the race.

What appealed to me was the possibility of devising a structural solution to a long-entrenched problem simply by creating an appropriate set of rules. That's as elegant as ethics gets. It was also an exhilarating exercise in the art of crafting compromise between opposing interests, always my first response to political division. The fact that I had always registered independently, without a party affiliation, enhanced my credibility as a dispassionate mediator. But the board's greatest asset in laying claim to evenhandedness and procedural transparency was its chairman, Father Joseph A. O'Hare. A Jesuit priest and the president of Fordham University, Father

O'Hare was a man of such unassailable integrity that fairness seemed assured. Under his leadership the board exemplified how a government agency could rise above partisanship to work for a general good.

The CFB was my introduction to the city and state political scenes. Many lawyers I met working there would go on to become power brokers whose awareness of me and eventual support would matter to my career in ways that I couldn't yet imagine. I had always thought my career would be devoted to principles that transcended politics, but the fact is there would have been no way to the federal bench except through such political channels. It would matter crucially that I was familiar to people of influence who, though recognizing that I did not involve myself in partisan efforts, could see that I was at least an honest broker. The integrity I had cultivated so jealously out of personal pride would be my calling card when the time came. Or so I was later told.

Sometimes, idealistic people are put off the whole business of networking as something tainted by flattery and the pursuit of selfish advantage. But virtue in obscurity is rewarded only in heaven. To succeed in this world, you have to be known to people.

Twenty-One

"This is difficult for me," my mother said. "He is like my son, Sonia. I watched him grow up. This is not easy for me."

"Please, Mami. You think it's easy for me?"

I can't deny my portion of the blame. The vortex of the District Attorney's Office was all-consuming, and I felt driven to do my utmost on every single case. How many nights had I spent poring over briefs I'd brought home, barely aware of his presence? But Kevin was also finding a new life of his own at Princeton, of which I had no part. One way or another, we had outgrown the first innocent bloom of love and its loyal attachment without having evolved new terms for being together.

On vacation together at Cape Cod in the summer of 1981, our first time there, an unseasonable chill hung in the air between us as tensions kept flaring up over nothing. It was a prelude to Kevin's cautious mention of the changes that had come over us and of how he no longer felt connected to me. Talking about our relationship, about feelings, was not something we did naturally. Even in the early days in high school, when we could talk for hours on end, it was always about some shared interest, or nothing in particular, but never ourselves.

It was late when we got home to the apartment in Princeton after a four-hour drive in uncomfortable silence. I tripped over the mail that had piled up. Tomorrow's business. I fell into bed.

In the morning, I opened an envelope from the DMV. It had taken the whole five years we'd been married for them to send me a new driver's license with my married name on it.

"You know, Kevin, if we break up, it will probably take another five years for them to change my name back again." I was joking, sort of.

"I'm sure they do it all the time."

There are things you may know in your heart for a long while without admitting them to conscious awareness, until, unexpectedly, something triggers an inescapable realization. In that unhesitating matter-of-fact reply was a truth that I could no longer shut out: our marriage was over. When Kevin left for work, I picked up the phone. I had never complained about him to Mami, never mentioned any problems between us. To me relationships are private. Unless something was really serious, my mother didn't need to know. As this was the first she had heard of any trouble, I was especially grateful that she didn't argue.

"Can I come home?"

"*Siempre*, Sonia." Always.

Kevin and I talked through the details without rancor. We agreed that I would assume our credit card debt, since I was the one bothered by it. In return I got custody of the Honda Civic. The only problem was that I didn't know how to drive a stick shift.

Never take driving lessons from someone while you're breaking up with him. Every time I popped the clutch, Kevin was apoplectic, and neither of us needed the added stress. But it was unavoidable, especially since I was running out of time. Marguerite and Tom would soon be coming to Princeton to help me move out. Though overwhelmed and sad and frustrated at still being unable to drive that stupid car, I was determined to get out of the apartment that same weekend, even if they had to tow me all the way to Co-op City. I packed late into the night before finally collapsing in a troubled sleep. I had an extraordinarily vivid dream: I'm in the car, engine idling. I put it in gear, lift my foot off the clutch very gently till it engages, a little more gas, the wheels are rolling. Nice . . .

The next morning, Marguerite and Tom arrived. It was clear from her sighs and the strained conversation that this was painful for them, too. We loaded up their car as well as the Civic with boxes of books and precious little else. I hadn't accumulated much of a life if you measured it in stuff. Five years of marriage and barely two carloads. Marguerite, it turned out, knew how to drive a stick, and so she offered to take the wheel. But I insisted on doing it and asked her just to ride with me. As I started the car, the knowledge I possessed in the dream seemed to be real. My sleeping brain must have learned the lesson my waking mind couldn't master because of the tension between Kevin and me. In a hyperalert state, I made it onto the highway and into fourth gear. From there it was a long, clear glide with plenty of time to gather my wits before I had to face traffic in the Bronx.

Mami greeted us with grim cheer as we unloaded boxes from the elevator. The house felt strange in spite of the old familiarity, empty somehow without Junior. He had graduated from medical school and moved to Syracuse for his residency. Mami cooked us a welcome dinner of *chuletas*, and the smells from the kitchen were more comforting than I could have imagined. Soon enough she and I would start pushing each other's buttons, but that night it was a relief to be home.

Kevin's mother, Jean, was heartbroken by our breakup. As rocky as my relations with her had been initially, her prejudice had been worn down by the fact of having a daughter-in-law, and a real friendship had grown up between us over the years. She would later tell me that she realized only after I'd gone how many gestures on Kevin's part—holiday gifts or a thoughtfully timed phone call—had been prompted by me.

In the end, I sold my wedding ring to pay the lawyer who handled our divorce. Saddened though I was at seeing Kevin

245

leave, I was no more sentimental about the formal trappings of marriage than I had been on our wedding day. When I told Judge Rothwax that I was getting divorced and wanted to revert to my maiden name, he started using it instantly and made a point of correcting anyone who still referred to me as Ms. Sotomayor de Noonan. The DMV would take longer to straighten out.

Twenty-Two

When summer of 1982 came around, I still hadn't figured out my next move, but I knew I needed a break from my mother. We would be at each other's throats if I couldn't get away at least for some weekends. Nancy Gold, now Nancy Gray, who had been my friend ever since taking the seat next to mine during orientation on our very first day at the District Attorney's Office, had a summer share on Fire Island. She wanted me to join her group house, and so I went to check it out. It was quite a scene: more people than rooms, parties, and late nights.

"It's not my style, Nancy."

But she insisted it would be a great way to kick-start my social life. "Never mind the crowd," she said. "I don't know most of them myself." I wasn't sure why she thought that made it more appealing.

"Just try it."

In the end, I refused to be convinced, saying I needed something more sedate. So Nancy introduced me to a college friend who was in another group house on the island, a very different scene, as she described it: shared meals, quiet evenings playing board games and reading. I threw caution to the wind and signed up for that one sight unseen.

My first trip out, the ferry abandoned me on the dock late at night in the middle of a storm that had knocked out the power and phone lines. I got hopelessly lost on the half-mile walk through the dunes from the ferry landing. When I finally found the house and burst in, Mark Serlen, a housemate who'd been dozing, looked as if he'd just seen a sea monster come through the door. But from there on it was a lovely, exquisitely peaceful summer. Every other weekend would find Valerie, her fiancé, Jack, Mark, and assorted other friends playing Trivial Pursuit and Scrabble, reading the Sunday *Times* or a good mystery, sailing the weathered little skiff, cooking marvelous meals with clams gathered from the bay, and smoking endless cigarettes. I confess that the first night I spent alone there, many things went bump in the dark and I armed myself with a kitchen knife and broomsticks. But I would eventually come to feel there was no place safer.

We repeated the house share for a few summers, each of us eventually moving on to other arrangements, but the friendships that began at Fire Island continue. The kids have grown up and have their own kids. The summer rituals have given way to other traditions, like season tickets to the ballet year after year with Mark. But at least one weekend every summer I still find my way back to the beach with my Fire Island family.

I began to open up to the possibility of dating again. It was tentative at first, I'll admit, but being outgoing and enjoying the process of getting to know a person in all his curious particularity, I grew to like dating. I wouldn't exactly fall hard for anyone, but I did meet some men who renewed my faith that I might be appealing and who even caused some of that nervousness of anticipation that I hadn't really felt since high school. Even a little romance can do wonders, if you are prepared to enjoy the moment and let the moments accumulate, whatever may come of it.

Probably nothing constrained my dating life as much as living at home with my mother. To hear her screaming from the bedroom "Sonia, it's midnight. You have to work tomorrow!" did not exactly make me feel like Mary Tyler Moore. If I was out late, she panicked. If she couldn't reach me by phone, she would call all my friends looking for me. We were making each other miserable.

Dawn Cardi told me her next-door neighbor in Carroll Gardens, Brooklyn, had an apartment for rent. By train it was twenty minutes from my office at 100 Centre Street, forty minutes on foot. The neighborhood was great, she said, a kind of Mayberry-on-the-Gowanus, only Italian. Many of the families on the block had been there for generations, and they watched out for one another, which sounded something like Abuelita's neighborhood when I was little. I went to see it that same evening. The building had real character, even an original tin ceiling, and the apartment was adorable. Naturally, the landlord wanted a security deposit. I said I could bring a check the next day, not yet knowing where I would get the money. But before I committed, I told him, my mother would have to see the place, not to make the decision, but for her own peace of mind, to be sure it was safe. The landlord liked that so much, he later told me, he called the real estate agent as soon as I left to delist the apartment.

When Dawn and I became neighbors, we developed a cozy routine. Getting off the train after a ridiculously long day, often after ten, I would stop at her place most nights before going home. Her husband, Ken, who got up very early for work, had usually gone to bed, but he always left a plate of dinner for me—he's still a great cook. Dawn would pour us a drink, and we'd talk over that day in the life of New York's criminal justice system.

Actually, by then we'd found much more than work to talk about, having discovered that our backgrounds had plenty in common. She was the daughter of first-generation immigrants who had weathered the sorts of challenges that can break a family, causing her to cultivate a certain self-reliance early on. And like me, she had a mother with extraordinary strength of character, one whom I would come to know and love like an extra mother of mine, just as I had Marguerite's.

I've always turned the families of friends into family of

my own. The roots of this practice are buried deep in my childhood, in the broad patterns of Puerto Rican culture, in the particular warmth of Abuelita's embrace and her charged presence at the center of my world, the village of aunts, uncles, cousins, in-laws, and compadres scattered across the Bronx. I'd observed how the tribe extended its boundaries, with each marriage adding not just a new member but a whole new clan to ours. Still, in Abuelita's family, blood ultimately came first, and she strongly favored her own. My mother, being more or less an orphan, poor in kinfolk, approached the matter less dogmatically. She treated my father's family as her own, and when he died, it was to her sister, Titi Aurora, that Mami would bind herself with an almost metaphysical intensity, not to mention filling the available space in the household. But she continued to expand the family of friends among our neighbors, whether in the projects or in Co-op City.

I have followed my mother's approach to family, refusing to limit myself to accidents of birth, blood, and marriage. Like any family, mine has its rituals and traditions that sustain my tie to every member, no matter how far-flung. My friend Elaine Litwer, for instance, adopted me for Passover, and though I otherwise see her family only rarely, joining her Seder nurtured our connection. Thanksgiving is Mami's and Dawn's in perpetuity. Christmas belongs to Junior and to Junior's kids, Kiley, Corey, and Conner, when they came. Travel becomes another source of tradition; friendships that might have faded with distance are preserved because every trip to a friend's city, for whatever reason of business, becomes an occasion to visit. In this way I stay meaningfully connected to old friends, like Ken Moy and his family, and establish new relationships that have sustained me.

Children elevate the art of found families to another level. I adore kids and have a special affinity with them, an ability to see the world through their eyes that most adults seem to lose. I can match any kid's stubbornness, hour for hour. I don't baby anyone; when we play games, I play to win. I treat kids as real people. Sometimes I think I love my friends' kids even more than I love my friends. Over the years, I have gathered more godchildren than anyone I know, and I take the role seriously.

Kiley is mine in a special way.

When I first set eyes on her, she was little more than a tangle of stick-thin limbs and tubes in the neonatal intensive care unit: one pound, eleven ounces. She was impossibly frail, and then very unlikely to survive, but I stood there awestruck at the sight of her drawing little breaths, a miracle of both life and science. I thought I knew everything about family before that ringing phone woke me up in the middle of the night: Junior, calling from Detroit to say that he had rushed Tracey to the hospital. I got on the next plane.

Junior had met Tracey during his residency at Syracuse, where she was a nurse. She'd followed him to Philadelphia for a fellowship, where they married before moving to Michigan. Now Junior stood beside me before the glass partition of the ICU, reciting the clinical details in his best doctor's voice. It was how he kept himself from going to pieces, but I could tell he was very scared. I felt closer to him in that moment than I ever had. It was not just the effect of seeing my little brother going through the worst experience of his life. It was also seeing what fatherly strength and devotion he had learned. Junior, who couldn't even remember Papi, had figured out for himself what it was to be a man.

Kiley's prognosis was not good, but she would be spared the seizures that can lead to complications. Tracey spent hours and hours every day sitting beside the incubator, watching, until the amazing day when she was first able to hold her daughter in her hands. Almost daily, it seemed, the doctors were intervening to solve some new problem. But slowly, very slowly, we allowed hope to take root. And then one day, sitting alone beside her, I somehow knew with absolute certainty that Kiley would make it.

It was almost a year before she first laughed, every milestone seeming to come at an excruciatingly slow pace. She'd remain a tiny child, my mother horrified at how little she ate. But I would be the one to get her to have mashed bananas laced with brown sugar and to introduce her to White Castle hamburgers, watching with delight as she actually finished her very first. But not until she was five could I persuade Junior to let her spend the day alone with me. Kiley needed no persuading. We explored the Children's Museum, ate ice cream at Serendipity, saw the Christmas show at Radio City Music Hall and the crèche at St. Patrick's—all on our first solo outing. After Junior moved the family from Michigan to Syracuse, Kiley never missed a chance to come stay with Titi Sonia.

Seeing my enthusiasm for being something of a crazy aunt—Titi Sonia might drive for hours to deliver on a promise to a child, or show up in an elf costume—many loved ones naturally asked whether I would one day have kids of my own. The question was never uncomplicated, even when my marriage seemed secure.

The prospects of my having a baby, or rather the potential for complications caused by diabetes, terrified my mother. She let Kevin know that if we had any intention of having children, she was counting on him to become a doctor first, not so as to be able to support a family, but to understand fully the risks involved. It wasn't my mother's decision, but I was not indifferent to her fears. In fact, a part of me felt them too. I knew, of course, that type 1 diabetics did have kids. It wasn't impossible, but the incidence of maternal complications was sobering, especially since I'd spent most of my life imagining I'd be lucky to live past forty. My projected longevity and the chance for a safe pregnancy had certainly improved alongside the methods of disease management since I'd been diagnosed, but I still feared that I wouldn't see old age. Even if that risk did not dictate my decision entirely, it seemed inarguable that having kids would be tempting fate.

Adoption was an attractive alternative. Eight years after

Kiley's birth, Junior and Tracey adopted a pair of twins, Conner and Corey. Tracey likes to point out that they are Korean boys with Irish names, a Polish mother, and a Puerto Rican father—the perfect American family. My nephews are all the proof I could have needed of how emotionally satisfying adoption might have been. Still, there remained the fear that I might not be around long enough to raise a child to adulthood. Ultimately, the satisfaction of motherhood would be sacrificed, though I wouldn't say it was sacrificed to career.

It is interesting to me how, even after all the strides of the women's movement, the question of whether we can "have it all" remains such a controversy in the media, as if the ideal can be achieved. Most women of my generation who entered professional life did not forgo motherhood, and many did succeed at both. But they paid a price, one still paid by most women who work outside the home (and men too, I believe, if they parent wholeheartedly): a life of perpetual internal compromise that leaves you always feeling torn. Though in some corner of my heart I am still sulking about Mami's absence during my childhood, I nevertheless credit the powerful example she set me as a working woman. But we would do well to abandon the myth of "having it all," career and family, with no sacrifice to either, together with the pernicious notion that a woman who chooses one or the other is somehow deficient.

During my time at the District Attorney's Office, women were only beginning to enter the legal profession in significant numbers. Fewer still were practicing criminal law. Men and women got equal pay at the DA's Office, but promotions came far less easily for most women. I saw many women who were no less qualified wait much longer than men for the same advance. And they would have to work twice as hard as men to earn it, because so much of what they did was viewed in the light of casual sexism.

There were many times a defendant's lawyer would enter the courtroom before a session and ask each of the male clerks and paralegals around me, "Are you the assistant in charge?" while I sat there invisible to him at the head of the table. My response was to say nothing, and my colleagues would follow suit. If it rattled him a bit when he eventually discovered his error, that didn't hurt our side, and perhaps he'd be less likely to repeat it.

Could I have managed to negotiate this culture as well as the crushing caseload with a child tugging at my awareness in the background of every moment? I think not. The idea of another life utterly dependent on me, the way a child needs his mother, didn't seem compatible with the professional necessity of living at this punishing pace. As it was, there was already too little time to accomplish the things I envisioned.

Having made a different choice from that of many women, I occasionally do feel a tug of regret. But families can be made in other ways, and I marvel at the support and inspiration I've derived from the ones I've built of interlocking circles of friends. In their constant embrace I have never felt alone.

Twenty-Three

Joining the DA's Office had represented a chance to be a practicing lawyer right away and to play a tangible part in protecting the public. There was no denying the allure of the mission, or the thrill I derived from accomplishing it, but while I was working fifteen-hour days, I wasn't giving much thought to the daily experience of confronting humanity at its worst, any more than I was noticing the subtle signs of the rift developing at home. It was Kevin who had made me see what was happening between us, but eventually, when the divorce was behind me, I would have to discover for myself what my job was doing to me.

There are those in law enforcement who manage to remain unaltered by the work in their private selves, but they stand out with the rarity of saints. All around me I saw personalities darkened by cynicism and despair. Trained in suspicion, skilled at cross-examining, you will look for the worst in people and you will find it. I'd felt from the beginning that these impulses were at odds with my essential optimism, my abiding faith in human nature and its enduring potential for redemption. But now I could see the signs that I, too, was hardening, and I didn't like what I saw. Even my sympathy for the victims, once such an inexhaustible driver of my efforts, was being depleted by the daily spectacle of misdeeds and misery. I began to ask myself whether there weren't other equally worthy jobs. Meanwhile, I would persevere at the DA's Office, convinced at least I was doing something valuable.

It was a relatively minor crime that caused me to doubt even that. I was working in the complaint room one day, my eyes, as usual, skipping over the names, when I picked up a new file, going straight to the facts of the case. Names don't appear in the arresting officer's narrative: it's always the defendant did this; the victim did that. But as I read to the bottom of the page, I said to myself, I've already seen this episode. We caught this guy. We tried him. We locked him up. I swear, it's Mr. Ortiz!

Sure enough, it was. He had served his time, but no sooner had he landed back on the street than he was caught in a carbon copy of the earlier crime. What had been a misdemeanor in the first instance became a felony now by virtue of repetition, but otherwise the cases were identical. He was, of course, not the first repeat offender I'd come across, but somehow his unremarkable case crystallized a certain sense of futility in my efforts. If this was the system, maybe I should be working to improve it rather than simply enforcing it on the front lines.

It was now that the old dream of becoming a judge seemed, if still not within reach, at least something that I might reasonably start working toward, and I was aiming for the federal bench. The federal bench was where matters of broad consequence, cases affecting far more lives than those of a victim and a defendant, were decided. I'd been aware of this since law school, when I studied with particular fascination how the landmark rulings of southern judges like the legendary Frank M. Johnson Jr. had done so much to advance civil rights and bring an end to Jim Crow. The idea that a single person could make such a difference in the cause of justice was nothing less than electrifying, and having more or less accepted the primacy of career in my life, I saw no reason to stint on ambition.

By now I had seen enough of the world to imagine what a path to such a goal might look like. Most federal judges come to the bench with one of two accomplishments behind them: partnership in a prominent law firm or an important stint, at some point in their careers, in government. There are exceptions, of course, and the only invariable requirement is a record of excellence—in academia or elsewhere—that rises to the attention of a senator's selection committee or the president's staff. Nowadays many federal judges have served first as federal prosecutors, and though this was a less likely path when I was at the DA's Office, I knew that I needed a rest from criminal law. Throughout my time there I had interviewed occasionally when I spotted an opening in public service, but it became clear that I would need more varied experience if I was going to aim higher than a line attorney in a government bureaucracy.

In any case, I wanted to gain experience in civil law, a challenge I welcomed, having certainly enjoyed my courses in business law at Yale (how many people got honors in Commercial Transactions or really took an interest in tax law, anyway?). Those courses had also taught me how much of legal work involved representing corporations and economic power. To be a judge, I'd need to learn to move comfortably in that world. And so I decided that my next job would be an immersion in civil law.

When I announced my intention to jump, Bob Morgenthau tried harder than I might have expected to dissuade me. He indicated I would likely become a bureau chief if I stayed and that post could lead to a state court judgeship; he was unaware that my gaze was set on the federal bench. He did manage to delay my departure for well over a year by assigning me to a handful of exceptionally challenging cases that were very much in the public eye.

It was very soon after that exchange that my bureau chief called me. "Sonia, this is a very sensitive situation. The Boss wants you to be the one to handle it." The office needed to investigate an accusation of police brutality made by a church leader in Harlem. Relations between police and the black community were already severely strained. A year before, a man picked up for graffiti vandalism had gone into a coma and died in custody. Now a Harlem reverend was claiming to have been beaten after being stopped for a traffic violation. The two officers countered that he had assaulted them. "I'm not going to tell you what the outcome should be," the Boss said. "Just make sure the office doesn't look bad in the press." I would hear from him once again during the investigation, asking for a status report. Otherwise, he left me to it and kept his distance.

C. Vernon Mason, the well-known civil rights lawyer, was representing the minister. Visiting my alcove office, Mason lectured me at length on the alienation of the community, its anger at the police, its distrust of the prosecutor's intentions, and his own belief that justice could not and would not be done, and he declared his client's unwillingness to cooperate. I in turn lectured him back: assuming the corruption of everyone in law enforcement was a self-fulfilling prophecy, I said, whose effect was only to sabotage the system, ensuring that justice could not be done. I made an emotional plea for him to give me a chance, but he would give me neither the benefit of the doubt nor any help at all in the investigation.

Mason didn't understand where this prosecutor was coming from. As much as I respected the police and appreciated the difficulty of their job, I had seen for myself how the frustrations of a massive crime wave and a woefully underfunded response could change people who'd started out with the best of intentions. But if the community could have no faith in law enforcement, the job of policing would be infinitely harder, the mission ultimately doomed. If I found that wrong had been done that day, I would prosecute it.

For three months I scoured the streets of Harlem daily for witnesses. I knocked on every door within blocks of where the encounter had taken place, plastering the neighborhood with my card, begging anyone who would listen to talk to me if he or she had seen what happened. I parked myself on a stool at Sylvia's famous soul food counter and chatted with anyone coming or going. But no one ever came forward. If anyone had seen something, no one was saying.

One thing was accomplished, however: a genuine effort was observed. Ultimately, there would be no indictment, but there would be no explosive headlines, either. Tensions had been defused, at least this time. But the larger story would not end any day soon. The cops would need special training. The community would need to learn the value of helping the force recruit, instead of branding anyone of their own who joined a traitor.

The second big assignment that Bob Morgenthau sent my way would be my first murder trial. It was a huge case, very complex, and real tabloid fodder. As a homicide novice, I couldn't have led the prosecution, but Hugh Mo, the senior assistant DA in charge, ensured that my second-seat role was far from pro forma. Hugh was a slightly built figure with a booming voice and a big personality to match; a hard-driving prosecutor, he was also a gentle family man—an all-around confounder of stereotypes. Our offices were side by side, and we developed an easy, seamless teamwork and camaraderie.

He generously allowed my visible participation in the prosecution of Richard Maddicks, who was charged with being the Tarzan Murderer.

The press had so dubbed the perpetrator because his modus operandi included swinging through a victim's apartment window from a rope secured to the roof. In a marathon of armed burglaries over a few months, he had terrorized one small area of Harlem, shooting three people to death and seriously wounding seven others. He would shoot anyone he found at home, whether or not the person resisted or posed any threat. He even shot one victim's small dog. If anything prevented him from finishing a job, he might return to the same building on another day or just lurk on a nearby rooftop or in an air shaft for a few minutes until he could resume.

Maddicks's rap sheet told the tale: a twenty-five-year career in assault and robbery. He was on parole when he was arrested and supporting a two-hundred-dollar-a-day drug habit. His hauls as a thief suggested what sorts of people he preyed on: a pocketful of subway tokens, a wad of bills that had been stuffed in a shoe or a bra, the food in the kitchen. One of his big jackpots was a few thousand dollars one couple had kept at home, their life savings. His victims were barely hanging on to begin with, and their lives were usually destroyed by his visit, if they survived it.

Hugh and I had discovered twenty-three separate incidents, eleven of which had strong enough evidence to bring to trial and which we consolidated into one indictment. We figured the only way a jury could see the big picture of

Maddicks's villainy was to try all eleven together. Easier said than done: the law does not allow you to try unrelated crimes together, and it was no surprise that the defense filed a motion to sever the various counts.

"It's not a conspiracy," said Hugh. "There's only one of him." I dug into the library looking for an appropriate way to frame the common elements that linked the crimes, and we requested a *Molineux* hearing, a New York State proceeding in which a judge decides whether the facts of the case justify allowing evidence that is normally inadmissible. We argued that our purpose was to show not criminal propensity but rather proof of identity: given the rare level of physical strength and agility required for the acrobatics common to all the incidents, we could reasonably claim that this element, not unlike a signature modus operandi, identified Maddicks as the perpetrator.

Judge Rothwax handled the pretrial motions. As usual, I made sure to be prepared, and he was perfectly reasonable. We would prosecute all eleven incidents in one trial. I felt the very real satisfaction of having devised an argument persuasive enough to show that the facts of our case fell within the boundaries of this corner of the law. The critical faculty that had remained an abstraction to me at Yale, and eluded me at Paul, Weiss, and wasn't even necessary to prosecuting most cases was now in my sure possession: I was undeniably thinking like a lawyer.

We located forty witnesses who were willing to testify, Hugh and I each taking twenty to interview and prepare for trial. This being my first murder, much of the legwork was new to me. So was the huge volume of records—autopsy, fingerprint, and ballistic reports, multiple witness statements given to different officers—to be assimilated. But with Hugh's guidance I learned how to sift them for the crucial details to fashion our case. He instructed me too in the preparation of charts and maps and diagrams by which the evidence could be visually represented to prevent the jury from being overwhelmed by the dizzying minutiae, always a danger in complex prosecutions.

The effort also required Hugh and me to become intimately familiar with those few blocks in Harlem where Maddicks had conducted his spree. It's essential for a prosecutor to visit the scene of the crime. You have to root yourself in the space, internalize it, and absorb details that you would invariably miss in a secondhand description. You have to make the scene come to life in the minds of the jurors, and so it has to live in your mind first.

Azilee Solomon had come home from work to find her door unlocked, her home ransacked, her longtime companion—her husband, really, by common law—dead in the blood-soaked chair where he had been napping. They had both worked at the Hilton hotel for twenty years, she as a chambermaid, he as a janitor. Every last penny that they had saved for retirement was stolen. The meat and coffee from their refrigerator were gone, along with the shopping cart that Mrs. Solomon used to wheel her groceries home.

At Maddicks's girlfriend's apartment, detectives found the same meat and coffee, but that proved nothing: anyone could have bought those brands. Outside the building, however, there were six shopping carts lined up by the trash, among which Mrs. Solomon instantly recognized her own. It was true that shopping carts were also mass-produced. But only one could have had the piece of yellow tape that Mrs. Solomon had used to mend a broken rung. "Take out those old clothes," she told the detectives, "and you'll find that yellow tape underneath." At trial we staged a dramatic shopping cart lineup in Judge James Leff's court to re-create the moment of discovery.

I spent a lot of time with Mrs. Solomon in the process of preparing for her testimony. I got to know her well. She was a deeply religious woman who radiated kindness. My gift of faith was not as great as hers, but I was deeply touched to see the solace it brought her. Though the murder of her partner was senseless and had turned her life upside down, she somehow accepted it as God's will. She wanted Maddicks removed from the proximity of anyone else he might harm, but she expressed no desire for vengeance. Her tears flowed but without self-pity as she told her story in a matter-of-fact tone, first to me and then to the jury. I could tell that she had been loved.

The Tarzan Murderer himself was, by disturbing contrast, my first real-life encounter with a human being beyond salvage. Throughout the trial, I watched him obsessively, searching his face for the least trace of feeling. Something in me badly needed to see even a glimmer of empathy or regret, as witness after witness told one more horrifying story of loss. I would be disappointed. He sat there, utterly impassive, hour after hour, and I couldn't help thinking: The devil is alive right here. I've always had a fundamental faith in rehabilitation, always believed that education and effort, if applied intelligently, could ultimately fix anything. Richard Maddicks taught me that there are exceptions, however few. What we do with them is a separate question, but after he was sentenced to sixty-seven and a half years in prison, I was glad to know that he was unlikely to be free in my lifetime.

Later, when we said good-bye after the trial, Mrs. Solomon turned back to me as she left my office and added, "Miss Sonia"—she couldn't manage my last name—"there's something very special about you. You've been blessed. I'm glad we met." She was gone before I could answer, but I thought: Mrs. Solomon, there's something very special about you, too. I am humbled and honored to have known you. There are people who make me believe, in ways that I can't fully explain, that I have something important to accomplish in this life. Sometimes it's a seemingly random encounter. The inscrutable words of a stranger that somehow say to me: Sonia, you have work to do. Get on with it.

The last of the really tough cases that I perceived as Bob Morgenthau's challenge to me carried a different stench of evil. Nancy and Dawn were both concerned about how it would affect me. "Can you handle it?" they asked. I knew I could, though I would surprise even myself with the ferocity of determination this one provoked, a steelier side of me than I'd ever known.

I was working late one night when I reached my limit for the day. I turned off the projector, flipped the lights on, took a deep breath, and tried to will away the nausea. You can understand that child pornography is abominable, you can appreciate the harm that's done to the children used to make it and to the morals of a society, but you can't begin to imagine the depth of revulsion you'll feel.

There were two defendants. Scott Hyman was small-fry, the retail front end who'd sold a few films to an undercover cop and was supposed to connect him with the wholesaler for the big purchase. He was young, even vulnerable looking, showing up for court every day with the same oversized sweater hanging on his scrawny frame. His partner Clemente D'Alessio cut a much less sympathetic figure, stocky with slicked-back hair and a pockmarked face, a garish gold crucifix hanging on his chest. If he wasn't the brains of a bigger operation, he was at least smart enough to stay out of sight. Everything we had on him was circumstantial and hinged on identifying his voice in a single recorded phone call. My plan was to implicate them both in the same transaction, focusing on the link between retail and wholesale.

The first day and opening arguments were more nerve-racking than any I had experienced in a while. I remembered how a bureau chief had advised another female ADA. "Handle it like a man," he told her. "Go to the bathroom and throw up." The laugh was sufficient to quell my stomach. I've since accepted that all trial lawyers get nervous, even some judges, and the day you find being in court routine enough that you feel relaxed will probably be a day you'll regret.

The defense might have argued entrapment, but they chose not to. Instead, Hyman's attorney went for "diminished capability." Apparently, Hyman was addicted to quaaludes.

Diminished capability is always a flimsy argument at best. It has no legal standing, and I could see maybe five different ways to knock it down.

D'Alessio's attorney, a high-priced criminal defense lawyer with more than twenty years of trial experience, often on high-profile cases, decided on a mistaken-identity strategy: there was another Clem who worked in the same building, and he, the defense claimed, was obviously the one Hyman was speaking to in the incriminating phone call. So D'Alessio had found a way to remain invisible, even as he sat there at the defense table. I would have to find a way of using to our advantage that cloak of secrecy he'd wrapped around himself. That he'd evidently taken such pains to keep his hands clean despite a mountain of circumstantial evidence was entirely in keeping with our view that we had netted quite a big fish.

I presented my evidence over six long, methodical, painstaking days. There was so much stuff—piles of films, tapes, documents—that we had to wheel it into the courtroom on carts. I mapped the locations in detail, painting a scene of seedy storefronts. This wasn't just atmosphere. I needed the territory laid out clearly so as to lead the jury along the disjointed trail of evidence that came from the surveillance teams: Hyman coming and going to D'Alessio's office; the brown paper bag seen here, seen there, seen going in and not coming out; the locations where conversations were caught on hidden mics . . .

Was I pushing the jurors too far by subjecting them to the tedium of listening to the undercover cops' recordings? They had to suffer through long silences, incongruous music from the car radio while the clock hand swept slowly, and wait for a few damning words. But the tapes left no doubt about the nature of what was happening. You could hear Hyman boasting about other sales he'd made. He also talked about the wholesaler's concern for secrecy. And then, finally, we get the link between Hyman and D'Alessio: "Just like the last time, yeah, same guy."

My summation didn't need rhetoric. The facts were damning enough. All I needed to do was to show how they were connected with relentless logic, step by step, leaving no piece out. I tried to put myself in the jurors' shoes and anticipate any possible misgiving or misunderstanding. Would they balk at the circumstantial nature of the evidence against D'Alessio? Keep it simple, straightforward, I reminded myself.

My closing ran two and a half hours. The judge took another two hours to charge the jury, reviewing all the elements of the law. It was early evening by the time they began their deliberations. But by the end of the next day, the jury forewoman was reading the verdict, pronouncing "guilty" eighty-six times—forty-three counts for each defendant. Hyman and D'Alessio had expected this; they had bail on hand.

But there remained the matter of the sentencing. I had seen cases in which defendants found guilty on all counts had evaded the full weight of justice because a single jurist was, for one reason or another, unwilling to impose it. In the conversations we had taped, when Hyman bragged about other crimes—drug deals and credit card scams—he said he never worried about getting caught. When it came time for sentencing, he said, you just had to keep postponing until you got the right judge. I could not let that happen. When we reconvened a month later, I pressed and argued for the maximum.

D'Alessio got three and a half to seven years; Hyman got two to six.

Earlier, Bob Morgenthau had offered me a promotion to head the Juvenile Office. My work on this trial had got him thinking that this might be a specialty area for me. My refusal of his offer was instantaneous, an instinctive gesture of self-preservation. It was time for me to move on.

When the child pornography case was wrapped up, I took a brief vacation in Puerto Rico, but my mind was back in New York, and in particular on my cousin Nelson, who had reentered my life. After disappearing for about eight years through the worst of his addiction, he had somehow managed to join the military and clean up. There would still be ups and downs, but he didn't lose touch with the family again, and so gradually we had been able to reestablish our connection. The worst had seemed long past when he married Pamela. She had a daughter whom he cherished as his own. They had just learned that a second child was on the way when Nelson was diagnosed with AIDS. His was one of the very first cases linked to needle use, just before awareness of the disease exploded in the public consciousness.

Nelson, like me, had had a special connection with Abuelita, and it didn't end when she died. His old premonitions of an early death were haunting him now. He told me he could hear ghostly trumpets. "Abuelita is calling me, and I'm telling her I'm not ready. I want to live to see my child born." He would, but not much longer than that, the end coming before his thirtieth birthday. In his last weeks, we would have many talks for hours at a stretch, slipping into the transparent ease we'd had in childhood, as if making up for lost time. I hadn't understood until then that one could be addicted to drugs and yet function normally in the world, holding a job and supporting a family. Nelson wasn't robbing people to get his fix; he wasn't shooting up in stairwells. He managed his addiction like a chronic disease, not unlike my diabetes.

I told him how I had been dazzled by his brilliance and his limitless curiosity about how the world works. And how I despaired of ever matching up to him. He looked at me and shook his head. "You really don't understand, do you? I've always been in awe of you. There was nothing you couldn't learn if you set your mind to it. You would just study until you figured it out. I can't do that; I never could. That's why I couldn't finish college, why I couldn't stick with a job. I didn't have the will. That determination that you have is special. It's a different kind of intelligence."

One day after little Nelson had arrived, we talked about Nelson's happiness at his son's birth and his sadness at the prospect of not being there for his children. We talked as well about the time a couple of months earlier, before his condition had gotten really bad, when he'd asked me to give him a ride to run an errand. He could no longer get around easily, and there was someone he needed to see, just for a little while. He asked me to wait, and so I sat in the car, parked outside the run-down tenement in Hunts Point, just a few blocks from where Abuelita used to live. I figured this was an old friend to whom he wanted to say his good-byes while he still could. But as he now confessed, inside he'd been scoring heroin. I wanted to kick myself—how could anyone, let alone an assistant district attorney who'd seen everything I'd seen, be so naive? I recited that essential lesson of Papi's, simplistic but also simply true: Good people can do bad things, make bad choices. It doesn't make them bad people.

As Nelson begged me to forgive him, there was a hint of delirium fueling the shame and sadness in his voice. But I knew forgiveness was beside the point. I myself was carrying a load of survivor's guilt. Who was going to forgive me? Why was I not lying in that hospital bed? How was it I had escaped when my soul's twin, my smarter half, once joined to me at the hip, had not? His request only made the load heavier. My God, what a waste.

July 1983, I'm at the house on Fire Island. I wake very early from a deep sleep. It's still dark out, but I'm completely alert, even though I was up late last night. The clock says 4:30. I throw on jeans and a T-shirt and walk out to the bay. I sit on the dock and watch the deep blue draining from the sky in the early dawn. The sun is still hidden behind the island. It's probably just breaking the edge of the Atlantic. Nelson is here, I can feel him. He's come to say good-bye. Morning erases the last stars and dissolves the remaining night.

I walked back to the house to find the phone ringing: Nelson's dad. "Sonia, it's Benny," he started. I knew how difficult it was for him to make this call.

"*Yo ya sé.* I already know. I'll be on the first ferry home."

Twenty-Four

I struggle to understand how two children so closely matched could meet such different fates.

What made the difference between two children who began almost as twins, inseparable and, in our own eyes, virtually identical? Almost but not quite: Nelson was smarter; he had the father I wished for, though we shared Abuelita's special blessing. Why did I endure and thrive, where he failed, consumed by the same dangers that had surrounded me?

Some of it can be laid at the door of machismo, the culture that pushes boys out onto the streets while protecting girls, but there's more. Nelson had mentioned it that day at the hospital: the one thing I had that he lacked. Call it what you like: discipline, determination, perseverance, the force of will. It had made all the difference in my life. If only I could bottle it, I'd share it with every kid in America.

But where does it come from? Good habits and hard work are part of the story, but they are how it expresses itself, effects rather than the cause. I know that my competitive spirit—my drive to win, my fear of failure, my desire constantly to outdo myself—bubbles up from very deep within my personality. It's rarely directed at others; I compete with myself.

What Nelson saw driving me arises from a different kind of aspiration: the desire to do for others, to help make things right for them. I learned it from others, too. My best and most immediate examples of that kind of selfless love were those who were closest to me: Abuelita, healer and protector, with her overflowing generosity of spirit; and my mother, visiting nurse and confidante to the whole neighborhood.

My understanding of my survival was bound up with my grandmother's protection. It was more than a refuge from the chaos at home; I was under her safekeeping, physically and metaphysically. It gave me the confidence to manage my illness, to overcome my insufficiencies at school, and ultimately to imagine the most improbable of goals for my life. That feeling of Abuelita's protection continued to grow after her death. I was lucky, but it always seemed like luck with a purpose.

My childhood ambition to become a lawyer had nothing to do with middle-class respectability and wealth. I understood the lawyer's job as helping people. I understood the law as a force for good, for protecting the community, for upholding order against the threat of chaos, and for resolving conflict. The law gives structure to most of our relationships, promoting all of our interests together in the most harmonious way. All kids have action heroes: astronauts, firemen, commandos. My idea of heroism in action was a lawyer, and a judge was a superlawyer. The law for me was not a career but a vocation.

My earliest exposure to helping professions had been to those of medicine and teaching: Dr. Fisher, the staff at Prospect Hospital and the clinic at Jacobi, and the Sisters of Charity, who taught us at Blessed Sacrament. The law, I understood at a very young age, was different in scope. Doctors and nurses and teachers helped individuals, one by one. But through the law, you could change the very structure of society and the way communities functioned.

The civil rights movement was the backdrop for my generation growing up.

There are no bystanders in this life. Our humanity makes us each a part of something greater than ourselves. And so my heroes were never solitaries. My heroes were all embedded in community. And the will to serve was first stirred by the wish to help my community.

When I got to Princeton, I found my sense of community where I could, working with Acción Puertorriqueña, the Third World Center, and the Trenton Psychiatric Hospital. Near as it was to Princeton, Trenton was a world apart from the certainties of privilege. The patients I served there were vulnerable in the extreme: confused; distanced from whatever ties of family or friendship might have once sustained them; and, for want of a common language, cut off even from those looking after them. In my outrage at their abandonment, I realized that my community extended well beyond the place I came from, the people I knew.

Some of those who came to Princeton and Yale from places such as I had come from resolved never to look back. I don't judge them. A degree from an Ivy League college or a top law school is assumed to guarantee entry to a world of plenty, and nothing obliges you to look back on what you've worked hard to escape. But I didn't see good fortune as a chance to write my own ticket; it was something entrusted to me, not given outright, and I needed to find a worthy use for it. My chance encounter with Bob Morgenthau over the cheese table would have led nowhere if I hadn't been deeply primed for what he offered. It was not what most of my classmates were looking for, but it fit into the scheme I imagined. Now, having completed that part of the journey, I was only more convinced that nothing had happened by chance.

All that remained to be seen was how far along the next step would take me.

Twenty-Five

Shea Stadium, the 1986 World Series. The Mets and the still-cursed Red Sox are tied in a tense tenth inning of play that has the crowd on their feet cheering, first for one side, then the other, like kids on a wild seesaw ride.

The real drama, however, is happening in the parking lot, where I'm on the back of a motorcycle, wearing a bulletproof vest, a walkie-talkie screeching in my ear, in pursuit of a truck full of counterfeit goods. We're doing fifty, then sixty, circling the lot like a racetrack, when the truck dodges around a corner. It's a dead end, a concrete cul-de-sac, and in just a moment he's spun around and is barreling straight for us. My driver's about to bolt, but I tell him, "Stay put, he won't hit us. We'll stop him right here." This guy's not crazy, I'm thinking. But he could be, or maybe just panicked. Whatever the case, he's speeding up. Next thing I know, he's got half his wheels up on the concrete wall beside us, like a stunt man riding the wall of death—can you even do that in a truck? Before I know it, he's slipped past us, doing almost ninety in the opposite direction. Enough. Does someone have to die for a load of fake Mets caps, cheap shirts, and souvenirs?

What am I even doing here?

Good question. After I worked through the cases that Bob Morgenthau assigned me as inducement to remain at the DA's Office, it was finally time to leave. One thing I knew for certain: I wanted to continue doing trial work, having learned to love my days in the courtroom.

I also knew very well what I didn't want: the life of a cubicle-encased cog in the machinery of a large firm. So as I had when looking at opportunities after Yale, I would aim for a smaller firm where I might grow more quickly into a substantial role. But as I interviewed, I found that size was no guarantee of ethos. Small firms were often spin-offs that not only poached clients from but also reproduced the culture of the larger firms where their partners had started their careers.

One that stood out as an exception was Pavia & Harcourt, a tiny firm by New York standards, barely thirty lawyers when I was interviewing in 1984. Its founder, a Jewish refugee from Italy during World War II, had built its reputation on representing elite European business interests in the United States. Much of the firm's work related to finance and banking, to licensing of trademarks and distribution of products, and the diverse range of legal tasks attending international trade and business operations.

Arriving for my first interview, I was struck by the aura of the place—a midtown oasis of restrained elegance. George Pavia, the founder's son and now managing partner, was said to be fond of continuity, and the decorum of the offices befitted a roster of clients whose names were synonymous with European luxury and high style: Fendi, Ferrari, Bulgari . . . Conversations shifted constantly between English, Italian, and French. It was hard to imagine an atmosphere more remote from that of the DA's Office.

In spite of the old-world ambience, the firm was ahead of its time in welcoming women. There were two among the nine partners at a time when it was rare to find even one in the upper echelons of big Manhattan firms. This one was exceptional in its organization, too: associates worked directly with partners in two-person teams that made mentoring natural. It was a situation where I could learn quickly and, I hoped, quickly advance.

I interviewed many times over, meeting with each of the nine partners and all of the litigation associates. The positive impressions I was forming seemed to be mutual. It was clear that my trial experience appealed greatly and would fill an immediate need. A degree from Yale didn't hurt. But at some point my progress seemed to lose momentum inexplicably, and I found myself waiting for a call that didn't come. Meanwhile, interviews with other firms only made it clearer where

I really wanted to be. Pressing the headhunter who had connected us, I learned that George Pavia feared I would quickly get bored with the work of a first-year associate—the position they were hiring for—and move on.

Be diplomatic but direct, I told myself. I don't tend to bang people over the head, but some situations require a bit of boldness. I asked for another meeting and once again found myself ushered into that serene nest lined with Persian carpets and delicately etched views of old Genoa.

"Mr. Pavia, I understand that you have some hesitations about hiring me. Are you comfortable talking about it?"

"Yes, of course." He explained his concerns. They were valid, I acknowledged, and then laid out my own position: Never having practiced civil law, I had a lot to learn. As long as I was learning, there was no chance of boredom. As I became more familiar with the work, one of two things would happen. Either I'd still be struggling to keep up—still no chance of boredom, although I probably wouldn't last at the firm. Or else they would recognize what I was capable of and give me more responsibility. I didn't see how they could lose. I made clear that I had no reluctance about accepting the starting salary of a first-year associate—a fraction of what I could expect from a large firm—as long as he was willing to increase it when my work warranted it.

The bonus and raise that followed my first year-end review were huge, and by the second review my salary was up to standard.

☆

My first cases at Pavia & Harcourt involved customer warranty disputes and problems with real estate leases. The work of a beginning associate typically involved eclectic and sometimes marginal legal work for clients the firm represented in more crucial aspects of their business. It did, however, draw on skills that were second nature to a prosecutor. Within my first couple of days on the job, a colleague who sat within earshot of my phone calls let it be known to another litigation associate, who then spread the word, that I was tough and could not be pushed around by an adversary.

I was shaken to hear myself so harshly categorized. Trying case after case by the seat of your pants at the DA's Office, you develop a bravado that can seem abrasive to lawyers who have no acquaintance with that world. It was a kind of culture shock in both directions. The great distance from the grimy halls of Centre Street to our genteel bower on Madison Avenue made itself known in other small ways too. A gift from a grateful client, for instance, did not have to be returned in the presence of a witness—a nice perk I didn't expect.

"You're in private practice now, Sonia. There's no threat of corruption," counseled David Botwinik, the partner I turned to—indeed, we all turned to—for advice on any question of ethics. I called him the Rabbi. It was okay to accept a gift, he said, though allowing that "in the ten years I've had them as clients, they never gave *me* a gift."

The more I observed Dave in action, the more profoundly his sense of integrity, fairness, and professional honor impressed me. Just as I had done with John Fried at the District Attorney's Office, I turned to Dave instinctively as a guide. His presence was comforting, avuncular, and expansive. Blinking owlishly behind his glasses, he stuttered slightly. The hesitation only made his words seem more thoughtfully considered.

It was through his instruction that I became versed in a complex and little-understood area of the law. Dave had specialized for thirty years in representing foreign commodity traders who bought in the American grain markets. He had worked hard to institute more evenhanded arbitration practices that tempered the influence of the big grain houses. Observing how I prepared witnesses and conducted cross-examinations, he asked me to assist him in grain arbitrations, which, though less formally structured than a trial, involved similar strategies.

"I'm too old for this now, you can do it," he said, but I could never have managed without his vast knowledge. He could read between the lines of any contract and see immediately why it was drafted as it was, what issues were important, respectively, to the parties involved. He knew all the players in the industry, which was a man's world entirely. Even with my knowledge of admiralty law, I struggled at first to grasp the logic of the business. Finally, it clicked, though it took a late-night cry for help to cut through the Gordian knot of interwoven contracts: We were not actually tracking shipments of grain.

Only once did I even see the grain. Our client had sent a sample for tests, and it was clear to me that the lab results had been falsified. I knew that a sealed plastic pouch from a private laboratory is no guarantee of a chain of custody when anybody can buy a heat-sealing kit for plastic bags at the supermarket. So I did. During arbitration, at the end of my cross-examination, I asked the witness to open the supposedly inviolate sample of grain. He tore the seal off the plastic bag and found inside it a note in my handwriting: "Bags can be tampered with."

I had learned over the years never to reveal that I could type. In the days before everyone had a personal computer, it was a sure way for a young lawyer to find herself informally demoted to secretary, and I stuck to that rule rigidly. Only once, in the wee hours approaching a morning deadline, did I ask Dave Botwinik to cover his eyes so I could type a final draft. Dave I could trust. He had a deft way of turning aside other lawyers' requests for the only woman in the room to get coffee.

Fran Bernstein, on the other hand, was far above this fray in the gender wars. She could sit for unbroken hours at her Smith-Corona while it rattled like a machine gun, as if her brain were plugged directly into the machine. I was astonished by her writing process, how the pages of elegant prose in no apparent need of polishing just rolled off the typewriter. But it was only one of her remarkable qualities. When she spoke, the flow of her ideas was just as irrepressible. As a law student, Fran was one of the first women to edit the law review at Columbia, where she later became a lecturer. She had also been among the first women to clerk for a judge on the Second Circuit. Having left work for several years to raise her children, she had returned only part-time. If that had put a crimp in her career, she didn't seem to mind. Though I was at first intimidated in her presence, she would become a true friend and another of my mentors at Pavia & Harcourt.

Fran's effortless eloquence so humbled me that when she first asked me to write a brief, I was paralyzed. For all my success in the courtroom, writing still terrified me. At the DA's Office, I had often volunteered for the overspill of appeals work that the trial bureaus were obliged to help with, just for the chance to work on my writing. Working on Fran's brief, I stayed up all night, my brain contorted in uncomfortable positions, suffering flashbacks to that traumatic summer at Paul, Weiss. The draft that I managed to finish past dawn was subpar. But when I confessed how utterly incompetent I felt, Fran was more than gracious. As a professor, she noted, she had been writing prolifically her whole career. The same role furnished her with an instinctive sense of how to encourage someone trying to learn.

"What do you know about handbags?" Fran asked me one day.

"Nothing. What's to know?" I was about to become an expert. To start with, Fran explained, a Fendi bag sold for eight hundred to several thousands of dollars. That deserved a double take. My cash, keys, and cigarettes were stashed in a bag that cost all of twenty dollars. She showed me one of the legendary pocketbooks, explained the finer points of stitching technique, how to recognize the quality of the fabric and the hardware—all the details that distinguished the real thing from a knockoff.

Fran had been tracking the development of intellectual property law for several years. It was a new field, as yet barely mentioned in law schools. Although patent and copyright laws were a well-established area of practice, trademarks drew less attention in those years. Meanwhile, fake Gucci and Fendi handbags, counterfeit Rolex and Cartier watches, and gallons of faux Chanel No. 5 were an exploding business on the sidewalks of Manhattan.

Fran presciently understood that the ultimate danger of not defending a trademark was loss of the precious rights to its exclusive use. She set about educating our clients, many of whom were in the business of fashion, creating luxury products whose worth was as tightly bound to the prestige of a name as to the quality of production. Fendi was the first to appreciate the importance of what Fran was trying to do. Cheap knockoffs of Fendi handbags were being sold not only in Chinatown and at flea markets all over the country but on the shelves of a reputable retail chain. Eventually, they showed up on the sidewalk right in front of Fendi's Fifth Avenue store.

Fran decided to educate me as well, because she wanted my help in taking that big retail chain to court.

Leading up to the trial, I was in the conference room watching Fran prepare a witness when she was called away to the phone. She asked me to continue in her stead. The Fendi fashion house was very much a family business. Candido Speroni, our expert on the intricacies of Fendi's production processes, was married to one of the five Fendi sisters, each of whom was responsible for a different aspect of the business. Candido's nephew Alessandro Saracino, a young lawyer himself, was acting as interpreter.

Preparing witnesses is an art form. As a prosecutor, you learn that you can't tell witnesses what to say or not to say: they will blurt out the strangest things when they're put on the spot in court. Instead, the purpose of coaching is to help them understand the reason behind each question so that you're working as a team to communicate their relevant knowledge to jurors. I was deep in the process with Candido, completely focused on the task at hand, when I looked at my watch and realized that Fran had been gone for a very long time indeed. I wondered aloud what had happened to her, and she answered from the corner by the door, "I'm here. I've been watching." After suggesting that we break for lunch, she said to Alessandro, "Please talk to your uncle and ask if he'll agree . . . Sonia should be the one to take this to trial, not me. It will cost you much less, but ultimately it's not the money. She's just that good at it!"

And so began my friendship with the Fendis, and the unlikely experience of going to court in front of the esteemed judge Leonard Sand as the only young associate calling the office at the end of each day to tell a senior partner what papers I needed prepared for the next morning.

Fran's handing me the Fendi case as my first crack at civil litigation was a tribute not only to her personal generosity but to the nature of Pavia & Harcourt, where collaboration was ingrained in the culture. That spirit of transparent teamwork was a joy to me, and I strove to be as open and helpful to others as Fran and Dave were to me. One young associate who struggled with dyslexia was as awed by my reading speed as I was by Fran's rapid-fire writing skills. "Sonia, you just inhaled that article as fast as you could turn the pages!" he moaned. But he had a reliable knack for spotting what was likely to be most useful, and so we often worked in tandem, hacking through the dense undergrowth of required reading, swapping observations and ideas.

In this comradely environment, I learned to be more attentive to how I was perceived by colleagues. That initial impression of being a tough person had mostly faded with experience but would resurface now and again when someone new joined us. Theresa Bartenope was hired as a secretary for a different department on the far side of the building, but I lured her into becoming my paralegal in the intellectual property practice. That meant I was often calling over the crackly intercom, "Theresa, I need you in my office." She would appear at my door a few minutes later, panting from the sprint, hands shaking, hives spreading up her neck. What's with her? I wondered. After she'd withdrawn to her side of the building, people in the hallway burst out laughing at the spectacle. Finally, someone clued me in, and I called Theresa in again, this time more gently: "Theresa, why are you so scared of me? I don't bite."

When I'm focused intensely on work, I become oblivious to social cues, or any cues for that matter. I block out the entire universe beyond the page in front of me or the issue at hand. Colleagues who knew me well didn't take it personally. In fact, they sometimes found it convenient. Hallway conversations could be carried on right outside my door, because I was the only person impervious to distraction, completely unaware. The same tendency as a prosecutor gave me a reputation—undeserved, I believe—for ruthlessness in cross-examinations. It's not how I mean to be; when I'm concentrating hard and processing information quickly, the questions just shoot out unceremoniously.

Theresa, thank heaven, overcame her fear, and she has since accompanied me on every step of my career. She remains my right hand and protector, the dearest of friends. When I miss something, she's the one who sees it. She's the one who holds a mirror up when she notices me getting intimidating or too abrupt, an effect only amplified by the trappings of my current office. When I am too wrapped up in something, she pulls me up for air and reminds me to be kind.

As it happened, the case I argued against the big retailer was settled mid-trial, but I would continue working closely with Fran Bernstein on intellectual property cases for the Fendis, as well as other clients. Litigation, however, was not an effective remedy to the problem of counterfeit goods sold on the street and in Chinatown; there was no point bringing petty vendors to trial. Instead, trademark owners decided to join forces in applying for a court order permitting us to confiscate the goods and the records related to their production and distribution. In building the case for a seizure order, we worked with private investigators to track down the suppliers funneling knockoffs into New York from several manufacturing points in Asia as well as moonlighting craftsmen in Italy. Investigators would purchase items from vendors at different locations, and we could map connections by matching hardware or fabrics from different lots. Keeping an area under surveillance, they could often identify a warehouse by spotting the runners who moved between that location and the vendors. If we could intercept the contraband at that distribution point, we might even find customs and shipping documents that would lead further up the supply chain.

I showed Fran how to work up an affidavit. She wrote most of the briefs. I loved the investigative work, the challenge of the puzzle, and the thrill ride of the seizure operations.

Within two years of recruiting me to the work on intellectual property, Fran suffered a recurrence of the breast cancer that she had beaten into remission a few years before. The news weighed heavily: her mother, sister, grandmother—virtually every female in her family—had succumbed to the same disease. As her treatment, and the illness itself, progressed, she was less and less present. For a time, I depended on her guidance over the phone and tried to cheer her on through that same thin connection, but she was failing rapidly.

When I was up for partner in my fourth year at the end of 1988, she came into the office for the first time in months to cast her vote. She had lost a lot of weight and was very frail, but her spark was still there. That night, she and her husband, Bob, took me to dinner at La Côte Basque. It was my first time at a restaurant of such stellar opulence, and I was thrilled by the experience, though sad to see that Fran could barely eat. The outcome of the partnership vote was still under wraps, so it wasn't obvious yet that there was reason to party, but Fran couldn't wait. "You'll have to pretend that you don't know what I'm going to tell you, but tonight we celebrate!"

Later, as we stood at the curb while Bob was getting the car, Fran looked me up and down. "If you're going to become a partner, you'll have to dress the part. Fendi is your client now. You should represent them appropriately. You need to buy a Fendi fur coat."

"Fran, I don't want a fur coat!" She sounded like my mother complaining about the way I dressed. I already had a wonderful relationship with the Fendi family, and it didn't depend on my wearing haute couture. Alessandro, the young lawyer who was apprenticing to the family business, had become a good friend over months of daily phone calls between New York and Rome, at all hours, irrespective of my time zone or his.

It was Alessandro's grandmother Adele who, with her

husband, had established the Fendi name as the epitome of Italian luxury, quality, and design. It was she, too, who had groomed each of her five daughters to assume a different facet of the financial or creative management, their husbands in turn also drawn into the family business. Alessandro was therefore perfectly at ease working with assertive women, and I instinctively warmed to a business environment bound together by strong family ties. It was a natural collaboration.

The Fendis' friendship pulled back the curtain onto a very private world of luxury and exquisite taste. When I visited their place in Rome and vacationed with them across Europe, my eyes were opened not only to the finest of modern Italian design and a glorious classical legacy but to an entirely different sensibility. Spirited through celebrations of theatrical enchantment, I collected dreams to last a lifetime. Perhaps also a certain understanding, and with it the confidence that comes of having seen life from all sides.

What mattered most of all, though, was that they became family. Alessandro is a brother to me. He'll jump to my defense ferociously—I daresay he'd offer to meet you with pistols at dawn if my honor was at stake. I, in turn, wouldn't pause to draw breath before boarding the next flight to be by his side in a moment of need. Just as I never hesitated to invite his parents, Paola and Ciro, to Co-op City for Thanksgiving dinner at my mother's.

Twenty-Six

$\mathbf{A}$ couple of weeks after my celebratory dinner with Fran and her husband, George Pavia called me into his office so he and Dave Botwinik could tell me, this time officially, that the firm's partners had elected me to membership. The good news came with a curious proviso, words that have stuck in my mind. "It's clear that you won't stay in private practice forever," George said. "We know you're destined for the bench someday. Dave is even convinced you'll go all the way to the Supreme Court. But with this offer, we ask only that you remain with us as long as you continue in private practice."

To offer a partnership to someone not planning to stick around was unusually generous, especially in a firm so small that each partner is an integral part of the team. I accepted with enormous gratitude but also obvious mortification at Dave's fantastical prophecy. If he could have known that I'd dreamed of becoming a judge since childhood, I might have taken it as an affectionate but overheated compliment. In fact, though, I had long refrained from verbalizing the ambition, understanding that any federal judgeship would require a rare alignment of political forces, as well as no small bit of luck. Dave may have intuited the direction of my dreams, but even so, his talking about the Supreme Court like that made me wince. I felt strangely exposed standing there as colleagues alluded casually to my secret pipe dream in the same breath in which they were marking the professional milestone of my making partner, and even more so with the shadow of Fran's death looming.

When she finally lost her fight the following spring, the loss devastated everyone. Each death of someone close to me has come as a slap, reminding me again of my own mortality, compelling me to ask: What am I accomplishing? Is my life meaningful? When Abuelita died, I felt spurred to study even harder in college. When it was Nelson's time, I could no longer put off thinking about life beyond the DA's Office. Fran had entrusted me with the groundbreaking work in intellectual property that would become her legacy, and when she died, I threw myself into it with my best single-mindedness. Still, to see her go at fifty-seven fired my habitual sense that I might not have enough time to make a real run at my ultimate goal.

I've lived most of my life inescapably aware that it is precious and finite. The reality of diabetes always lurked in the back of my mind, and early on I accepted the probability that

I would die young. There was no point fretting about it; I have never worried about what I can't control. But nor could I waste what time I had; some inner metronome has continued to set a beat I am unable to refuse. Now diabetes has become more manageable, and I no longer fear falling short in the tally of years. But the habit of living as if in the shadow of death has remained with me, and I consider that, too, a gift.

On a glorious day at the end of June, a group of friends were celebrating my thirty-seventh birthday with a barbecue in my backyard. I was lucky to have stumbled on the apartment right down the block from my old place and Dawn's, lucky to have grabbed it at a discount before the co-op conversion was even concluded, and luckier still that Dave Botwinik helped me find an unusually affordable loan for the down payment. Best of all, the backyard was perfect for parties.

Everyone was taken care of. All their glasses were filled. Let them dance, I thought. Exhausted, I needed to lie down for a few minutes. I didn't feel right, light-headed, but once supine I couldn't get my body to move. Eventually, I managed to drag myself off the bed, opening the screen door to the backyard. But that was as far as I could get. I needed to sit down right there. Fortunately, there was a step. And there was Theresa. She was talking to me, but I couldn't make out the words. She came closer, still talking gibberish. There was something in her hand that I wanted badly. I needed it. I grabbed for it, but my aim was shaky. I smashed the piece of birthday cake into my mouth. Theresa stood there with her own mouth open in shock. I must have looked pretty disconcerting with frosting smeared all over my face.

When I recovered and we talked about what had happened, Theresa told me that although she was vaguely aware that I was diabetic, she had no knowledge of what a sugar low looked like. Friends who saw me lie down just assumed that I'd had a few too many. But I was so busy playing host that I hadn't had even one yet. The card I'd been given as a child was still in my wallet, carried around for all these years. I'd made it to my thirty-seventh birthday with no occasion for someone to pull it out. It said:

I Have Diabetes

I AM NOT drunk. If I am unconscious or acting strangely, I may have low blood sugar.

Emergency Treatment

I need sugar immediately. If I am able to swallow, give me candy, soda pop, fruit juice, or table sugar. If I cannot swallow or do not recover within 15 minutes, call a doctor or the closest emergency medical help and tell them I have diabetes.

Very few of my friends were aware of my being a type 1 diabetic and completely dependent on insulin shots. Not that I was aware of hiding it. I would have said that I was being politely discreet, but the truth is my secrecy was a deeply ingrained habit. I was averse to any revelations that might have seemed a play for pity. And managing this disease all my life had been the hallmark of the self-reliance that had saved me as a child, even if it may have partly cost me a marriage. I didn't need anyone's help with it. But in truth, I was more vulnerable than I was willing to admit.

The secrecy wasn't simply in my nature. When I was young, disabilities and illnesses of all sorts were governed by a code of silence. Such things were private matters, and you didn't speak about them outside the family. I wouldn't have dreamed of giving myself a shot in public, though I rarely had to worry about that because I was only taking one shot a day, first thing in the morning. If the situation somehow arose, traveling or spending a night away from home, my mother would tell me to go do it in the bathroom.

All through college, law school, and my years at the DA's Office, I would stick with essentially the same regimen I'd had as a child. It wasn't until I reached thirty and settled in Brooklyn that I decided to seek out a specialist in type 1 diabetes. The advances in treatment that had passed me by were significant. I started to catch up, using improved forms of insulin and taking shots twice a day. When my first doctor moved, she referred me to Andrew Drexler, one of the foremost diabetic endocrinologists in the country. Under Andy, now a cherished friend and confidant, my treatment is as good as it gets.

I still use the tried-and-true approach of injecting insulin, though many diabetics today have switched to convenient insulin pens or pumps with computerized controls to adjust dosages continuously during the day. I now keep track of my blood sugars with a continuous glucose monitor that uses a sensor implant in my stomach to tell me my blood sugars. The sugar numbers reflected on my monitor help me calculate how much insulin I give myself in my five or six shots a day. When deciding what I'm going to eat, I calculate the carbohydrate, fat, and protein contents. I ask myself a litany of questions: How much insulin do I need? When is it going to kick in? When was my last shot? Will I walk farther than usual or exert myself in a way that might accelerate the absorption rate? If I weren't good at math, this would be difficult.

This regimen certainly takes a lot more attention than I gave to the disease when I was young, but it also allows for a much more fine-tuned regulation of my blood sugar levels. The benefit adds up, since the dire complications of diabetes—heart disease, blindness, neuropathy that can lead to amputation of limbs—are mostly the effects of long-term damage caused by chronically high levels. Meticulously keeping mine within normal range gives me an excellent chance of a normal life span. No matter how careful I am, though, a fever or infection can send my sugars soaring. Trauma or extreme stress has the same effect.

Even with the most conscientious monitoring, blood sugar can swing suddenly in a way that is a threat to one's life not in the future but in the immediate present. That's what happened the day I grabbed that hunk of birthday cake from Theresa. Surprises can insinuate themselves insidiously. I knew, for instance, how much carbohydrate was in a meal at a typical Chinese restaurant, but one time my calculations were thrown perilously off by a very different style of cooking at a Szechuan place of great refinement. Jet lag or losing track of shifts in time zone probably figured in another crisis. I'd flown to Venice for the wedding of a friend, an Italian lawyer who had worked for a time at Pavia & Harcourt. Somehow, after I checked into my hotel room, my blood sugar dropped precipitously, and I passed out.

Fortunately, Alessandro and his wife, Fe, had come to Venice for the wedding too. They realized something was wrong when I didn't show up on time. After trekking across the city to my hotel, Alessandro threatened to break down my door if the concierge didn't put aside hotel policy and unlock it. Orange juice was administered, an ambulance was called, which was in fact a boat and too big to squeeze into our back-alley canal. So a Venetian stretcher, which is to say a chair on poles, was provided, and I was conveyed, variously in and out of consciousness, to a hospital that was really a nursing home in an ancient convent, with facilities to match. I tried to show the doctor how to use my fancy glucose meter, but he was having none of it. "I am the doctor; you are the patient," he insisted, as Alessandro translated with chagrin.

We laughed at the story afterward, especially as recounted with Alessandro's gloriously expressive Italian gestures, conjuring images of Fe in a stunning blue evening gown and himself in black tie preparing to batter my door down, or the ultimate indignity of having the Italian hospital staff refer to the two of them as "the Americans."

Although they stick out in my memory, such episodes didn't happen very often and have been rare in the last decade, as technology has improved and my body has settled into middle age. Still, each time I found myself in a blood sugar crisis, I couldn't help but notice that some unlikely intervention had saved my life, whether a friend just happening by or phoning out of the blue, or, one time, Dawn's little Rocky, who, finding me unconscious, barked furiously, refusing to be calmed, until he drew attention where it was needed. Contemplating such good fortune reinforced my sense that Abuelita was still watching over me. But I decided that was no basis to push my luck. Though the Fendis and I would, for years to come, dine out mirthfully on the story of the Venetian affair, the bald truth is that if Alessandro had not been aware of my diabetes, I'd be dead. It was the final confirmation I needed that for safety's sake I had to be open about my condition. And since taking my present job these many years later, when the danger seems to have receded, I have another good reason to claim the disease publicly. I don't know whether they still give diabetic children a list of professions they can't aspire to, but I'm proud to offer living proof that big dreams are not out-of-bounds.

There is one person with whom I have deferred opening up as long as possible. The stories of those close calls suggestive of my nine lives have never been mentioned to my mother. I'll have to deal with the fallout when she reads this book. Her guilt, pity, sadness, and ultimately fear of my disease are still beyond all reason, and at times have driven me nuts. But then, any problem of mine she has discovered belatedly has resulted in the same hysteria. Junior reports she once called him to complain that I don't tell her what's happening. He answered her far better than I could have: "Sonia's never going to tell you anything, Mami, because you always over-react." Even more important, he told her, he didn't know a happier person than his sister. "Sonia lives her life fully. If she dies tomorrow, she'll die happy. If she lives the way you want her to live, she'll die miserable. So leave her alone, okay?"

I love my brother dearly. He knows me in ways the rest of the world never could. We've always watched out for each other. His kids still crack up whenever they hear me calling him Junior—he's Juan to everyone else now—but he'll always be Junior to me, even if he's no longer such a nuisance.

Mami hung up on him that time, he said. I could picture her sitting there in Co-op City, fuming in her jungle of house-plants, stems shooting up to the ceiling, the vines clinging to the corners, fringing the picture windows. That message would not go over easily, but eventually it would be received.

The story of my secrecy and the self-reliance that produced it does not begin and end with my diabetes. But I've come to see that it does begin and end with my mother, who became my most constant emotional paradigm, informing my character for good and for ill, as well as the character of my relations with her.

Many times I felt there was a wide moat separating me from the rest of the world, in spite of my being, by all accounts, a great listener to all my friends. They felt free to tell me their troubles. Like my mother, I would suspend judgment, feel their pain, perhaps even point out a fact they might have overlooked: I have a knack for translating the mysteries of other people's minds and could open their eyes to what the world looked like to their husband, their boss, or their mother. The only trick I couldn't manage was to ask the same of them.

Sharing was not my style; my problems were mine to deal with. Ever since fifth grade, ever since putting behind me the misery and isolation visited upon an alcoholic's family, ever since that cute boy, Carmelo, convinced me that being smart could be cool, I'd surrounded myself with a crowd of friends. And yet inside I remained very much alone. Perhaps even within my marriage, which, for all our mutual regard and affection, had suffered from a certain self-sufficiency of mine that frustrated Kevin. It was not until these years after the DA's Office, as I started making more purposeful strides toward the person I wanted to be professionally, that I could begin to dream of reshaping the person I was emotionally, too. My faith in my potential for self-improvement, which had been the foundation for all my academic and professional success so far, would now be tested in more inaccessible regions of the self. But I was optimistic: if I could help fix your problems, surely I could fix my own.

I'd always believed people can change; very few are carved in stone or beyond redemption. All my life I've looked around me and asked: What can I learn here? What qualities in this friend, this mentor, even this rival, are worth emulating? What in me needs to change? Even as a child, I could reflect that my anger was accomplishing nothing, hurting only myself, and that I had to learn to stop in my tracks the instant I felt its surge. Learning to be open about my illness was a first step, and it taught me how admitting your vulnerabilities can bring people closer. Friends want to help, and it's important to know how to accept help graciously, just as it's better to accept a gift with "Thank you" than "You shouldn't have."

If there's a measure of how well I've succeeded in this self-transformation, it's that very few of my friends—even those who have known me the longest—can remember the person I was before undertaking the effort. Such is the nature of familiarity and memory. They also swear that they've always known about my diabetes and claim memories of seeing me give myself shots long before I ever did so openly. But there is no better indicator of progress, or cause for pride, than the thaw in relations with my mother.

Mami gone, checked out, the empty apartment. Her back to me, just a log in the bed beside me as a child. Mami, perfectly dressed and made up, like a movie star, the Jacqueline Kennedy of the Bronxdale Houses, refusing to pick me up and wrinkle her spotless outfit. This was the cold image I'd lived with and formed myself in response to, unhappily adopting the aloofness but none of the glamour. I could not free myself from its spell until I could appreciate what formed it and, in its likeness, me.

There was so much about my mother I simply hadn't known. When she was struggling through her nursing degree at Hostos Community College, terrified of failure, facing every written exam like a firing squad, she had told me a little about her school days in Lajas and San Germán. About her fear of being ridiculed by classmates, scolded by teachers, her certainty that she was stupid. Beyond that I knew practically nothing about her childhood. Her most telling stories would trickle out slowly, in dribs and drabs, but it was only when I had the strength and purpose to talk about the cold expanse between us that she confessed her emotional limitations in a way that called me to forgiveness.

"How should I know these things, Sonia? Who ever showed me how to be warm when I was young? I was lonely; I was angry at Mayo. What else did I see?"

My anger at her would still surge from time to time, and when it did, I would call on this awareness: she had her own story, pieces that were missing in her own life. I called too on a talisman of memory, one I could grasp like the smooth beads of a rosary. I'd return to it like some childhood storybook I knew by heart but of which I never tired. It was the memory of those summer nights when I woke in a terrible sweat, and Mami would towel me down with a cool wet cloth, whispering softly, so as not to wake Junior, because this was for me, my time. The little fan whirring away; my neck turning cool as the moisture evaporated; my mother's hand on my back.

I wouldn't suffer the same lack of examples as my mother. Friends would show me how to be warm, and I would learn by allowing others a chance to do for me as they had let me do for them, until no one remembered a time when it was not that way. As I learned, I practiced on my mother—a real hug, a sincere compliment, an extra effort to let down my guard—and miraculously she softened in turn, out of instinct long dormant, even if she didn't quite know what was going on. Opening up, I came to recognize the value of vulnerability and to honor it, and soon I found that I wasn't alone even on this journey. My mother was taking every step alongside me, becoming more affectionate and demonstrative herself, the person who, given a chance, she might have been.

Kiley runs to greet me, jumps into my embrace. She throws her skinny little arms around my neck, squeezes her tiny, birdlike three-year-old body to mine in crazy disproportion. And without warning my heart bursts, tears well in my eyes. A tenderness I have no name for rushes like a drug through my veins, as I realize that the absence of human touch has been, for so long, a burden carried unwittingly.

I wrote myself a prescription for hug therapy. I told each of the children in my life that I wasn't getting enough hugs. Tommy, Vanessa, Zachary . . . "Would you help me out by giving me a hug whenever you see me?" Kiley didn't need telling, of course, but every one of the others got it instantly. In this, the wisdom of toddlers is unassailable. The hugs came. And feeling flowed that had never come so easily before. Even as the kids grew into gangly teenagers, the hugs never stopped. Younger siblings, John and Kyle, would join the cause as the years went by.

What I've learned from children I've been able to give back to adults. The stroke on the arm that says I understand, the welcome hug, the good-bye kiss, the embrace that lingers that much longer in a time of sorrow. I've discovered the palpable difference between such acts as mere gestures and as sluices of true feeling between two people.

We were in the dressing room, and I was getting out of my jeans, ready to attack the pile of possibilities that my friend Elaine had gathered off the racks, when she dropped the armful of clothes and doubled over, hooting hysterically. I was afraid she would bring down the flimsy partition walls.

A client of Pavia & Harcourt's who'd become a very close friend, Elaine Litwer was a gutsy and street-smart survivor of extreme poverty and a colorful family from the Lower East Side. She talked nonstop, was never wrong, and suffered no fools in wielding her merciless wit. Many weekends we'd prowl the shops and hang out like a pair of teenage girls.

"Sonia! My God! Who buys your underwear? Your mother?"

"As a matter of fact, in this case, yes."

307

"We have to fix that right away!"

Any offense I might have taken at Elaine's uncensored mockery was offset by a discreet satisfaction at the thought of Mami's having, for once, been knocked off her pedestal as a fashion authority. I was happy to let Elaine help me choose some age-appropriate undergarments.

This was part of a much bigger project. Elaine was teaching me to shop, to recognize what looks good on me, how color works with skin tone, the drape of a fabric, how the eye follows a line. Alas, it was one subject in which I was not to prove a quick study. But little by little I developed confidence in my own judgment, and Elaine, bless her, found a way to make this process fun. Until she took me in hand, I'd hated shopping and confined myself to mail-order catalogs rather than suffer the smirks of salesgirls and the taunts of full-length mirrors. And even when I did something right, my mother's idea of encouragement was scarcely encouraging. Any compliment would be immediately qualified: "That looks nice, Sonia, but now you need to paint your nails."

But to be perfectly honest, it wasn't all my mother's fault. Dressing badly has been a refuge much of my life, a way of compelling others to engage with my mind, not my physical presence. I'm competitive enough that I'll eventually withdraw from any consistently losing battle. Elaine gave me the precious gift of showing me that it didn't need to be that way. I am a woman; I do have a feminine side. Learning to enjoy it would not diminish any other part of me.

She looked at me with her wide-eyed, wicked grin. "I

would never in a million years have chosen that for you, Sonia, but it looks great on you. You see? You're becoming your own person."

Not every relationship ends with such mutual respect and dignity as Kevin and I somehow salvaged from our youthful mistakes. I would discover what it is to go down in flames romantically, disappointment that shakes your foundations. The despair would pass, but until it did, friends came to my rescue, just as they had after my divorce. Being left alone in my misery was never an option. Elaine's taking me shopping every weekend was part of a campaign undertaken in the aftermath of one ill-fated romance. Alessandro and Fe, too, have been known to jump into the breach of a breakup: "Mama says you must come to Ibiza with us for vacation."

One remedy for heartache I concocted on my own was learning how to dance. I scheduled the lessons, rolled up the carpet, and committed myself to learning salsa. No longer would I sit there like a potted plant watching others on the floor. The gawky, uncoordinated Sonia would make peace with herself in motion. I may never have a natural rhythm, but I know that the knees make the hips move, and I would learn to read a partner so well that I can now follow like an expert.

I still can't sing to save my life—a slight hearing impairment doesn't help matters—but after unnatural amounts of rehearsal to memorize where each syllable falls, I can now get up onstage at a holiday party and hold my own in a musical skit.

I finally learned how to swim, too. Okay, maybe not with athletic grace, but I can swim twenty laps without stopping. I can jump off the boat with the best of them, and no one will ever need to rescue me. I never imagined that even later in life I would learn to throw a baseball, but really you never know. During my first term on the Supreme Court, I practiced twenty minutes every afternoon for weeks so I could be ready to throw the first pitch at Yankee Stadium. Not from the mound, of course, but I did send it straight down the middle. Exercise of all kinds has been a joyous discovery, and I've even biked a century tour. It would take years, but now when I look in the mirror, what I see is really not bad. It's true, I love food too much; my weight goes up and down. But when time permits, I actually enjoy the effort of keeping it off.

One reckoning with my physical self would prove harder than all the others. I had been a smoker since high school, burning through three and a half packs a day for much of my life. I made my first serious attempt at quitting in my final year at law school: every time I felt the urge, I ran around the block, often with Kevin and Star chugging alongside in solidarity. Going cold turkey during exams may sound like a needlessly brutal rigor, but in retrospect it seems less perversely self-punishing than lighting up again two years later when Kevin and I split. There would be further attempts, using various methods, including hypnosis, but nothing worked for good until I saw little Kiley holding a pencil be-

310

tween two fingers, blowing imaginary smoke rings. The guilt of endangering the health of a loved one is by far the best motivation I've discovered.

I checked into a five-day residential program and even wrote a long love letter, saying farewell to what had been my most constant companion for so many years. It was another heartbreak, but I comforted myself by imagining that if I were ever to become a judge someday, I couldn't very well be calling a recess every time I needed a cigarette. And it worked. I remain a nicotine addict, a fact that inspires a certain compassion for the addictions of others, but I haven't had a cigarette since. I no longer worry about slipping, but I do fantasize that I might indulge one last smoke on my deathbed, just as Abuelita did.

Twenty-Seven

In 1990, I flew to London with Alessandro, Fe, his parents, and his sister for a Boxing Day celebration. When I got back to work after the Christmas holiday, my office looked like the office of someone who had been let go. The towers of paper that normally obscured my desktop had vanished, exposing a dark polished wood grain I'd all but forgotten about. Upon it sat only one document for my attention: an application form for the position of a federal district court judge. This was obviously Dave Botwinik's doing. I grabbed the form and charged the short distance down the hallway to his office.

"Dave, come on."

"It's from Senator Daniel Patrick Moynihan's judicial selection committee. They vet the recommendation he makes to the president. Fill it out."

"Are you crazy? I'm thirty-six years old!"

"Humor me, Sonia. They're looking for qualified Hispanics. You're not only a qualified Hispanic but eminently qualified, period." He promised to give me back my files if I filled it out, which I promised to do before counting the pages: it was endless. But Dave would not be deterred: he volunteered his assistant as well as my own, plus the help of a paralegal, whatever I needed to get the job done. I had long suspected that Dave Botwinik's ambitions on my behalf were partly a displacement of ambitions he'd once had for himself. Until then, I'd just ignored it whenever he raised the topic. But this time he was showing a whole new level of determination, and he was not the only one on the case.

A few weeks earlier, I had shared a cab with Benito Romano after a PRLDEF board meeting. Having served as interim US attorney when Rudy Giuliani quit the post to run for mayor, Benito had himself been approached by a colleague on Senator Moynihan's search committee. He had declined the offer, he said, but given them my name.

"Why not you?" I asked.

"I have a wife, Sonia. I have kids. How am I going to put them through college on a judge's salary?" It's a very real problem that has discouraged many a talented person from considering the bench. The pay cut I would suffer as a young partner wouldn't be as severe as a more experienced lawyer's, and having no children spared me the impossible choice. But this calculus didn't alter my feeling of reaching for too much too soon.

Even with help, the application took the better part of a

week to complete. I had to account for every jot of my adult life, it seemed, as well as furnishing current addresses for each landlord, supervisor, judge, and legal adversary who had ever crossed my path. At least the financial information was easy; I still had little to report on that front. Beyond the summary of professional experience typical of job applications, this document would be the starting point for an investigation scouring my past for any ethical lapse. But I wasn't daunted by that. I soon realized that, perhaps more than I would ever have admitted, most of the choices I'd made over the years had anticipated this very moment.

I heard back from the senator's committee very quickly after submitting the application, the interview scheduled within a couple of weeks. If I still couldn't take the whole business quite seriously, I nevertheless prepared as if my life depended on it. When I had gone for recruiting interviews at Yale, it never occurred to me to do research in advance or rehearse the answers to likely questions.

I prepared as thoroughly as I would have done for a criminal prosecution, reading whatever I could find and seeking out colleagues and any friends and family of theirs with the least experience of the judicial nomination process: What kinds of questions could I expect to be asked? What objections might I need to rebut? I was no longer afraid of the obvious one I myself first anticipated: "Aren't you too young to be applying for this position?" I'd certainly presumed so, but a bit of digging revealed I would not be the youngest to hold it. Becoming a judge in one's thirties was uncommon but not unheard of, and I would have the names of those exceptions at my fingertips. And also one ready truth: although wisdom is built on life experiences, the mere accumulation of years guarantees nothing.

Judah Gribetz, a childhood friend of David Botwinik's and long-time adviser to Senator Moynihan, chaired the committee, with whom I met in the conference room of a downtown law firm. I was facing some fifteen people around the table, most but not all of them men and lawyers. One of the few I recognized was Joel Motley, son of Constance Baker Motley, the first African-American woman to be appointed a US district court judge. As questions flew at me from all sides, the answers were flowing easily, and I was pleased with how well I'd prepared. Then Joel asked one I'd never predicted. "Don't you think learning to be a judge will be hard for you?" I took a breath to gather my thoughts, and then the answer poured out: "I've spent my whole life learning how to do things that were hard for me. None of it has ever been easy. You have no idea how hard Princeton was for me at the beginning, but I figured out how to do well there and ended up being accepted to one of the best law schools in the country. At Yale, the DA's Office, Pavia & Harcourt—wherever I've gone, I've honestly never felt fully prepared at the outset. Yet each time I've survived, I've learned, and I've thrived. I'm not intimidated by challenges. My whole life has been one. I look forward to engaging the work and learning how to do it well."

When the discussion turned technical, my trial experience held up very well under scrutiny. As a state prosecutor,

I'd tried many more cases than an attorney working in the federal system would have done. We talked at length about the child pornography and Tarzan Murderer cases, and I explained those investigations and the legal strategies employed.

We talked about my community service, which I knew was especially important to Senator Moynihan. My work at PRLDEF was clearly a point in my favor, as was the Campaign Finance Board and my other pro bono activities. As I sat there fielding questions, I dared to believe that the interview was actually going very well. With each question, I could see the pitch coming toward me as if in slow motion. I was relaxed but also alert, centered but agile, ready to move in any direction. If I was not picked, I knew it wouldn't be because I had blown the interview. And that sense alone made the experience worth it.

But the whole process still seemed like make-believe, even when Senator Moynihan's office phoned soon after, inviting me to meet him in Washington. He turned out to be so forthright and gregarious that I warmed to him at once. We talked about Puerto Rico and the challenges facing the Puerto Rican community in New York, our conversation ranging widely from Eddie Torres (a judge who also wrote crime novels that the senator admired), to getting out the Latino vote, to the eternal question of the island's status. Here, clearly, was a scholar as well as a politician, someone who understood the sociology as well as the policy issues while also possessing the social skills of a master diplomat.

After more than an hour, I sensed that we were coming

to an end and prepared to thank him before going off to wait out the predictably interminable period of deliberation. But the senator had one more surprise in store, saying, "Sonia, if you accept, I would like to nominate you as a district court judge in New York." He warned me that the confirmation process would not be easy. The Bush administration was not in the habit of smiling on recommendations from a Democrat; on principle, it would fight any candidate he proposed. "It may take some time," he said, "but I'll make you a promise: If you stay with me, I'll get you through eventually. I won't give up."

Then he asked if I was willing to hold up my side of the bargain: Was I prepared to spend a good portion of my remaining professional life as a judge? I was stunned. Until that moment, I had still not allowed myself to believe lest I awaken from this daydream. But here was Senator Moynihan looking at me, waiting for an answer. "Yes!" With all my heart, yes.

I floated out of the Russell Senate Office Building and wandered down the street in a daze. After a couple of blocks I saw a monumental flight of stairs, familiar white columns: the Supreme Court Building glowing serenely, like a temple on a hill. There could not have been a more propitious omen. I felt blessed in that moment, blessed to be living this life, on the threshold of all I'd ever wanted. There would be plenty of time soon enough to deal with my insecurities and the hard work of learning this new job. For the moment, though, I just stood there, dazzled at the sight and glowing with gratitude.

☆

My mother and Omar had been together for a few years at that point. At first she'd told me only that she was renting my old bedroom to this man. Then, meeting him a couple of times on visits home, I sensed that there was more to the story than they were saying. Arriving late one night, I surprised them kissing in the lobby. "Do you have something to tell me?" I asked. Mami was flustered, beaming, embarrassed, and clearly very happy.

"We were going to tell you, Sonia. I just didn't know how." As I got to know Omar over time, I fully approved of my mother's choice. Now they were sitting side by side on the couch in my living room in Brooklyn, and I was the one who had to figure out how to break the news.

"Mami, Omar, I'm going to tell you something, but you have to promise to keep it a secret. There won't be a public announcement for a couple of weeks, but I've been given permission to tell you." I asked if they knew who Senator Patrick Moynihan was. Tentative nods. "The senator is going to nominate me to become a US district court judge in Manhattan."

"Sonia, how wonderful! That's terrific news!" As always, Mami's initial reaction was enthusiasm. She didn't always understand fully what my news meant, but as a matter of maternal principle she was a loyal cheerleader. Omar, too, congratulated me earnestly. Then the questions started.

"So, you're going to earn more money, right?" my mother said.

"Not exactly, Mami. A judge's salary is much less than I'm earning now."

She paused for a long moment. "Well, I guess you'll be traveling a lot, seeing the world?"

"Not really. The courthouse is in downtown Manhattan, and I can't imagine I'll be going anywhere else. Not the way I have at Pavia."

The pauses were growing a little longer. "I'm sure you'll meet interesting people and make friends as nice as the ones you've met at the firm."

I was determined not to laugh. "Actually, the people who appear before a judge are mostly criminal defendants in serious trouble or people fighting with each other. There are ethical reasons, too, why I wouldn't be socializing with them."

Silence, and then: "Sonia, why on earth do you want this job?"

Omar, who knew me well by now, came to my rescue. "*Conoces tu hija*. You know your daughter, Celina. This must be very important work." The look on Mami's face carried me back to that moment under the rumbling El train when we shared our uncertainty about what lay ahead of me at Princeton: "What you got yourself into, daughter, I don't know . . ." In truth, I'd had no idea then that Princeton would be only the first stop on a magical ride that by now had already taken me farther than I could have ever foreseen.

The eighteen months that it took my nomination to clear were an education in the arts of politics and patience. I knew that the delays had nothing to do with me personally. Two interviews with the Justice Department, investigations by various government agencies, and eventually the Senate confirmation hearings had all gone smoothly. No one had voiced doubt about my qualifications or otherwise objected to my appointment. I was simply caught in the biggest game in town—one in which procedural delay is a cherished tactic. Through it all, Senator Moynihan was as good as his word, never flagging in his effort or allowing me to give up hope.

Meanwhile, I would become aware of a chorus of voices rising in my support. The Hispanic National Bar Association lobbied the White House steadily and rallied grassroots support from other Latino organizations. If confirmed, I would be the first Hispanic federal judge in the state's history, a milestone the community ardently wished to achieve (José Cabranes had very nearly claimed the honor in 1979 but was simultaneously nominated for a judgeship in Connecticut and chose to serve there instead, though much later he would take a New York seat on the Second Circuit Court of Appeals). Even before Senator Moynihan had settled on my name for the nomination, a veritable *This Is Your Life* cast of backers came forward: my fellow board members at PRLDEF, Bob Morgenthau and others at the DA's Office, Father O'Hare and colleagues on the Campaign Finance Board, lawyers I'd known through mutual clients. They wrote letters, made phone calls, and volunteered to make the sorts of informal appeals to colleagues that can be persuasive when echoing from many sides. I was astonished to see all the circles of my life telescoping on this one goal of mine, making it seem all the more as if everything until now had been a prelude to this moment.

Finally, on August 12, 1992, the US Senate confirmed my nomination to the District Court for the Southern District of New York, the mother court, the oldest district court in the nation. The public induction ceremony followed in October. Though brief—perhaps all of five minutes—it was far from perfunctory. Every moment of it moved me deeply: donning the black robe, swearing solemnly to administer justice without respect to persons, equally to the poor and the rich, and to perform my duties under the Constitution faithfully and impartially. So help me God. I took, for that occasion only, the traditional newcomer's seat between the chief judge, Charles Brieant, and Judge Constance Baker Motley, the next most senior of the estimable colleagues I was joining. Such ritual was profoundly humbling, signaling as it did the paramount importance of the judiciary as an institution, above the significance of any individual, beyond the ups and downs of history. Whatever I had accomplished to arrive at this point, the role I was about to assume was vastly more important than I was.

The sense of having vaulted into an alternative reality was compounded by no less disorienting changes in my personal life. I moved to Manhattan, because I needed to live within the area of my jurisdiction. Dawn was appalled that I would shatter our neighborhood idyll on account of some minor rule, frequently bent. I feared she would never forgive me for abandoning her in Brooklyn, but for me there was a deep sense of honor at stake. I was becoming a judge! How could I not follow the rules?

My mother, meanwhile, had plans of her own. She decided to move to Florida. She and Omar had gone there on vacation the Monday after my induction, and the next thing I knew, Mami was on the phone, telling me in a giddy voice that she'd rented an apartment.

Within days of their return to New York, the apartment in Co-op City was packed up. When the cartons were removed, I stood with Mami in the empty apartment, our voices bouncing off the scuffed walls, the hollowness echoing with so many years, amid a confluence of our tears and memories. We hugged, and then it was good-bye, Mami and Omar driving away.

Before they even reached Florida, I got a phone call from Puerto Rico: Titi Aurora had died. She had gone there to move her husband to a nursing home—the second husband, who was even crazier than the first and who'd entangled her already hard life into still further knots of sadness and exhausting labor. This was not news I could break to Mami over the phone. I needed to get on the next flight to Miami and be with her when she heard it. Titi had fought bitterly with Mami over the move to Florida. They squabbled often over all sorts of small things, but this had become a much deeper rift. To learn that death had cut off any possibility of reconciliation would, I well knew, cause Mami unbearable pain.

I marveled at how two such very different women could live so tightly bound to each other. Affection was not part of the recipe, nor was any emotional expression beyond their habit of snapping at each other. There was no confiding of secrets, no sharing of comfort visible to others. Titi could be disagreeable because her life had been harsh, but she lived it honorably, firmly grounded on a rock-solid foundation of personal ethics that I deeply admired. For her part, Mami, though more compassionate with strangers, brought to this relationship gratitude beyond measure for mercy shown in hardship a very long time ago. It was a gratitude time hadn't faded, and that, too, I deeply admired.

I rented a car at the airport and arrived at the unfamiliar apartment complex very late at night after getting lost, driving in tearful circles. My mother must have phoned Junior before I arrived; however it happened, when she opened the door, it was clear that the news had already reached her. She fell into my arms sobbing.

We traveled together to Puerto Rico to bury Titi Aurora. I didn't break down until I was handed the envelope of cash that she had set aside with my name on it. We'd kept the old ritual: whenever she was going to Puerto Rico, I would lend her the money for the plane ticket. In recent years, I desperately wanted to give her the money, considering I could now afford it and she was living on Social Security. But she wouldn't have it: if she simply accepted the cash as a gift, she could never ask for it again, as, of course, she would surely need to.

Back in New York, I helped sort out the few wisps of a material life that Titi had left behind. There was precious little for someone known to us as a pack rat. Most of what remained was a closetful of gifts that she couldn't bear to part with or to use.

"What are you so scared of?" Theresa asked. "What could possibly go wrong?" She had come with me from Pavia & Harcourt, her reassuring presence in chambers perhaps the only thing keeping me tethered to any semblance of sanity. My first month as a judge I was terrified, in keeping with the usual pattern of self-doubt and ferocious compensatory effort that has always attended any major transition in my life. I wasn't scared of the work. Twelve-hour days, seven-day weeks, were normal for me. It was my own courtroom that scared me. The very thought of taking my seat on the bench induced a metaphysical panic. I still couldn't believe this had worked out as dreamed, and I felt myself almost an impostor meeting my fate so brazenly.

At first, I worked around my anxiety by scheduling every single conference in my chambers. Until a case actually came to trial, I could skirt the problem. Finally, there came before me a case involving the forfeiture of the motorcycle gang's Hells Angels clubhouse in Alphabet City, the neighborhood in New York's East Village named for its Avenues A, B, C, and D, and the marshals in charge of security drew the line. I could not meet with this bunch except in open court.

"All rise." The trembling would pass in a minute or two, I told myself, just as it always had since the first time I'd mounted the pulpit at Blessed Sacrament. But when I sat down, I noticed that my knees were still knocking together. I could hear the sound and wondered in complete mortification whether the microphone set in front of me on the table was picking it up. I was listening to the lawyers, too, of course, as the telltale tapping under the table continued, a disembodied nuisance and reproach. Then a first question for the litigants occurred to me, and as I jumped in, I forgot about my knees, finding nothing in the world more interesting than the matter before me right then. The panic had passed; I had found my way into the moment, and I could now be sure I always would. Afterward, back in the robing room, I confessed my satisfaction: "Theresa, I think this fish has found her pond."

Epilogue

Looking back today, it seems a lifetime ago that I first arrived at a place of belonging and purpose, the sense of having heard a call and answered it. When I placed my hand on the Bible, taking the oath of office to become a district court judge, the ceremony marked the culmination of one journey of growth and understanding but also the beginning of another. The second journey, made while I've been a judge, nevertheless continues in the same small, steady steps in which I'd taken the first one, those that I know to be still my own best way of moving forward. It continues, as well, in the same embrace of my many families, whose vital practical support has been bestowed as a token of something much deeper.

With each of my own small, steady steps, I have seen myself grow stronger and equal to a challenge greater than the last. When, after six years on the district court, I was nominated to the Second Circuit Court of Appeals, and to the Supreme Court twelve years after that, the confirmation hearings would be, at each step, successively more difficult, the attacks more personal, the entire process faster, more brutally intense. But at each step, too, the numbers of family and community encircling me and coming to my defense would be exponentially greater.

Over a thousand people would attend my induction ceremony for the Second Circuit. A more intimate group of over three hundred friends and family stayed on to celebrate that occasion and to witness my very first official act as a judge of the Second Circuit, performed that very night: marrying Mami and Omar. Combining the festivities not only doubled the joy, making the party even livelier, but also permitted me to honor those closest to me and acknowledge a debt to them—to Mami especially—for their part in what I'd become. My awareness of that debt would not be felt so keenly again for years, until the moment when I unexpectedly saw Junior's face on the big television screen, crying his tears of joy at my nomination to the Supreme Court; the searing tears that image drew from my own eyes in turn would leave no doubt about how much the love of family has sustained me.

Just as I had to learn to think like a lawyer, I would have to teach myself to think like a judge. In my small, steady steps I have mastered the conceptual tools of a trial judge wrestling with fact and precedent and of an appellate judge dealing with the theory of law on a more abstract level. I have been a happy sponge, soaking up whatever lessons I could learn from mentors generous with time and spirit. I have been thrilled by the learning that came from the opportunities I've had to teach and the energy drawn from interaction with my law clerks and the freewheeling exchange of ideas I have nurtured in my chambers. Now my education continues on the Supreme Court as I reckon with the particular demands of its finality of review. Almost daily, people ask me what I hope my legacy will be, as if the story were winding down, when really it has just begun. I can only reply that my highest aspiration for my work on the Court is to grow in understanding beyond what I can foresee, beyond any borders visible from this vantage.

In this connection, one memory from high school days comes to mind. During my junior year, I was chosen to attend a conference of girls from Catholic schools all over the city. Over a weekend of discussions on religious and social issues, I found myself sparring again and again with one individual, a Hispanic girl with an impressive Afro of the sort I had seen before only on television; nothing so radical ever appeared in the halls of Cardinal Spellman High School.

The two of us were engaging with far more energy than

anyone else at the table, a vigor that, on my part at least, derived not from the certainty of my convictions but from my love of the push and pull of ideas, the pleasure of flexing the rhetorical muscles I had been building in Forensics Club, and an eagerness to learn from the exchange. I argued, as I would so often with lawyers years later, not from a set position but by way of exploring ideas and testing them against whatever challenge might be offered. I love the heat of thoughtful conversation, and I don't judge a person's character by the outcome of a sporting verbal exchange, let alone his or her reasoned opinions. But in my opponent's responses I sensed an animosity that over the course of the weekend only grew. After the final roundup session, at which we reflected on our experience of the meeting, I told her that I had very much enjoyed our conversation, and I asked her what had inspired the hostility that I sensed from her.

"It's because you can't just take a stand," she said, looking at me with such earnest disdain that it startled me. "Everything depends on context with you. If you are always open to persuasion, how can anybody predict your position? How can they tell if you're friend or foe? The problem with people like you is you have no principles."

Surely, I thought, what she described was preferable to its opposite. If you held to principle so passionately, so inflexibly, indifferent to the particulars of circumstance—the full range of what human beings, with all their flaws and foibles, might endure or create—if you enthroned principle above even reason, weren't you then abdicating the responsibilities of a thinking person? I said something like that.

Our conversation ended on that unsettled note, but I have spent the rest of my life grappling with her accusation. I have since learned how these considerations are addressed in the more complex language of moral philosophy, but our simple exchange that day raised a point that remains essential to me. There is indeed something deeply wrong with a person who lacks principles, who has no moral core. There are, likewise, certainly values that brook no compromise, and I would count among them integrity, fairness, and the avoidance of cruelty. But I have never accepted the argument that principle is compromised by judging each situation on its own merits, with due appreciation of the idiosyncrasy of human motivation and fallibility. Concern for individuals, the imperative of treating them with dignity and respect for their ideas and needs, regardless of one's own views—these, too, are surely principles and as worthy as any of being deemed inviolable. To remain open to understandings—perhaps even to principles—as yet not determined is the least that learning requires.

With luck, there will be plenty of time ahead for me to continue growing and learning, many more stories to tell before I can begin to say definitively who I am as a judge.

Who I am as a human being will, I hope, continue to evolve as well, but perhaps the essence is defined by now. The moment when, in accordance with tradition, I sat in Chief Justice John Marshall's chair and placed my hand on the Bible to take the oath of office for the Supreme Court, I felt as if an electric current were coursing through me, and my whole life, collapsing upon that moment, could be read in the faces of those most dear to me who filled that beautiful room. I looked out to see my mother with tears streaming down her cheeks and felt a surge of admiration for this remarkable woman who had instilled in me the values that came naturally to her—compassion, hard work, and courage to face the unknown—but who'd also grown with me as we took our small steps together to close the distance that had opened up between us in the early years. I might have been little Mercedes as a child, but now I was equally my mother's daughter. I saw Junior beaming proudly, and my family who traveled from New York and Puerto Rico to be there, and so many friends who have stood by me through the years. The moment belonged as much to them as to me.

I sensed the presence, too, almost visible, of those who had recently passed: my friend Elaine, who had suffered a series of strokes but to the very end managed to leaven both her own dying and the drama surrounding my nomination with her humor; Dave Botwinik, who had set this whole dream in motion toward reality.

Then I caught the eye of the president sitting in the first row and felt gratitude bursting inside me, an overwhelming gratitude unrelated to politics or position, a gratitude alive with Abuelita's joy and with a sudden memory, an image seen through the eyes of a child: I was running back to the house in Mayagüez with a melting ice cone we called a *piragua* dripping sweet and sticky down my face and arms, the sun in my eyes, breaking through clouds and glinting off the rain-soaked pavement and dripping leaves. I was running with joy, an overwhelming joy that arose simply from gratitude for the fact of being alive. Along with the image, memory carried these words from a child's mind through time: I am blessed. In this life I am truly blessed.

Acknowledgments

I am indebted to the many children who have shared their hearts, thoughts, and dreams with me. You inspire me.

I am grateful to my dear friend Zara Houshmand, who has once again helped refine my work.

Beverly Horowitz, with the entire team of Delacorte Press/ Random House, have expertly guided the editing and production of this book. Thank you.

I am appreciative to my team of advisers: Peter and Amy Bernstein of the Bernstein Literary Agency, and my lawyers, John S. Siffert and Mark A. Merriman. They are always incredibly helpful.

Finally, my assistants Susan Anastasi, Anh Le, and Victoria Gomez are always indispensable in all my efforts.

I have a treasure trove of many people who guide and support me, and I thank them all for their love.

Glossary of Spanish Words

abuelita: Grandma.

Bendición, Abuelita: Bless me, Grandma.
bisabuela: Great-grandmother.

café con leche: Coffee with milk.
chiflado: Literally, "crazy," a looney; used to translate "stooge" in the title and show *The Three Stooges*.
chuletas: Pork chops.
como una maldición: Like a curse.

Dame un cigarrillo: Give me a cigarette.

el jurutungo viejo: The boondocks; the end of the world.
el luto: Mourning.
embusteros: Liars.
"En Mi Viejo San Juan": "In My Old San Juan." A bolero written by Puerto Rican composer Noel Estrada in 1943. It is considered by many Puerto Ricans to be a kind of unofficial anthem. It describes the narrator's desire to go back to his longed-for city by the sea, and the melancholy realization that this will never happen.

Es el precio de hacer negocios: It's the price of doing business.
espera: Wait.

ficha: Playing piece; usually a domino.

guagua: Bus.
güiro: Musical instrument made from an elongated, hollowed-out gourd with notches on one side, played by rubbing a stick with tines along the notches.

jíbaro: Straw-hatted peasant farmer or laborer who plays a significant role in Puerto Rican culture and identity. This almost mythical figure is said to be traditional, hardworking, plainspoken, and wise.

la nata: Cream; also, the skin on milk.
la tetita: Literally, "the tit"; also used to denote the crunchy end of a loaf of Puerto Rican *criollo* bread.

Mercedes chiquita: Little Mercedes.
merienda: Midday meal; light lunch; snack.
mi'jita: My dear; honey.

Nacimiento: Nativity scene.
nena: Girl.
¡No me molestes!: Don't bother me!
No tengas miedo: Don't be afraid.

para: Here; stop.
picadillo: Seasoned ground beef.

Que Dios te bendiga, te favorezca y te libre de todo mal y peligro: May God bless you, favor you and deliver you from all evil and danger.

¡Qué guapo!: He's so handsome!
¿Quieres una china?: Do you want an orange?

recao: Herb also known as *culantro,* or Thai parsley, which is one
    of the basic ingredients of the spice mixture known as *sofrito*
    used in many Puerto Rican recipes.
rosario: Rosary.

sofrito: Sauce made of tomatoes, chopped peppers, onions, garlic,
    and *recao,* or *culantro.*

¡Te vas a enfermar!: You'll get sick!
tío: Uncle.
titi: Term of endearment for *tía,* or aunt.
tostones: Fried green plantains.
¿Tú estás ciego?: Are you blind?

vendedor: Salesman.
vivero: Livestock market.

Yo soy Celina: I am Celina.

A Brief History of the Supreme Court

The Supreme Court of the United States is the highest and most influential court in the nation. The Supreme Court was established by Article III of the United States Constitution and is the only court that was established by the Constitution. It is one of the three co-equal branches of the U.S. government, composed of the Executive Branch, the Legislative Branch, and the Judicial Branch. The Executive Branch includes the office of the President and various federal agencies, the Legislative Branch is made up of the Senate and House of Representatives, and the Judicial Branch is the Supreme Court and lower federal courts. These three branches of government were created so that no one part of the government would have absolute authority. With the power of judicial review, the Supreme Court is able to ensure that the actions of the other two branches stay within the limits set by the Constitution.

The purpose of the Supreme Court is to hear cases and controversies arising under the Constitution or the laws of the United States. The Supreme Court has two areas of jurisdiction: original and appellate. Original jurisdiction means that a case is filed directly in the Supreme Court and does not have to first pass through any lower court. This includes cases arising between two states, or between a state and a foreign government. The majority of cases heard by the Supreme Court are appellate cases, which means the Court reviews and makes decisions on cases that have originated in lower courts. These cases are brought to the Supreme Court through the appeal process. Unlike in other courts, there are no witnesses or evidence present in most Supreme Court cases because the cases have already been tried and documented in lesser courts.

The Supreme Court is composed of nine Justices: one Chief Justice and eight Associate Justices. The Court has not always been composed of nine Justices, and the number has fluctuated since the Court's first meeting in 1790. The Court was initially composed of a Chief Justice and five Associate Justices; this number changed six times before settling at the present total of nine Justices in 1869.

In the courtroom, the Justices sit in order of seniority, with the Chief Justice in the center and the most senior Justices sitting closest to him on either side. Over the history of the Supreme Court, there have been 17 Chief Justices and 101 Associate Justices.

To become a Justice, there is no specific list of requirements, such as age, education, or career field. Even though a law degree is not an explicit requirement, the vast majority of Justices have attended law school.

There is no term limit for Justices; the position is generally considered to be a life appointment. The Constitution states that "Judges, both of the supreme and inferior Courts, shall hold their Offices during good Behaviour. . . ." A Justice may choose to resign or retire, but the only way to remove a Justice from the Supreme

Court is through impeachment, a highly uncommon occurrence. The only Justice to be impeached was Associate Justice Samuel Chase in 1805. The House of Representatives passed Articles of Impeachment against him; however, he was acquitted by the Senate. When there is a vacancy on the Court, the President nominates a new Justice, who then must be confirmed by the Senate. To provide a sense of turnover, the average term length for Justices is sixteen years.

The term begins each year on the first Monday in October, continuing until late June or early July, when the Court breaks for summer recess. The Justices grant review in approximately seventy to eighty of the more than seven to eight thousand petitions filed with the Court each term. During the term, the Court operates with alternating periods of sittings, when the Justices hear pending cases, and recesses, when the Justices read briefs, decide which cases to hear in the future, and write opinions.

The Supreme Court's primary task is to interpret the Constitution and federal laws in the cases that come before the Justices. The Court has exercised these duties for more than two centuries, proving its importance and longevity as an institution.

For more information about the Supreme Court, visit supremecourt.gov.

About the Author

SONIA SOTOMAYOR is the author of the national best-seller *My Beloved World* and the middle-grade adaptation *The Beloved World of Sonia Sotomayor*. She also wrote the picture-book autobiography *Turning Pages: My Life Story*, illustrated by Lulu Delacre. She graduated summa cum laude from Princeton University in 1976 and from Yale Law School in 1979. She worked as an assistant district attorney in New York and then at the law firm of Pavia & Harcourt. She served as a judge of the US District Court, Southern District of New York, from 1992 to 1998, and from 1998 to 2009 she served on the United States Court of Appeals for the Second Circuit. In May 2009, President Barack Obama nominated her as an Associate Justice of the Supreme Court; she assumed this role on August 8, 2009.